For Lis & James

May 2009
Olaf

Ordinary People as Mass Murderers

The Holocaust and its Contexts

Series Editors: Olaf Jensen, University of Leicester, UK and Claus-Christian W. Szejnmann, University of Leicester, UK.
Series Editorial Board: Wolfgang Benz, Robert G. Moeller and Mirjam Wenzel

More than sixty years on, the Holocaust remains a subject of intense debate with ever-widening ramifications. This series aims to demonstrate the continuing relevance of the Holocaust and related issues in contemporary society, politics and culture; studying the Holocaust and its history broadens our understanding not only of the events themselves but also of their present-day significance. The series acknowledges and responds to the continuing gaps in our knowledge about the events that constituted the Holocaust, the various forms in which the Holocaust has been remembered, interpreted and discussed, and the increasing importance of the Holocaust today to many individuals and communities.

Titles include:

Olaf Jensen and Claus-Christian W. Szejnmann (*editors*)
ORDINARY PEOPLE AS MASS MURDERERS
Perpetrators in Comparative Perspectives

Forthcoming titles:

Olaf Jensen (*editor*)
HISTORY AND MEMORY AFTER THE HOLOCAUST IN GERMANY, POLAND, RUSSIA AND BRITAIN

Tanja Schult
A HERO'S MANY FACES
Portraits of Raoul Wallenberg in Contemporary Monuments

The Holocaust and Its Contexts Series
Series Standing Order ISBN 978–0–230–22386–8 Hardback
978–0–230–22387–5 Paperback
(*outside North America only*)

You can receive future titles in this series as they are published by placing a standing order. Please contact your bookseller or, in case of difficulty, write to us at the address below with your name and address, the title of the series and the ISBN quoted above.

Customer Services Department, Macmillan Distribution Ltd, Houndmills, Basingstoke, Hampshire RG21 6XS, England

Ordinary People as Mass Murderers

Perpetrators in Comparative Perspectives

Edited By

Olaf Jensen
Lecturer in Holocaust Studies, School of Historical Studies, University of Leicester

and

Claus-Christian W. Szejnmann
Professor of Modern History, Loughborough University

palgrave
macmillan

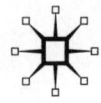

Editorial matter, selection © Olaf Jensen and Claus-Christian
W. Szejnmann 2008.
All remaining chapters © their respective authors 2008.

All rights reserved. No reproduction, copy or transmission of this
publication may be made without written permission.

No portion of this publication may be reproduced, copied or transmitted
save with written permission or in accordance with the provisions of the
Copyright, Designs and Patents Act 1988, or under the terms of any licence
permitting limited copying issued by the Copyright Licensing Agency,
Saffron House, 6-10 Kirby Street, London EC1N 8TS.

Any person who does any unauthorized act in relation to this publication
may be liable to criminal prosecution and civil claims for damages.

The authors have asserted their rights to be identified
as the authors of this work in accordance with the Copyright,
Designs and Patents Act 1988.

First published 2008 by
PALGRAVE MACMILLAN

Palgrave Macmillan in the UK is an imprint of Macmillan Publishers Limited,
registered in England, company number 785998, of Houndmills, Basingstoke,
Hampshire RG21 6XS.

Palgrave Macmillan in the US is a division of St Martin's Press LLC,
175 Fifth Avenue, New York, NY 10010.

Palgrave Macmillan is the global academic imprint of the above companies
and has companies and representatives throughout the world.

Palgrave® and Macmillan® are registered trademarks in the United States,
the United Kingdom, Europe and other countries.

ISBN-13: 978–0–230–55202–9 hardback
ISBN-10: 0–230–55202–1 hardback

This book is printed on paper suitable for recycling and made from fully
managed and sustained forest sources. Logging, pulping and manufacturing
processes are expected to conform to the environmental regulations of the
country of origin.

A catalogue record for this book is available from the British Library.

Library of Congress Cataloging-in-Publication Data
Ordinary people as mass murderers : perpetrators in comparative
    perspectives / edited by Olaf Jensen, Claus-Christian W. Szejnmann.
        p. cm. — (The Holocaust and its contexts)
    Includes bibliographical references and index.
    ISBN 978–0–230–55202–9 (alk. paper)
        1. Holocaust, Jewish (1939–1945) 2. World War, 1939–1945—
    Atrocities. 3. Mass murderers—History—20th century.
    I. Jensen, Olaf. II. Szejnmann, Claus-Christian W., 1965–
    D804.3.O734 2008
    940.53′18—dc22   2008030098

10 9 8 7 6 5 4 3 2 1
17 16 15 14 13 12 11 10 09 08

Printed and bound in Great Britain by
CPI Antony Rowe, Chippenham and Eastbourne

This book is dedicated to all those who have been the victims of mass murder and genocide

Contents

List of Photographs and Figures   ix

Preface   xi

Notes on the Contributors   xiii

Glossary   xvii

Introductory Thoughts and Overview   1
Olaf Jensen

Part I   Perpetrators of the Holocaust

1   Perpetrators of the Holocaust: a Historiography   25
Claus-Christian W. Szejnmann

2   Male Bonding and Shame Culture: Hitler's Soldiers and the Moral Basis of Genocidal Warfare   55
Thomas Kühne

3   The Men of *Einsatzgruppe D*: an Inside View of a State-Sanctioned Killing Unit in the 'Third Reich'   78
Andrej Angrick

Part II   Female Perpetrators of the Holocaust

4   Women under National Socialism: Women's Scope for Action and the Issue of Gender   99
Christina Herkommer

5   Female Concentration Camp Guards as Perpetrators: Three Case Studies   120
Irmtraud Heike

Part III   Psychological and Sociological Approaches

6   The Ordinariness of Extraordinary Evil: the Making of Perpetrators of Genocide and Mass Killing   145
James E. Waller

7 On Killing and Morality: How Normal People Become Mass
   Murderers   165
   Harald Welzer

Part IV Perpetrators and Genocide

8 The Organisation of Genocide: Perpetration in Comparative
   Perspective   185
   Donald Bloxham

9 International Law after the Nuremberg Trials and Rwanda:
   How Do Perpetrators Justify Themselves?   201
   Gerd Hankel

Index   221

List of Photographs and Figures

The views or opinions expressed in this book, and the context in which the images are used, do not necessarily reflect the views or the policy of, nor imply approval or endorsement by, the United States Holocaust Memorial Museum.

Cover photo

Czechstochwa [Katowice], Poland, 3–8 September 1939: 'German soldiers round up a group of Jewish men on Strazacka Street in Czestochowa' (#26822, copyright United States Holocaust Memorial, USHMM). (The image has been distorted to protect the dignity of the victims.)

(The photograph stems from a series of photos in an album belonging to a Wehrmacht soldier)

Photos in the book

Photo 5.1	Concentration camp Bergen-Belsen, Germany, 17 April 1945: Some captured female SS camp guards (#18323, USHMM, Photograph courtesy of the Imperial War Museum, London)	121
Photo 5.2	Concentration camp Bergen-Belsen, Germany, circa 21 April 1945, after the liberation of the camp by British soldiers (#78248, copyright USHMM)	122
Photo 5.3	Concentration camp Bergen-Belsen, Germany, 21 April 1945, after the liberation of the camp by British soldiers (#74929, copyright USHMM)	123

Photo 9.1 One of the traditional courts near Butare, in the south of Rwanda in Autumn 2002 (private collection, courtesy of Gerd Hankel) 216

Figure

Figure 6.1 A model of how ordinary people commit genocide and mass killing 149

Preface

This book, *Ordinary People as Mass Murderers: Perpetrators in Comparative Perspectives*, launches a series that seeks to explore the Holocaust and its contexts. The emphasis both here and in subsequent volumes is placed as much on context as on Holocaust. This recognises the continuing gaps in our knowledge about the events that constituted the Holocaust, the variety of ways in which the Holocaust has been remembered, interpreted and discussed, as well as the increasingly important role the Holocaust plays for various individuals and communities. Researchers and students now reflect on the Holocaust as a system of events and issues that has historicised the world we live in. As the current volume shows, it is now clear, as perhaps never before, that ordinary people can be induced to be mass murderers. Ordinary has lost its ordinariness.

This is one reason why, more than sixty years on, the Holocaust remains an issue of intense debate. The series, The Holocaust and its Contexts, aims to show how the Holocaust reaches into various different aspects of life and raises issues relevant to understanding current society, politics and culture. The issues that come up in Holocaust history and in Holocaust Studies generally both broaden the understanding of the Holocaust and illuminate its current ramifications.

This book is largely based on papers given at the conference 'Perpetrators of the Holocaust and other Genocides' held by The Stanley Burton Centre for Holocaust Studies at the University of Leicester on 9 May 2006. The editors would like to express their gratitude to the Burton family for their bequest without which the conference could not have been held.

The editors would also like to thank the keynote speaker, Professor Harald Welzer, who delivered the inaugural Aubrey Newman Lecture on 8 May 2006, along with the participants in the conference and the contributors to this book for their interest and their cooperation.

We also gratefully acknowledge the support of Professor Norman Housley, Head of School of Historical Studies, and Professor Robert Burgess, Vice-Chancellor of the University of Leicester. Thanks also go to Professor Aubrey Newman, Sarah Whitmore, Lynne Wakefield, and to our student helpers Jenny Mitchell and Matt Neal.

The production of this book was greatly facilitated by Professor Richard Littlejohns with his translations of four essays, and by the support and assistance given by librarian Brigitte Blockhaus and research student Holger Nies at the Institute for Advanced Studies in the Humanities, Essen: we are very grateful to them. A very special thanks goes to Martin L. Davies who proof-read the complete manuscript meticulously and made invaluable linguistic suggestions.

The editors and publishers also wish to thank the following for permission to reproduce copyright material: Caroline Waddell and the Photo Archive of the United States Holocaust Memorial Museum (USHMM), Washington; The Imperial War Museum (IWM), London and Crown Copyright; and Gerd Hankel (Rwanda). Every effort has been made to trace rights holders, but if any have been inadvertently overlooked the publishers would be pleased to make the necessary arrangements.

Finally, the editors are grateful to Michael Strang, History Editor, and to Ruth Ireland, History Editorial Assistant, at Palgrave Macmillan for taking this book project on, and for starting an exciting collaboration between Palgrave Macmillan and ourselves as editors of the new book series The Holocaust and its Contexts.

Olaf Jensen and Claus-Christian W. Szejnmann
Leicester, August 2008

Notes on the Contributors

Andrej Angrick is a historian at the Foundation for Science and Culture (Stiftung zur Förderung von Wissenschaft und Kultur) in Hamburg. His publications include: with Peter Klein, *Die 'Endlösung in Riga'. Ausbeutung und Vernichtung 1941–1944* (Darmstadt, 2006); *Besatzungspolitik und Massenmord. Die Einsatzgruppe D in der südlichen Sowjetunion 1941–1943* (Hamburg, 2003); and he is co-editor of *Der Dienstkalender Heinrich Himmlers 1941/42* (Hamburg, 1999).

Donald Bloxham is Professor of Modern History at the University of Edinburgh and winner of a 2006 Philip Leverhulme Prize. He is author of *The Great Game of Genocide: Imperialism, Nationalism, and the Destruction of the Ottoman Armenians* (Oxford, 2005); *Genocide on Trial: War Crimes Trials and the Formation of Holocaust History and Memory* (Oxford, 2001); and, with Tony Kushner, *The Holocaust: Critical Historical Approaches* (Manchester, 2005). He is co-editor of the forthcoming Oxford University Press monograph series *Zones of Violence*.

Gerd Hankel is a philologist and lawyer and since 1998 research staff member at the Hamburg Institute of Social Research. From 2000 to the end of 2001 he was a member of the research team curating the exhibition 'Crimes of the German Wehrmacht: Dimensions of a War of Annihilation 1941–1944'. His current research focuses on the legal aspects of the genocide and the reconciliation process in Rwanda. His most recent publications include: *Die UNO. Idee und Wirklichkeit* (Hamburg, 2006); 'Justice in Transition: the Case of Rwanda', in Gerhard Werle (ed.), *Justice in Transition: Prosecution and Amnesty in Germany and South Africa* (Berlin, 2006), 175–83; 'Verleugnung oder Auseinandersetzung? Zum Umgang mit Völkermord und staatlichen Gewaltverbrechen', in Verena Radkau et al. (eds), *Genozide und staatliche Gewaltverbrechen im 20. Jahrhundert* (Vienna, 2004), 40–52; *Die Leipziger Prozesse. Deutsche Kriegsverbrechen und ihre strafrechtliche Verfolgung nach dem Ersten Weltkrieg* (Hamburg, 2003). With Gerhard Stuby he has also co-edited *Strafgerichte gegen Menschheitsverbrechen. Zum Völkerstrafrecht 50 Jahre nach den Nürnberger Prozessen* (Hamburg, 1995).

Irmtraud Heike is a historian in Hanover, Germany. Her work focuses on female guards in concentration camps and on female forced labour. She is currently working on the topic of 'Zwangsarbeiter in Hannover' (Forced Labourers in Hanover) in connection with the research project 'Hannoversche Lager' (Camps in Hanover), Stadtwerke Hannover AG. Her publications include: with Janet Anschütz et al. (eds), *Gräber ohne Namen. Die toten Kinder Hannoverscher Zwangsarbeiterinnen* (Hannover, 2006); 'Ehemalige KZ-Aufseherinnen in westdeutschen Strafverfahren', *Beiträge zur Geschichte der nationalsozialistischen Verfolgung in Norddeutschland*, 9 (2005), 89–102; with Janet Anschütz, *'Wir wollten Gefühle sichtbar werden lassen'. Bürger gestalten ein Mahnmal für das KZ Ahlem* (Bremen, 2004); with Janet Anschütz, *'Man hörte auf, ein Mensch zu sein'. Überlebende aus den Frauenkonzentrationslagern in Langenhagen und Limmer berichten* (Hamburg, 2003); 'Johanna Langefeld – Die Biografie einer KZ-Oberaufseherin', *WerkstattGeschichte*, 12 (1995), 7–21.

Christina Herkommer is a Research Assistant and Lecturer in the Department of Sociology at the Free University, Berlin. She is working on a dissertation about 'The Public Perception of Women's Roles in National Socialism 1945–2005'. She studied Sociology, Psychology and History at the Universities of Marburg, Bath and Berlin and worked as a Research Assistant at the Centre for Research on Anti-Semitism at the Technische Universität Berlin. Her publications include: *Frauen im Nationalsozialismus – Opfer oder Täterinnen. Eine Kontroverse der Frauenforschung im Spiegel feministischer Theoriebildung und der allgemeinen historischen Aufarbeitung der NS-Vergangenheit* (Munich, 2005); 'Der Diskurs zur Rolle von Frauen im Nationalsozialismus im Spiegel feministischer Theoriebildung', in Christine Künzel and Gaby Temme (eds), *Täterinnen und/oder Opfer? Frauen in Gewaltstrukturen* (Münster, 2007) (forthcoming); 'Rettung im Bordell', in Wolfgang Benz (ed.), *Überleben im Dritten Reich. Juden im Untergrund und ihre Helfer* (Munich, 2003), 143–52.

Olaf Jensen is a Lecturer in Holocaust Studies at the School for Historical Studies, University of Leicester, and Director of the Stanley Burton Centre for Holocaust Studies. From 2001 to 2005 he was Research Fellow at the Centre for Interdisciplinary Memory Research at the Institute for Advanced Studies in the Humanities in Essen, and worked on different interdisciplinary research projects on autobiographical memory and historical consciousness. His research has focused on National Socialism and the Holocaust, particularly on the impact of memory on contemporary German society, and on how the past is transmitted from one generation to the next. Recent publications include: *Geschichte* *machen. Strukturmerkmale des intergenerationellen Sprechens über die NS-Vergangenheit in deutschen Familien* (Tübingen, 2004); and '"One goes left to the Russians, the other goes right to the Americans" – Family Recollections of the Holocaust in Europe', in Martin L. Davies and Claus-Christian W. Szejnmann (eds), *How the Holocaust Looks Now: International Perspectives* (Basingstoke, 2007), 19–29. He is currently editing *History and Memory after the Holocaust in Germany, Poland, Russia, and Britain* (Basingstoke, 2009) for the Holocaust and its Contexts series.

Thomas Kühne is Professor of History and Strassler Family Chair in the Study of Holocaust History at Clark University, Worcester, Massachusetts. His book *Dreiklassenwahlrecht und Wahlkultur in Preussen 1867–1914* (Düsseldorf, 1994) won the German Bundestag Prize. Since changing his focus to twentieth-century gender, military and Holocaust history, his recent work deals with the mythical ideal of comradeship among German soldiers: *Kameradschaft. Die Soldaten des nationalsozialistischen Krieges und das 20. Jahrhundert* (Göttingen, 2006). His five edited books include *Männergeschichte – Geschlechtergeschichte* (Frankfurt/Main and New York, 1996) and, with Benjamin Ziemann, *Was ist Militärgeschichte?* (Paderborn, 2000). He has been a Member at the Institute for Advanced Studies in Princeton and has served as chair of the German Historical Peace Research Society.

Claus-Christian W. Szejnmann is Professor of Modern History at Loughborough University, and led the Stanley Burton Centre for Holocaust Studies between 2004 and 2007. His research interests lie in Nazism, the Holocaust, the GDR, unified Germany, identities in Germany, regionalism, biography, fascism and the extreme right. His major publications are *Vom Traum zum Alptraum. Sachsen während der Weimarer Republik* (Leipzig, 2000); *Nazism in Central Germany: the Brownshirts in 'Red' Saxony* (Oxford, 1999), and (co-edited with M. L. Davies), *How the Holocaust Looks Now: International Perspectives* (Basingstoke, 2006). He is currently writing *Contesting the Rise of the Nazis* (Oxford, 2009); *Nazism in Germany: a Comparative Regional History* (Berghahn Books, 2011); and editing *Rethinking History, Dictatorships and War*.

James E. Waller is Edward B. Lindaman Chair and Professor of Psychology at Whitworth University (Spokane, WA). He has published thirty-five articles in peer-reviewed professional journals and contributed ten chapters in edited books. In addition, he is the author of *Becoming Evil: How Ordinary People Commit Genocide and Mass Killing* (New York, 2002; 2nd edition 2007); *Prejudice Across America* (Jackson, MS, 2000); and *Face* *to Face: the Changing State of Racism Across America* (New York, 1998). For twenty years, he has taught courses on intergroup relations, prejudice, and genocide studies.

Harald Welzer is Head of the Center for Interdisciplinary Memory Research at Essen and Research Professor of Social Psychology at the University of Witten/Herdecke. His research focuses on memory and remembrance, violence, and research methodology. His most important recent publications are *'Opa war kein Nazi!' Nationalsozialismus und Holocaust im Familiengedächtnis* (with K. Tschuggnall and S. Moller) (Frankfurt/Main, 2002); *Das Kommunikative Gedächtnis. Eine Theorie der Erinnerung* (Munich, 2005); *Täter. Wie aus ganz normalen Menschen Massenmörder werden* (Frankfurt/Main, 2005); and *Klimakriege. Wofür im 21. Jahrhundert getötet wird* (Frankfurt/Main, 2008). His books and articles have been translated into English, French, Dutch, Hebrew, Hungarian and Chinese.

Glossary

Außenkommandos	External commandos
CUP	Committee of Union and Progress (ruling faction in the Ottoman government)
Einsatzgruppen	Special killing units
Ek	Einsatzkommando (task commandos of Einsatzgruppen)
EP	Evolutionary psychology
Erstaufseherin	Head Guard
EUM	Directorate for General Security (Ottoman Empire)
Frauenschaft (NSF)	National Socialist Women's League
Freikorps	Free Corps
Gestapo	Geheime Staatspolizei (Secret State Police)
Gruppenführer	Platoon leader/group leader
HSSPF	Higher SS and Police Leaders
IAMM	Directorate for the Settlement of Tribes and Immigrants (Ottoman Empire)
NCO	Non-commissioned officer
NKWD	Narodnyj Komissariat Wnutrennych Del (People's Commissariat of Internal Affairs, USSR)
Nazi	National Socialist (Nationalsozialist)
NSDAP	National Socialist German Workers' Party (Nationalsozialistische Deutsche Arbeiterpartei)
Oberaufseherin	Senior Guard
Operation Barbarossa	Codename for German attack on the USSR in 1941
Reichsarbeitsdienst	National Labour Service
Reichsbanner	Republican defence force (trans.: Imperial Banner)
Reichsführer	Reich Leader
Reichswehr	German armed forces between 1921 and 1934
RSHA	Reichssicherheitshauptamt (Reich Security Head Office)

Schutzhaftlagerführer	Protective Custody Camp Leader
SD	Sicherheitsdienst (Security Service)
Sipo	Sicherheitspolizei (Security Police)
Sk	Sonderkommando (special commandos of Einsatzgruppen)
SS	Schutzstaffel (Protection Squads)
SS-Sippengemeinschaft	SS-kinship community
Stasi	Staatssicherheitsdienst der DDR (Security police of the German Democratic Republic)
SS-WVHA	SS Wirtschafts-Verwaltungshauptamt (SS Economic-Administrative Main Office)
Unterführer	Sub-leader
USSR	Union of Soviet Socialist Republics
Vergemeinschaftung	National Socialist collectivisation
Vernichtungskrieg	War of extermination/annihilation
Volk/völkisch	People/racial-nationalist movement of the Nazis
Volksgemeinschaft	People's community
Volksgenosse	Member of the 'racial' community
Waffen-SS	Armed SS
Wehrmacht	German armed forces between 1935 and 1945

Introductory Thoughts and Overview

Olaf Jensen

Abu Ghraib and the shock response to 'sadistic' perpetrators

When it comes to reports of violence, torture, murder, mass murder and genocide, the public is always shocked. In most cases the immediate reaction is to claim the perpetrators were 'insane' or 'abnormal', in short: not 'like us'. The scandal provoked by the treatment of prisoners in Abu Ghraib in Iraq by US soldiers in 2003 revealed this again;[1] later, similar incidents involving British soldiers were discovered.[2] Particularly scandalous were the sheer number of digital pictures and videos the US soldiers took of their 'activities' inside the prison: 1,325 images and 93 video files of suspected detainee abuse, and 546 images of suspected dead Iraqi detainees.[3] In the end only a few soldiers were sentenced – most prominent among them Private Lynndie England, Specialist Charles A. Graner, and Staff Sergeant Ivan L. Frederick II.

Drawing on a secret military report, Seymour Hersh showed in *The New Yorker* that the abuse and torture in Abu Ghraib were part of the 'loosen up' technique of Military Intelligence (MI) to get 'information' from prisoners. Accordingly the defence strategy of the lawyers of the soldiers was to claim that they only carried out the orders of their superiors.[4] The extent of the scandal in Abu Ghraib became even clearer after it was discovered that medical doctors were also involved in the torture by covering up torture-related killings.[5] The psychologist Robert Jay Lifton, famous for his work on the Nazi doctors, commented: 'They made choices. No doctor would have been physically abused or put to death if he or she tried to interrupt that torture. It would have taken courage, but it was a choice they had.'[6]

However, according to the reports, there was one person with courage in Abu Ghraib: Specialist Joseph M. Darby received from Charles Graner a CD with many pictures and videos of the torture and soon after slipped an anonymous letter underneath the door of the Criminal Investigation Division (CID). Later he gave a sworn statement and the investigation started.[7] 'What Would You Do?' asked Anne Applebaum in the *Washington Post* two days after Hersh's report, pointing out that simple explanations would not work because Lynndie England was an average, well-adjusted girl from Virginia who 'joined the army to pay for college', and Darby was the one known for his aggression in his home town. Applebaum concludes that 'no one's behaviour in extreme situations is predictable... Evil is a mystery. So is heroism.'[8]

But why is 'evil' a mystery? Why are we surprised again and again that soldiers are doing such things? Why does the public expect from soldiers the same scheme of values and norms as are set for 'normal' people in a 'normal' – i.e. not-war – societal setting where one is prosecuted for torturing or killing one's neighbour? Couldn't it be possible that soldiers (or people who think they are soldiers, 'freedom fighters', etc.) and their superiors are convinced they are doing what they are doing for a 'greater good'? On British television, for example, advertisements for the British Infantry show soldiers kicking in doors and storming a house without reasoning but with the slogan 'Forward as one!'[9] And one could ask: what houses are these supposed to be? Where? Who is living there and what happens to the people?

In my own research I interviewed a former member of the Waffen-SS who told me that some 'Russians' committed the 'asininity' (*Idiotie*) of surrendering to his tank-unit after a battle. 'Of course', he said, 'they didn't live a minute longer. You know, we couldn't carry them on our tanks and maybe one of them could have kept a hand grenade or something.'[10] What makes it so difficult for us to face the fact that people who are not that different from us and who are more or less 'normal' are able to commit crimes like torture, murder and genocide?[11]

Of course we could immediately question the concept of 'normality' here, claiming that what we consider 'normal' in modern societies is already pathological, or that the boundaries between individuals being 'normal' and being 'pathological' are blurred given the amount of 'undetected' neurosis or even psychosis we could probably find in most societies. For our context and the essays in this volume one could say that the label 'normal' or 'average' is meant to relate to people who were not noticeably transgressing the norms and legal limitations of violence before (and after) the violent incident occurred. How is it possible, after everything the world went through especially in the twentieth century and given all the knowledge about perpetrators that we have, that we still think human beings are first and foremost 'good'? Rick Hampson wrote in May 2004 that 'One of the most surprising things about the abuse of Iraqi prisoners is that so many Americans are surprised' after 'decades of research and eons of history' make it very clear that 'Under certain circumstances, most normal people will treat their fellow man with abnormal cruelty.'[12]

The social psychologist Philipp Zimbardo, famous for his Stanford Prison Experiment in 1971,[13] was immediately drawn into the centre of attention because of the parallels with his experiment with students as guards and prisoners in the mock prison in the basement of the psychology department at Stanford University. From the very beginning of the scandal Zimbardo refused to describe the perpetrators as 'rogue soldiers' or as the 'few bad apples' in the US army as the US government had. He claimed instead that it was the 'bad barrel' that corrupted 'good apples' and analysed in detail the situation and living conditions in Abu Ghraib and the people involved.[14]

After having interviewed and studied Staff Sergeant Ivan 'Chip' Frederick, Zimbardo came to the conclusion that there is absolutely nothing 'dispositional' to find in his record that would explain Frederick's participation in the torture in Abu Ghraib. He (and some peer reviewers) could not find any hints towards a pathology he could have brought into the situation in the cell block Tier 1A.[15] Zimbardo is convinced that situational factors are most important: the lack of training for the work in a prison, the unbearable and dangerous conditions in Abu Ghraib and the chaotic structure of command – and sometimes the total absence of it, to name just a few. The feedback Sergeant Frederick received when complaining about the situation in his block and the dehumanisation of the prisoners was: 'This is the way military intelligence wants it done', and Zimbardo gives evidence that the photos were also ordered and taken as material for future interrogations to scare prisoners. These are all reasons why he argues for attributing responsibility to the top of the chain of command instead of only sentencing the lower ranks.[16] However, is it not too easy just to blame the situational factors or the superiors?

The 'rush to the dispositional'

In a volume on the *Social Psychology of Good and Evil* edited by Arthur Miller, Zimbardo calls the tendency to link evil behaviour to pathological origins a 'rush to the dispositional'.[17] It is no wonder, he says, that public opinion tends to overemphasise dispositional factors when from the time of the witch hunts of the Inquisition societies have attributed 'evil' to individuals, focusing on people who were different from the majority and marginalised from the society. Later on, traditional psychology also singled out dispositional factors – 'defective genes, "bad seeds," or premorbid personality structures' – as the sources of violence. Based on his research of the last thirty years, Zimbardo is convinced that 'this view overlooks the fact that the same violent outcomes can be generated by very different types of people, all of whom give no hint of evil impulses.'[18]

Zimbardo is very explicit in his view that a dispositional concept of violence serves first and foremost to let society and its political leaders 'off the hook' of responsibility where the factors 'that create racism, sexism, elitism, poverty, and marginal existence for some citizens' are concerned. It also implies a strict dichotomy between 'good' people and 'evil' people and the 'illusion that such a line constrains crossovers in either directions'. This also means a lack of willingness to analyse and understand the process that leads people to behaviour that is defined as evil.[19] As we know, the human mind can adapt to almost every environment 'in order to survive, to create, and to destroy, as necessary', because we are 'not born with tendencies toward good or evil but with mental templates to do *either*'.[20]

In Nuremberg in 1946 the 'rush to the dispositional' was visible in the treatment of the main war criminals on trial. As James Waller describes in his book *Becoming Evil*:

> The only lesson the world wanted to learn was simple: keep insane people out of high office and the atrocities of Nazi Germany will never happen again. In fact, for most of the mental health professionals assigned to Nuremberg, the question was not *if* they would find psychopathology among the defendants, but simply *how much* psychological disturbance they would find. The notion that any of the defendants would test as seemingly normal and ordinary people was simply not considered.[21]

However, the psychological tests and analysis of the internees were quite disappointing from the perspective of the prosecutors because against all assumptions it mainly showed that these remaining Nazi leaders were not mentally disordered from a medical point of view.[22]

Ordinary men

It is astonishing that even after Raul Hilberg's groundbreaking study in 1961 of the destruction process of the Holocaust, its organisation, and its institutional and personnel structures the myth of the pathological killers continued. Like every military structure the Nazis avoided recruiting dysfunctional and, therefore, unreliable and undisciplined people. The Nazis were very aware of the psychological damage the 'Final Solution' could have on their men, and 'commanders in the field were ever watchful for symptoms of psychological disintegration' because they realised the danger of producing masses of 'neurotics and savages'. Because 'excesses' attracted unwanted attention, 'the personnel of the machinery of destruction were not supposed to look to the right or to the left; they were not allowed to have either personal motives or personal gains.' That a very particular genocidal morality was involved is illustrated by the notorious Posen speech by Heinrich Himmler on 4 October 1943. There he claims that those involved in the mass killings 'remained decent' (*anständig*) thereby revealing the self-righteousness of the perpetrators of the Holocaust. Hilberg also shows that orders were disobeyed and that individuals could refuse to take part in an *Einsatzkommando* or prohibit a killing operation without being seriously punished.[23]

Important impulses of research into violence have been Hannah Arendt's political philosophy in the 1960s, Stanley Milgram's and Philip Zimbardo's research in the 1970s, and the important book by Christopher Browning on the 'ordinary men' of the Police Battalion 101 and the 'Final Solution' in Poland in 1992.[24] Browning's book has had a huge impact on research into perpetrators and is also a main focus of this volume (the chapters by Szejnmann, Kühne, Angrick, Herkommer and Hankel all refer to it). Browning not only showed additional evidence that some perpetrators were officially given the choice of not taking part in mass shootings of Jews in the East without punishment, but also adapted results of social psychological experiments by Zimbardo and Milgram to his analysis of primary sources on the 101 Police Battalion. Browning writes:

> Zimbardo's spectrum of guard behaviour [in the Stanford Prison Experiment] bears an uncanny resemblance to the grouping that emerged within Reserve Police Battalion 101: a nucleus of increasingly enthusiastic killers who volunteered for the firing squads and 'Jew hunts'; a larger group of policemen who performed as shooters

and ghetto clearers when assigned but who did not seek opportunities to kill (and in some cases refrain from killing, contrary to standing orders, when no one was monitoring their actions); and a small group (less than 20 percent) of refusers and evaders.[25]

Browning is of course aware of the limitations and problems of comparing psychological research from the laboratory with Holocaust situations. Nevertheless, he concludes that the results of Milgram's experiments on obedience to authority also 'find graphic confirmation in the behaviour and testimony of the men of Reserve Battalion 101'.[26] In these well-known experiments more than a thousand people were asked to take part in a short research project on 'memory and learning'. The typical subjects were male clerks, teachers, engineers, salesmen or labourers.[27] The experiment can roughly be described as 'learning through punishment'. The volunteering 'naïve subject' had to conduct a 'learning task' with the staged victim – the 'learner' – under the guidance and surveillance of the 'experimenter'. The victim was strapped to a chair, usually in another room, audible, and sometimes also visible through a window. The subject as a 'teacher' had to read lists of word pairs to the 'learner' which the latter had to memorise. In the testing sequence the 'teacher' read one word of the original list combined with four terms and the 'learner' had to remember which of the new words was paired with the first word of the original list (e.g. blue box). For every mistake of the 'learner' the subject was supposed to give him an electric shock until he had learned and repeated the combinations properly. The shock was delivered through a 'Shock Generator' to the learner's wrist from a 'Slight Shock' of 15 Volts for the first wrong answer to 'Danger: Severe Shock' of 450 Volts in 15 Volt steps; two additional switches 'after this last designation were simply marked XXX'. The 'learner' didn't of course receive any electric shocks: he just had to act as though he had, following a fixed procedure. The experimenter on the other hand had a fixed set of four answers in case the 'teacher' protested against the treatment of the 'learner', starting with: 'Please continue' or 'Please go on' at the first stage to 'You have no other choice, you must go on' at the last.[28]

Usually around forty subjects were tested in each setting to find out when they would stop obeying the orders of the experimenter. Milgram concludes, that 'despite the fact that many subjects experience stress, despite the fact that many protest to the experimenter, a substantial proportion continue to the last shock on the generator' which would have meant death, and 'that almost two-thirds of the participants fall into the category of "obedient" subjects', representing 'ordinary people'. They did so out of the 'sense of obligation [...] and not from any peculiarly aggressive tendencies [...] Ordinary people, simply doing their jobs, and without any particular hostility on their part, can become agents in a terrible destructive process.' Even if the purpose of their 'work' is against 'fundamental standards of morality, relatively few people have the resources needed to resist authority', and 'inhibitions against disobeying authority' are keeping the person 'in his place'.[29]

These experiments were criticised – like many others of this kind – for being conducted in a laboratory and, therefore, hardly comparable to the completely different setting and environment in which the Nazi crimes occurred, for their relatively small sample of subjects, or for the short amount of time the subjects were held in the setting.[30] Milgram also altered the setting a few times to find more evidence about what factors influence the obedience to, or disobedience of authority in the subjects, for example moving the victim into the same room as the 'teacher', leaving him with a free choice of shock level, acting as a bystander while two staged persons are conducting the experiment, or, especially interesting in our context: group effects. In the group-setting staged peers assisted with the lists but were protesting and leaving the setting at certain points – and almost all subjects as well: 36 of 40 compared to 14 out of 40 without this kind of positive group pressure.[31]

One of Milgram's main concerns was to challenge surveys conducted before, e.g. with psychiatrists, which would not have predicted that 'normal people' would ever go past the 150 Volts level.[32] In addition he was concerned about the fact that many people would have associated this kind of behaviour only with dictatorships like Nazi Germany but not with democracies like the USA. Having the war in Vietnam in mind, he was shocked that many of his students who were appalled by the behaviour of the subjects in the experiment and who claimed they would behave differently in such situations, 'in a matter of months, were brought into the military and performed without compunction actions that made shocking the victim seem pallid'.[33]

The 'behavioural freedom' of individuals is, following Zimbardo, dependent on their genetic, biological, physical and psychological make-up. The situation, however, created by 'agents and agencies' and their ideology, specific values and power, is the 'behavioral context that has the power, through its reward and normative functions, to give meaning and identity to the actor's roles and status'.[34] But the question remains: what is it in the end that makes people press the button for 450 Volts or higher, beating up a helpless prisoner until he dies, or pulling the trigger of a gun?

Self-control vs. problem solving

The social psychologists Baumeister and Vohs suggest that there is no easy answer why people are violent, mostly because of the difficult element that 'very few people perform what they themselves regard as evil actions'.[35] But they come up with a list of four main reasons as to why people do so.

First, there is 'instrumentality' or violence and evildoing as 'means to an end' – to get something (power, money, land or resources, etc.) or to influence someone else in a competitive situation where violence is one of the options for resolving the conflict. Baumeister and Vohs argue that this is usually only successful in the short run; in the long run, 'evil or violent means fail to produce the desired results'[36] – we will come back to this later.

Second, the reasons for attack could be 'threatened egotism', where the 'image of self' is threatened, or there is 'wounded pride' or honour. Research has shown that people with low self-esteem do not have the highest levels of aggression unlike those who 'scored high in narcissism and who had been insulted by their opponents'. This applies to groups of perpetrators like the Nazis defining themselves as 'the master race', or the Ku Klux Klan with their idea of 'racial supremacy'.[37]

Third is 'idealism' and 'doing good by doing bad'. This includes people or groups 'who are motivated by high-minded ideals' and who 'regard violence as a necessary means, often a distasteful and regrettable one, to accomplish something good and positive', sometimes even regarding it as their 'moral duty to perpetrate their violent acts'. Most revolutions, state-committed crimes, genocides and terrorist acts are in this category: the French Revolution, Stalinist USSR and Maoist China, Nazi Germany, the Khmer Rouge in Cambodia, or the Taliban and the radical Islamists of 11 September 2001.[38]

Finally 'sadism: the joy of hurting' is listed here as 'the most common account in victims' testimonies and fictional depictions but the least common in everyday life'. Often perpetrators are perceived as 'sadists' from the outside but in most cases perpetrators do not initially enjoy inflicting 'harm or pain on others'. Moreover, drawing on the example of the mass shootings of Jews in Poland committed by the Police Battalion 101 described in Christopher Browning's *Ordinary Men*, Baumeister and Vohs argue that perpetrators usually have to go through a long and painful process before they can overcome their inhibitions to kill and 'perform' in an efficient way.[39]

As the 'proximal cause' immediately before the violent act, Baumeister and Vohs identify a 'breakdown of self-control' as the 'final link in the chain of violence'. Self-control, they argue, is the only factor that can explain why there is 'not more evil than there is': 'Most people have a set of inner restraints, scruples, and inhibitions that prevent them from acting on every impulse they might feel.'[40]

Duntley and Buss in the same volume strongly disagree with the argument that violence is 'not an effective way to get what one wants', and that a failure of self-control is the key factor when it comes to violence and aggression. They argue on the basis of evolutionary psychology (EP) (see Waller in this volume), which may be roughly described as a specific approach to psychology that draws on evolutionary biology and tries to explain the brain, the mind and human behaviour in relation to their development over thousands of years. The key concepts in this approach are 'selection' and 'adaptation'. 'Our neural circuits were designed by natural selection to solve problems that our ancestors faced during our species' evolutionary history' write Leda Cosmides and John Tooby from the Centre for Evolutionary Psychology. These *adaptive* problems usually 'cropped up again and again during the evolutionary history' and their solution 'affected the *reproduction* of individual organisms'. The main adaptive problems are therefore linked to an organism's reproduction: 'what it eats, what eats it, who it mates with, who it socializes with, how it communicates, and so on'. Cosmides and Tooby conclude that 'the *only* kind of problems that natural selection can design circuits for solving are adaptive problems'.[41]

Duntley and Buss are also convinced that human psychology is 'the end product of a competitive evolutionary process' and they argue that it is possible that natural selection can treat a problem-solving strategy like 'homicide' as 'beneficial' even if it is not effective in '*every instance*' but outweighs the costs 'on average' and 'across the entire sample space of instances on which it is deployed'. This means the strategy could sometimes also be unsuccessful, i.e. the killer could be killed. But still, if the 'fitness benefits outweigh the net fitness costs of these adaptations for evil, relative to competing designs, then selection will favor their evolution, eventually making them fundamental components of human nature'.[42]

In addition, actions that appear 'impulsive' and out of control are actually developed and designed to solve certain problems in specific situations with impulsive *behaviour*. Sometimes immediate action is required and spending time by calculating the risks of an action could result in failure. That means, simply speaking, what we see is not what we get, 'impulsivity' is more a 'design feature of certain adaptations that promotes their tactical effectiveness... Speedy, immediate, real-time responses can be the product of adaptive design rather than "mechanism failure".'[43]

Humans inflict harm on other human beings because the competitive evolutionary process usually only has two options: to acquire benefits for their own fitness, or to 'inflict costs' on their competitors, for example by cutting off their access to resources. The more these cost-inflicting activities grow, the more 'evil' they get – stealing resources from rivals, damaging their reputation, stealing their mates, harming them physically, or even killing them.[44] Killing the rival has great risks as well – the perpetrators could be injured or killed themselves; relatives or group members of the victims may launch a campaign for revenge; society could demand retribution; or the 'reputation of the perpetrator' could be harmed, affecting potential resources of all kinds, etc. – risks that most perpetrators of recent genocides were well aware of. Duntley and Buss conclude that killing might not be 'always, or even often, beneficial to the fitness of the killer. Rather, *killing historically has been potentially beneficial in the currency of reproductive fitness under some delimited circumstances*',[45] i.e. when the benefits were higher than the risk. The study of the Second World War and the Holocaust has shown that Hitler and most Germans were fully aware of the fact that they were gambling with their total destruction because of their actions.

Nevertheless Duntley and Buss clearly state that all this does not mean that individuals are not responsible for their actions: 'humans are not lumbering robots insensitive to context'. The more we know about the evolved psychological processes, contexts and situations that trigger this specific behaviour, the better are our chances of effecting changes. Moreover, 'holding people responsible is one of the critical forms of environmental input that can be used to deter people from committing deeds we consider to be "evil" '.[46]

Lack of restraint and absence of empathy

In her recent book *Menschen Töten* (Killing People) Dorothee Frank not only asks why humans do kill but, unlike most other studies, she has actually interviewed a number of perpetrators, among them hangmen, soldiers, a mercenary, a war criminal from the war in Yugoslavia, an IRA member and a Muslim terrorist. She also argues against the common impression that there is a natural and unstoppable biological driving force that makes human beings kill each other.[47] As regards the actual killing, many factors have to be fulfilled. The de-individuation process for soldiers happens, for example, as part of their training to follow orders unquestioningly, even in the highest state of stress and exhaustion, and to hand responsibility over to the superiors. In addition the military authorities take the usual killing restraint ('you shall not kill') partially out of order – not everybody, but the defined 'enemy' is allowed to be killed. However, even with the killing restraint suspended and the responsibility passed on, the individual or the group still needs *reasons* for their actions that 'make sense' of what they are doing – like the reasons we have discussed before as well as reasons stemming from the dynamic of the group: camaraderie and conformity include the extreme situation of facing death, while relying on the group makes the members prepared to die for each other (see Kühne in this volume). This is usually supported by the small units (e.g. *Züge* or platoons) that soldiers are organised into. This increases group pressure, binds it together, and serves as justification for the killing action.[48]

Genocides and even massacres are usually planned and guided operations (see Bloxham in this volume). The elements used by leaders to start a genocidal and mass murder process usually follow a similar pattern. Hidden or available elements of hostility against the 'other' are centrally organised by a militarily structured task force, using professional propaganda over a long time-span to spread the ideology and to let everyone know what they should be afraid of. This includes all kinds of strategies, planning and administration, and Frank emphasises that death-lists of potential victims existed not only in the Holocaust but also in the Balkan war and in Rwanda.

She also argues that there are of course differences between genocides – like different motivations and constellations or the 'industrialised' killing in the death camps of the Holocaust and the level of bureaucracy involved. However, when it comes to the 'final excess of violence' they are usually quite similar. No matter how the killing is carried out the victims are always dehumanised or reified (*verdinglicht*), with 'rituals of humiliation through sadistic acts of violence in combination with verbal abuse accompanying the mass killing'.[49] The step from the thought, 'we don't like you, we would rather kill you', to the actual torture and killing is what is so difficult to understand.

The common first step is that the 'we' group is convinced that the 'other' side is going to launch an attack on their lives and safety. This usually works very well because of the fear that survival is in danger (*Überlebensangst*). This is evident in the repeated argumentation of 'just having defended the lives of their own' – as maintained in Nazi Germany, Kosovo and Rwanda. Step two is that one could get many resources for free – houses, furniture, cars, valuables, etc. – and the former friendly relationship towards one's neighbours quickly falls apart.[50] Step three: the 'we' group gets the signal that the 'others' have lost all their rights because of their behaviour and that they are allowed to do to them whatever they like – the establishment of a new 'genocidal' moral (see Welzer in this volume). Moral standards are not diminished overnight but they only relate to the 'in' group not to the 'out' group. Furthermore, the 'in' group's moral responsibilities are tightening because its members are expected to take part in the 'new' structure and to be in solidarity with the majority in hating the enemy. As we have seen this can also impose a huge 'sacrifice' for the new *Volksgemeinschaft* in taking part in the 'dirty job' of killing the defined enemy. The changeability of moral codes is visible in the example of torture and takes us back to the beginning of this introduction: these days, for many people torture is again acceptable for fighting terrorism in the 'war against terror'.[51]

Frank concludes by drawing on recent research on perpetrators and on her own findings that for mass killing to happen, the essential condition is that the killing constraint not only has to be officially abandoned, at least temporarily, but completely reversed. Killing becomes 'compulsory', and taking part in the genocidal process is now useful for one's career and one's social prestige.[52] The whole process from defining and dehumanising the victims to abandoning the killing constraint leads to the absence of empathy[53] – and many people who a short time before probably wouldn't have thought they could take part in something like that are now part of a genocidal process and most of them are convinced that they are doing the 'right thing', of creating something 'good', and without feeling guilty about it as numerous examples in this volume show. By quoting the former Protestant terrorist in Northern Ireland, Alastair Little, Frank reminds us that 'human beings can be victims in one situation, perpetrators in another and again victims. These positions are linked and are able to merge into one another.'[54]

Chapter overview

We believe that the structure and contents of this volume on perpetrators in comparative perspective are unique and innovative. Of course there are many other books and edited volumes on the Holocaust or genocides in general.[55] However, our impression is that they are still very much divided into separate fields and professions, whereas an interdisciplinary approach is needed. Following the approach in Hilberg's and Browning's work, this volume tries to focus on the acting individual and less on the overall structure of genocides or the desk murderers.

Part I gives an introductory overview of the research on perpetrators of the Holocaust since 1945 (Szejnmann), and two case studies (Kühne, Angrick) of different groups of male perpetrators of the Holocaust (the *Wehrmacht* and *Einsatzgruppe D*). Part II focuses on 'Female Perpetrators of the Holocaust' with an overview of the role and status of women in the 'Third Reich' (Herkommer) and a detailed study on three female concentration camp guards (Heike). Part III explores psychological and sociological approaches to the study of perpetrators in the Holocaust and other genocides (Waller, Welzer). Part IV focuses on the organisation of genocides, comparing the Armenian genocide and the Holocaust (Bloxham), followed by an analysis of the judicial consequences for perpetrators and their arguments of self-justification (Hankel).

Part I: Perpetrators of the Holocaust

Part I begins with a historiographical essay on 'Perpetrators of the Holocaust' by Claus-Christian Szejnmann. He shows the difficult process after 1945 of getting to grips with the scale of the atrocities committed under Nazism and the question of who was responsible for them. His discussion of the post-war period highlights aspects of suppression and denial, and the emergence of the stigma of pathological killers. He then explores the switch from the paradigm of 'mechanised' crime towards the analysis of 'ordinary people' and their motivations as perpetrators, accomplices or bystanders from the 1980s. Szejnmann sheds light on how a number of key events (especially the Nuremberg Trials, the Eichmann trial and the end of the Cold War), key works on perpetrators (e.g. the work by Kogon, Arendt, Hilberg, Browning, Goldhagen and Aly), and aspects such as generational change and new research methodologies have all shaped debates and interpretations in the field. His overview ends with the analysis of the so-called Perpetrator Studies from the 1990s. In his conclusion Szejnmann takes stock of our knowledge today, sheds light on continuing shortcomings in the field and suggests ways of overcoming them.

In Chapter 2, 'Male Bonding and Shame Culture', Thomas Kühne focuses on the German *Wehrmacht* and its involvement in war and the Holocaust and aims to answer the question of why the German soldiers were part of the war of annihilation and why they held out for so long even after their defeat was predictable. Kühne begins by reviewing recent work on the *Wehrmacht*, claiming that the leaders of the *Wehrmacht* were deeply involved in the planning and execution of the wars of annihilation. Even though many atrocities of the *Wehrmacht* were committed in conjunction with the SS *Einsatzgruppen*, the *Wehrmacht* was ideologically not as heterogeneous as the SS, and Kühne investigates the main approaches to the reasons and motivations for killing at that point. He identifies a combination of sociological (comradeship), and ideological (anti-Semitism) elements. Moreover, the National Socialists established a 'symbolic order' that 'combined stereotypes of the enemy with the experience of community' which built the basis for the 'mass involvement in Holocaust and war'. Kühne concludes that it was not group pressure alone that forced soldiers to join in but the development of a specific form of comradeship that made the 'inhuman' aspects of the war not only bearable for the *Wehrmacht* soldiers, but gave them also the 'awareness that they were above civilian morality' as well as above the international laws arising from previous wars.

In Chapter 3, 'The Men of *Einsatzgruppe D*', Andrej Angrick focuses on the 600 men under the command of Otto Ohlendorf, one of the notorious killing units operating in south-eastern Europe. He analyses in detail the establishment, the structure and the 'tasks' of this unit to reveal how this group of people was selected, what importance ideology or socio-cultural influences had, or whether being radicalised and brutalised because of the war or situational factors led them to commit the atrocities. Angrick emphasises that Ohlendorf was one of those 'unconventional intellectuals' in the National Socialist hierarchy, an economic expert and one of the highest profiles in the Reich Security Head Office (RSHA) to become leader of an *Einsatzgruppe*. As an opposite example, *Einsatzkommando* leader Bruno Müller is discussed as well. Angrick shows that the task of the *Einsatzgruppen* was of course 'murdering people' but was not from the beginning set up to execute the 'Final Solution'. For the shootings themselves, it is worth noting that the orders were mostly unclear and open to 'interpretation' and that in some instances the (platoon) leaders shot some victims first to show their rank and file what was expected of them. Related to this, Angrick gives examples of how members of the *Einsatzgruppe* coped with their killing task and of their individual motives.

Part II: Female Perpetrators of the Holocaust

Christina Herkommer's chapter, 'Women under National Socialism' is an overview of the main debates regarding the role of women in the 'Third Reich'. She suggests that it was not until the women's movement in the 1970s that (female) historians began to investigate the role women played in this part of history, and the traditional view that women 'did not count' in historical terms was slowly overcome. Herkommer outlines the dominant positions regarding the standing and involvement of women in the National Socialist system and the Holocaust. For a long time, women were defined as manipulated victims of the Nazi movement, and still seen as the 'better part of humanity'. That women could also be found in the position of perpetrators came into the debate only in the mid-1980s, but still with an emphasis on their more or less passive participation. Only later were women considered as having spent an active part of their career in the National Socialist system, e.g. as nurses or concentration camp guards. Eventually, the homogeneous concept of women under National Socialism – as victims or perpetrators – became a critical issue. It was followed by the recognition that women – like their male companions – could be found in various positions: 'as spectators, fellow-travellers and perpetrators' with their own specific 'scope for action'.

In Chapter 5, 'Female Concentration Camp Guards as Perpetrators', Irmtraud Heike offers three case studies of women as perpetrators. She focuses on guards in the camps of Ravensbrück, Neuengamme and Helmbrechts, and uses evidence and records from court cases to portray in detail the structure of the female units associated with the SS which served in the concentration camps. With the examples of Lotte M. and Ingeborg Aßmuß, but particularly with the case of Johanna Langefeld, Heike describes in great depth how their careers as camp guards unfolded, and what motives lay behind their decision to take on such a job. She shows that these women were not forced or ordered to do what they did but that they used their ambitions, their skills and strength to achieve what they were aiming for. This is particularly visible in the conflict between Johanna Langefeld and the notorious Rudolf Höss, commander of Auschwitz concentration camp. It shows, for example, that Langefeld considered herself as a decent person who had her own pedagogical 'ideas', based on National Socialist ideology, of how to deal with prisoners and how to lead a women's camp. Heike concludes that these 'biographies of female guards again and again reveal that they had extensive scope for action despite the male-oriented hierarchy in concentration camps'.

Part III: Psychological and Sociological Approaches

James Waller in his chapter 'The Ordinariness of Extraordinary Evil' gives an overview of the mass killings of the past century, from the genocide of American Indians to the genocide in Darfur. His diagnosis is that we know a lot about genocides and mass murder but mainly about the higher ranks. So far we haven't really focused on the mindset of the people carrying it out. Arguing from an evolutionary psychological perspective he offers a model explaining the factors involved that make ordinary people commit genocide and mass killing. Waller emphasises that the tendency of the wider public to distinguish between 'us' good people and 'them', the bad perpetrators, satisfies an emotional demand but the reasons for extraordinary evil cannot be found in an extraordinary personality type. The baseline in his explanatory model is the evolution of human nature as the ultimate cause, i.e. why a specific behaviour evolved by natural selection. But, more importantly, there are a number of sub-factors as proximate causes. The proximate causes, Waller explains, are the cultural, psychological and social influences that lead to factors like collectivistic values, authority orientation, the wish for social dominance, us–them thinking, blaming the victim, group identifications, or group binding factors. These proximate causes are sub-categories of constructions that influence individual behaviour: the Cultural Construction of Worldview, the Psychological Construction of the 'Other', and the Social Construction of Cruelty. Waller shows that even though our evolutionary development has caused our capacity for evil this does not mean that there are no choices. Perpetrators are not 'hapless victims of human nature, culture, psychology, or their social context. On the road to committing atrocities, there are many choice points for each perpetrator.'

In Chapter 7, 'On Killing and Morality', Harald Welzer focuses on the question of killing and morality related to the Holocaust. From a multi-disciplinary perspective, combining sociological, psychological and historical approaches, he asks whether the Nazi perpetrators considered their deeds as moral or immoral, and what significance situational factors had on the killing site. He argues that a dichotomy of 'good' and 'bad', moral or immoral might be comforting but that it does not work to explain why ordinary people committ mass murder. With a thorough analysis of members of Police Battalion 45 he shows the development of this unit within the killing process and the impact and importance of situational factors. Drawing on his own research and recent work from Germany, Welzer argues that most of the Nazi perpetrators were fully aware that their genocidal anti-Jewish policy was 'something unpleasant' but was 'considered necessary'. Once the group of potential victims was economically and socially separated from the majority and no longer part of the inner group, the pivotal 'coordinate' had changed towards genocide. Welzer concludes that we have to be aware of the perfidiousness of this process towards inhumanity and that by 'crossing the first threshold', and as each of the following thresholds is crossed, the 'threshold value sinks'. The first step opens the door to a potential, last, formerly unimaginable step and could lead to genocide and mass killing.

Part IV: Perpetrators and Genocide

Donald Bloxham's chapter on 'The Organisation of Genocide' focuses in a comparative and contrasting perspective on the Armenian genocide, which is described in detail, and the Holocaust. He follows the question of how it was possible to incorporate people into genocidal processes who were previously outside the 'circles of ideologues and leaders' and who were not necessarily influenced by the underlying ideology. By giving special attention to the context and the situational factors, he is aware that there is 'always more than one context in play in any given situation' and that no matter what approach we choose to explain perpetration, 'none on its own provides a total, generalisable explanation'.

Bloxham looks at the fact that genocides are usually organised according to a division of labour so that by analysing the 'macro' level of a genocidal process, we also get more insights into the 'micro' level: the 'social, cultural or psychological considerations' on the lower levels. But there are limitations: even though we have discovered general principles of how genocides occur and how they are organised we might only be able to develop a 'taxonomy or typology' and not a precise 'theory of the perpetrator of genocide' – a theme that unifies the essays in this volume.

Gerd Hankel's chapter on 'International Law after the Nuremberg Trials and Rwanda' adds a very important aspect to this volume: how the Holocaust and the intention to deal with the perpetrators influenced international law in relation to other mass killings. Hankel explains how difficult is was after the Holocaust to apply legal principles to determine 'the guilt of individuals' instead of 'collective guilt' for the involved countries, and how survivors and victims struggled with the 'difficult concept' of justice. Moreover he focuses on the justification perpetrators claim when prosecuted with genocide. He shows how difficult it was for survivors of the Holocaust to testify in court, and how easy it was at the same time for perpetrators to claim that they just acted under orders and that not following orders would have meant being killed themselves. Related to this, Hankel elaborates the similarities and differences between the situation of the perpetrators of the Holocaust and that of the perpetrators of the Rwandan genocide. Hankel concludes that justice may not really exist but that it is our duty to 'ascertain as precisely as possible what occurred and to do so with the greatest possible respect for the suffering and the interest of the victims and... to uncover the individual role of the perpetrators without denying their human dignity'.

Notes

1. For example, Amerikas Schande – Folter im Namen der Freiheit' (America's Shame – Torture in the Name of Freedom), *Der Spiegel*, 8, 20 February 2006.
2. 'Vile... but this time it's a British soldier degrading an Iraqi', *Daily Mail*, 1 May 2004; later on the pictures were dismissed as a hoax, details unknown (*Daily Mail*, 15 May 2004) (www.dailymail.co.uk; accessed 23 July 2007); but see also 'Soldiers guilty of "revolting" Iraqi abuse', *Daily Mail*, 23 February 2005: 'Two British soldiers were found guilty today of abusing Iraqi civilian prisoners at an aid camp in Basra' (www.dailymail.co.uk; accessed 23 July 2007). On a different level – pictures with human bones used for photo shoots in Afghanistan – with soldiers of the German Bundeswehr, which is a conscript army, in 2006, cf. 'Bundeswehr-Skandal: Ermittlungen gegen zwei Totenschänder' (Bundeswehr Scandal: Investigations against Two Corps Desecrators in Afghanistan), *Stern*, 25 October 2006 (www.Stern.de; accessed 23 July 2007); 'Schriftzug aus Leichenteilen' (Writing Made of Corpse Pieces), *Süddeutsche Zeitung*, 27 October 2006 (www.sueddeutsche.de; accessed 23 July 2007).
3. 'Abu Ghraib leaked report reveals full extent of abuse', *Guardian*, 17 February 2006 (www.guardian.co.uk; accessed 23 July 2007); see also Susan Sontag, 'Regarding the Torture of Others', *New York Times Magazine*, 23 May 2004 (www.nytimes.com; accessed 23 July 2007).
4. Seymour M. Hersh, 'Torture at Abu Ghraib – American soldiers brutalized Iraqis. How far up does the responsibility go?' *The New Yorker*, 10 May 2004 (www.newyorker.com; accessed 25 July 2007).
5. Ibid.
6. 'Docs Complicit in Prison Abuse?' *CBS News*, 20 August 2004 (www.cbs.com; accessed 23 July 2007); see also Robert J. Lifton, 'Doctors and Torture', 29 July 2004 (www.nejm.org; accessed 23 July 2007); 'Abu Ghraib doctors knew of

torture, says Lancet report', *Guardian*, 20 August 2004 (www.guardian.co.uk; accessed 24 July 2007).
7. Hersh, 'Torture'. It is worth noting that Darby was immediately called in the media 'the whistle blower' – a phrase with in fact quite a negative connotation, which made his parents fear for his safety ('Fears for safety of man who blew the whistle', *Washington Post*, 8 May 2004 (www.washingtonpost.com; accessed 24 July 2007)).
8. Anne Applebaum, 'What Would You Do?' *Washington Post*, 12 May 2004 (www.washingtonpost.com; accessed 24 July 2007).
9. See www.army.mod.uk/infantry/join_the_infantry/infantry_media.htm (accessed 7 August 2007).
10. See Olaf Jensen, *Geschichte machen. Strukturmerkmale des intergenerationellen Sprechens über die NS- Vergangenheit in Deutschen Familien* (Tübingen, 2004), 160ff.
11. For example, Lynndie England, who 'wouldn't even shoot a deer on family hunting trips'; Rick Hampson, 'Abuse less shocking in light of history', *USA Today*, 13 May 2004 (www.usatoday.com; accessed 24 July 2007).
12. Hampson, 'Abuse less shocking'; for a summary see Udo Bauer, 'Opfer des Systems oder willige Vollstrecker?' *Deutsche Welle*, 14 May 2004 (www.dw-world.de; accessed 24 July 2007).
13. Craig Haney, Curtis Banks and Philip Zimbardo, 'Interpersonal Dynamics in a Simulated Prison', *International Journal of Criminology and Penology*, 1 (1973), 69–97.
14. Philip Zimbardo, *The Lucifer Effect: How Good People Turn Evil* (London, 2007), 323ff.
15. Ibid., 344.
16. Ibid., 346–66.
17. Philip G. Zimbardo, 'A Situationist Perspective on the Psychology of Evil', in Arthur Miller (ed.), *The Social Psychology of Good and Evil* (New York, 2005), 21–50, here 24.
18. Ibid.
19. Ibid., 25.
20. Ibid., 26; emphasis in the original. Zimbardo also offers a 'Ten-step Program to Resist Unwanted Influences', and, moreover, is convinced that if bad circumstances can produce or trigger violence in individuals, it should be possible to 'use the power of the situation to produce virtue', and he defines and gives examples of all kinds of 'Heroes' who resisted the pressure of 'evil' circumstances, 451ff.
21. James Waller, *Becoming Evil: How Ordinary People Commit Genocide and Mass Killing* (Oxford, 2002), 58 (emphasis in the original).
22. Probably because this was unexpected, unwanted and difficult to explain, the test results were not fully published and disappeared for some time. Instead the picture of the deviate type of personality was maintained. See Ervin Staub, *The Roots of Evil: the Origins of Genocide and Other Group Violence* (New York, 1989), 67ff.; Waller, *Becoming Evil*, 58ff.; Harald Welzer, *Täter. Wie aus ganz normalen Menschen Massenmörder werden* (Frankfurt/Main, 2005), 7ff.
23. All quotes are from Raul Hilberg, *The Destruction of the European Jews* (New York, 1961), 646ff.; on the question of morality see Welzer in this volume.

24. Wieviorka, *Die Gewalt* (Hamburg, 2006), 135; see Szejnmann in this volume.
25. Christopher Browning, *Ordinary Men: Reserve Police Battalion 101 and the Final Solution in Poland* (orig. New York, 1992; this edn New York 1998), 168.
26. Ibid., 174.
27. Stanley Milgram, *Obedience to Authority: an Experimental View* (London, 1974), 16.
28. Ibid., 20–1.
29. Ibid., 4–6.
30. Wieviorka, *Die Gewalt*, 136; but Milgram was aware of that; *Obedience*, 175.
31. Milgram, *Obedience*, 117–18.
32. Ibid., 27–31.
33. Ibid., 180; see also Arthur G. Miller, 'What Can the Milgram Obedience Experiment Tell Us about the Holocaust? Generalizing from the Social Psychology Laboratory', in Arthur Miller (ed.), *The Social Psychology of Good and Evil* (New York, 2005), 193–239.
34. Zimbardo,*Lucifer Effect*, 446.
35. Roy F. Baumeister and Kathleen D. Vohs, 'Four Roots of Evil', in Miller (ed.), *Good and Evil*, 99.
36. Ibid., 91.
37. Ibid., 92–3.
38. Ibid., 93–5.
39. Ibid., 96–7.
40. Ibid., 99.
41. Leda Cosmides and John Tooby, *Evolutionary Psychology: a Primer*, Center for Evolutionary Psychology, University of California, Santa Barbara, 13 January 1997, emphasis in the original (online at www.psych.ucsb.edu/research/cep/primer.html; accessed 31 July 2007); see also: Cosmides and Tooby, 'Conceptual Foundations of Evolutionary Psychology', in David M. Buss (ed.), *The Handbook of Evolutionary Psychology* (New York, 2005), 5–67 (available at www.psych.ucsb.edu/research/cep/papers/bussconceptual05.pdf; accessed 31 July 2007).
42. Joshua D. Duntley and David M. Buss, 'The Evolution of Evil', in Miller (ed.), *Good and Evil*, 117–18.
43. Ibid.
44. Ibid., 106–7.
45. Ibid., 107–8, emphasis in the original.
46. Ibid., 119.
47. Dorothee Frank, *Menschen Töten* (Düsseldorf, 2006), 29ff.; see also Joanna Burke, *An Intimate History of Killing: Face-to-Face Killing in Twentieth-Century Warfare* (New York, 1999).
48. Frank, *Töten*, 188ff.
49. Ibid., 196.
50. See, for example, Götz Aly, *Hitlers Volksstaat. Raub, Rassenkrieg und nationaler Sozialismus* (Frankfurt/Main, 2005).
51. Frank, *Töten*, 203; see also Staub, *Roots of Evil*, 244ff.
52. Frank, *Töten*, 266.
53. Ibid., 267.

54. Ibid., 260, translation O.J.
55. See, for example, Leonard S. Newman and Ralph Erber (eds), *Understanding Genocide: the Social Psychology of the Holocaust* (Oxford, 2002); Robert Gellately and Ben Kiernan (eds), *The Specter of Genocide: Mass Murder in Historical Perspective* (Cambridge, 2003); Martin Shaw, *War and Genocide: Organized Killing in Modern Society* (Cambridge, 2003); Benjamin A. Valentino, *Final Solutions: Mass Killing and Genocide in the 20th Century* (Ithaca, 2005); Mark Levene, *Genocide in the Age of the Nation-State*, 2 vols (London, 2005).

Part I
Perpetrators of the Holocaust

Part I
Perpetrators of the Holocaust

1
Perpetrators of the Holocaust: a Historiography

Claus-Christian W. Szejnmann

Confronting the Holocaust: questioning humanity and facing insurmountable challenges

In late 1944 and early 1945 the British Foreign Office gave British soldiers a pocket guide to prepare them to conquer Germany and occupy it afterwards. The guide argued that Hitler had exploited Germany's tradition of authority and glorification of war, and had moulded a new generation of brutal killers. The Germans, the guide concluded, differed sharply from the British people: 'The likeness, if it exists at all, is only skin-deep. THE DEEPER YOU DIG INTO THE GERMAN CHARACTER, THE MORE YOU REALISE HOW DIFFERENT THEY ARE FROM US.'[1]

In the end, however, nobody seemed prepared for the horrors discovered by Allied soldiers. The depth and extent of what humans had suffered under the Nazi dictatorship questioned the core of humanity and posed serious challenges. Whilst it seemed imperative to tell what happened, to learn from it, to punish the perpetrators, and to explain why it happened, it emerged quickly that this was far from an easy task. It seemed obvious that the barbaric crimes called for a new departure in identifying and punishing those responsible. The Allied powers agreed that 'German militarism and Nazism will be wiped out' (Potsdam, August 1945) and publicly called for retribution for the crimes – at the time it was estimated that there were hundreds of thousands of perpetrators – set up military tribunals, and targeted 'German officers and men and members of the Nazi Party who have been responsible for or have taken a consenting part' in atrocities, war crimes and crimes against humanity.[2] However, in the western occupied zones the coming of the Cold War led to a dramatic transformation from a punitive approach to focusing on reconstructing a capitalist economic system with the help of the old elites. Whilst in the Soviet zone de-Nazification is often regarded as more successful – it was quicker and more rigorous – the Communists used the situation to carry out a general purge against everyone who opposed them, made compromises with former Nazis to stabilise the dictatorial rule, and pretended that the restructuring of their society had 'liberated' East Germany from Nazi oppression.

Finally, explanations about the relationship between Germans, Nazism and acts against humanity varied and proved to be far from straightforward. Whilst the British troops were taught that Germans had been shaped by sinister traditions and an evil dictator, direct contact with Germans suggested a more complex picture. Three years after the end of the Second World War the US psychologist H. L. Ansbacher published a study based on surveys of German POWs. When trying to explain why Germans had supported Nazism, and why, even after its defeat and after the 'discovery' of its horrific nature, half of the German population continued to believe that 'National Socialism was a good idea only badly carried out', Ansbacher concluded:

> What did the respondents mean by the 'idea' of National Socialism and the way in which it was carried out? Did they mean the idea of the master race, compulsions, aggression, and did they mean that this idea was not carried out with sufficient consistency? If this were the case, the German mind would indeed be a most perplexing problem and cause for alarm. Our results lead us to the strong belief that when half the Germans today assert the idea of National Socialism was good, but badly carried out, they mean primarily the idea of social and economic betterments, and find fault with its realization through oppression, aggression, and persecution. In this event the problem of the German mind is much less puzzling. No change of basic motives and goals is needed, only a more complete understanding on the part of the Germans of the real meaning of National Socialism, namely, that its vicious aspects were inseparably intertwined with its more constructive sides.[3]

The discourse about perpetrators of the Holocaust until the 1980s

The Nazi racial dictatorship was the most genocidal regime the world has ever seen. It is often forgotten that around 3 million Poles, 7 million Soviet civilians, and 3.3 million Soviet POWs were murdered because they were regarded as Slavic 'sub-humans'. The sociology of its perpetrators, who killed approximately 20 million unarmed people, occupies a central place in the study of the Holocaust and has a contemporary meaning.[4] How many people took part in the mass murder? What kind of people were they? What were their reasons for their murderous activities? And what were the consequences of their deeds? Some of these perpetrators still live with us or are known to us as family friends or acquaintances, fathers or mothers, uncles or aunts, grandfathers or grandmothers. These questions also deal with the uncertainty as to whether the mass murder of the Jews was a singular historic event, or, because potentially it may be rooted in the nature of humans, it can be repeated.

There have been sharply contrasting interpretations of whether and how these issues have been addressed in Germany.[5] Did German society suppress the past and conserve deep-rooted anti-democratic tendencies underneath the surface? Alternatively, did it readily engage with the Nazi past and transform into a vibrant democracy? Or, do these issues require differentiated answers that reflect failures and shortcomings as well as success? Thomas Kühne is in no doubt that the Nazi past was always present in the public life of Germany. However, he is also quick to point out that one has to distinguish carefully what aspects of the Nazi period and its aftermath were discussed, in what manner, with what objectives and to what effect within both German states, during the various periods of their history and by what groups, classes, generations, professions, confessions and political camps, and by which gender.

In countries that were dominated by Nazi Germany the discourse about the war focused on a small number of well-known agents of Nazi rule, the trauma suffered under Nazi occupation (Austria complained of having been the first victim of Nazi aggression), resistance (France, Poland), partisan warfare (Yugoslavia), or the 'great war of the fatherland' (Soviet Union) – all of which served as tools to integrate and legitimise their respective post-war societies. The painful and divisive issue of widespread collaboration, a crucial component of how the occupiers were able to establish their rule, and the role of local agents in the persecution of the Jews and other minorities, was swept under the carpet and received little attention.[6] Additionally, research on the Holocaust in the Eastern bloc was strongly ideologised before it became more or less insignificant.[7]

Considering the continuity in personnel in more or less all sectors of West German society after the defeat of the 'Third Reich' and the fact that many Germans had been perpetrators, accomplices or bystanders, it cannot be a surprise that most Germans were not keen on dealing with the topic of perpetrators, and kept secret or minimised the crimes of the past.[8] More than anything else, the Nuremberg Trials of War Crimes shaped the way in which perpetrators were dealt with and the discourses on perpetrators and memory in West Germany in the post-war period. Following the debates concerning the responsibilities for the crimes, only the Gestapo and the SS were classified as 'criminal organisations' whilst regular police, plainclothes police and the *Wehrmacht* successfully escaped the mantra of guilt: whilst Himmler's black corps was demonised, it isolated the crime institutionally and allowed large parts of the population to exonerate themselves from any guilt (according to Gerald Reitlinger, the SS became the 'alibi of a nation'[9]). Even Eugen Kogon, a Holocaust survivor and one who was highly critical of the way most Germans denied any guilt, in his influential book *The SS-State* (translation of the German title that appeared in 1946) described Hitler and his SS-henchmen as failed characters who suffered from inferiority complexes and were in 'naked pursuit of power':

> What we are dealing with here are not baffling mysteries of human nature, but violations of simple, basic, psychological laws in the evolution of inferior minds. It was inferiority – whether of minds, reason, willpower, imagination or the numerous social aspects of the human mind – that led these men into the SS.[10]

Other important developments also shaped collective perceptions and the specific discourse on perpetrators. Otto Ohlendorf, the leader of *Einsatzgruppe D*, claimed during the *Einsatzgruppen* trial in Nuremberg that the murder of Jews was based on a clear order from Hitler (i.e. that there was a central plan for the Final Solution) and therefore amounted to following 'Führer orders':

> BABEL [defence lawyer]: But did you have no scruples in regard to the execution of these orders?
>
> OHLENDORF: Yes, of course.
>
> BABEL: And how is it that they were carried out regardless of these scruples?
>
> OHLENDORF: Because to me it is inconceivable that a subordinate leader should not carry out orders given by the leaders of the state...

BABEL: Could any individual expect to succeed in evading the execution of these orders?

OHLENDORF: No, the result would have been a court martial with a corresponding sentence.[11]

This line of argument reduced perpetrators to mere executioners of an alien will steered by Hitler, Himmler and Heydrich (who were all dead but were treated as principal offenders) and emphasised that any resistance would have had deadly consequences. This defence strategy quickly became commonplace and helped many accused to go unpunished especially after 1949 when German courts judged the overwhelming majority of killers as 'assisting' in murders which they as individuals apparently did not want.[12] This interpretation turned the bearers of terror into victims of terror – i.e. ordinary Germans were prisoners of a specific historical period and structures and were condemned to obedience.[13]

The representation of female perpetrators and their defence strategy in various Nazi trials is a largely neglected topic but played an important part in the collective strategy of denying any guilt.[14] Accused women exploited their gender status by arguing that they had been exploited and had acted in subordinate positions as helpless assistants in a regime that was led by men. Furthermore, analyses of 'courtroom culture' and media representation of trials show that female perpetrators were stereotyped and demonised as complete deviations from femininity and exceptional 'female brutes', e.g., Ilse Koch, 'the witch from Buchenwald', Carmen Maria Mory, 'the devil' of Ravensbrück, or Herta Oberheuser, 'the sadist [doctor; CCWS] of Ravensbrück'. This discourse disguised the participation of a large number of women in Nazi crimes, and served to avoid a critical self-reflection on the past. In short, the picture of 'unnatural femininity' and dehumanised creatures with unbridled sexuality allowed society to construct a counter-model of itself as normal and innocent.

In the late 1940s and early 1950s there was no complete repression or denying of responsibilities for the crimes committed in the name of the German people in Germany. However, Germans practised what Robert Moeller described as 'selective memories'. In Germany the discourse focused not on the horrors the Jews had suffered under the Nazis, but on German victimisation and Soviet barbarism, i.e. crimes committed against German expellees and POWs.[15] Futhermore, according to Ulrich Herbert, public perception made connections with images of the liberation of the concentration camps Bergen-Belsen, Buchenwald, or Dachau – and not with the mass shootings in Riga or the mass gassings in Auschwitz. In this way, the process of mass murder was construed as a series of secret events that occurred in specially cordoned-off zones in 'the east' to which no witnesses were granted access.[16]

Perpetrator historiography uncritically followed the interpretation that blame and responsibility for the Holocaust lay with a few top Nazi leaders, in particular Hitler. The Führer was portrayed as a crazy, irrational and opportunistic demagogue, who ordered the Final Solution.[17] It took decades until some historians engaged more analytically with Hitler only to discover that he had a 'cohesive world view'.[18] The focus, however, remained on questions of order and timing – Was there a Führer order to the 'Final Solution'? Did Hitler decide on the mass murder of the Jews in the 1920s? When exactly was the decision made to kill all Jews? – all of which are important issues but ultimately do not address key humanitarian and moral questions raised by the Holocaust. The spotlight on Hitler simplified the dynamics and complexities of Nazism, and the notion of an 'evil monster' diverted attention from the responsibilities of others.

A number of high-profile court cases from the late 1950s 'broke the general silence about the perpetrators' and ignited debates about the mass crimes committed under Nazism, most importantly: the *Einsatzgruppen* trial in Ulm in 1958, the Eichmann trial in Jerusalem in 1961, and the Auschwitz trial in Frankfurt in the mid-1960s. A new generation of historians, whose well-known publication *Anatomie des SS-Staates* was expert evidence prepared for and in part delivered at the trial of war criminals in Frankfurt and published by the Institute for Contemporary History in Munich, provided solid 'analyses of the motives, structure, and methods of the leaders of the National Socialist regime'.[19]

Overall, however, Holocaust research at West German universities remained a marginal topic until the late 1980s. Instead, historians were preoccupied with searching for the background to why the Nazis came to power, and the turn to structural history in West German historiography meant that debates centred on system theory. This was an era when the concept of 'totalitarianism' blossomed (vilifying the socialist dictatorships as equivalent to National Socialism during the Cold War), and when historians were locked into a bitter stalemate between 'intentionalists' and 'structuralists'. Peter Longerich recently highlighted the narrow-mindedness of a debate in which apparent contrasts were, in fact, mutually conditional and reflected multi-layered and complex phenomena that cannot be grasped with one-dimensional explanations: humans who want to carry out mass murder depend on structures, whilst structures do not function on their own but need humans; regional initiatives were an integral part of centrally controlled policies; pragmatic explanations for the persecution of Jews were backed up by ideological justifications and vice versa.[20]

As it stood, influential books by Karl Dietrich Bracher focused on the intellectual origins and the organisational development of the Nazi dictatorship, and perpetrators did not feature in prominent anthologies about the Nazi dictatorship or the massive 'Bavaria Project' of the Institute for Contemporary History.[21] Notable exceptions in the 1970s were two studies that went largely unnoticed: Uwe Dietrich Adam investigated the coordination of various national institutions in the persecution of the Jews and was the first German historian who questioned the linear development that ended in genocide, and Christian Streit highlighted the central role of the *Wehrmacht* in the death of some 57 per cent of Soviet POWs.[22] Although the knowledge of the killing process was at best rudimentary, German scholarship largely ignored international developments in the field,[23] and the huge amount of rich material that had been generated by prosecutors in criminal proceedings against Nazi criminals. After all, the historical professions had played a crucial role in legitimising German claims to the East, the Nazi programme of ethnic cleansing and the genocide against European Jews. When, after 1945, the same historians and then their protégés continued to hold chairs at German universities, it made sense for them to pretend to be 'emotionally detached and "neutral" in [their] approach'.[24] It was indicative that a rare study based on court material by the criminologist Herbert Jäger in the late 1960s was largely ignored by historians although it was highly innovative on several counts.[25] It demolished the perpetrators' principal line of defence that they had acted under binding orders: Jäger could not find a single case in which someone who did not obey criminal orders was physically harmed. The book also emphasised the link between the war and genocide, and presented an important contribution about the individual motivation of Nazi perpetrators, a topic that other psychologists and criminologists had previously tackled but with little conviction. Jäger suggested a new typology that distinguished between excess crimes (crimes committed on one's own initiative and in disinhibitory conditions), crimes committed in a relative autonomous way, and crimes committed by following orders. Furthermore, some Holocaust survivors and critical authors responded to the horrors that were exposed by the court cases, the mild sentencing of mass murderers and the repression of the Nazi past: autobiographical accounts by Jean Améry and Primo Levi, and theatre plays by Rolf Hochhuth (*The Deputy*) and Peter Weiss (*The Investigation*) reached a mass audience.[26]

Meanwhile, highly influential non-German books on the Holocaust – e.g. works by Lucy Dawidowicz and Nora Levin that were largely based on secondary sources and put forward simplistic explanations which Raul Hilberg described bitterly as examples of 'manipulation in history'[27] – perpetuated the notion of evil leaders and popular irrational anti-Semitism.[28] There were, however, also scholars who produced outstanding and original scholarship that improved our understanding of the systematic mass murder of the Jews. The works of two scholars stood out. The philosopher Hannah Arendt was a leading voice amongst German-Austrian Jews and Holocaust survivors. In *The Origins of Totalitarianism* (1951) she attempted to explain why the relatively unimportant phenomena of the Jewish question and anti-Semitism became the catalytic agent leading to the rise and success of Nazism, a world war and finally the crime of genocide.[29] Her explanation suggested the emergence of the new form of totalitarian rule that was built upon irrational terror and ideological fiction. To Arendt, totalitarian regimes were capable of mobilising populations where a viable public life with conditions of liberty and freedom had been uprooted by devastating developments in the modern period (industrialisation, population movements, modern warfare, revolutionary upheaval, etc.). According to Arendt, 'absolute evil' emerged in totalitarian societies – 'absolute because it can no longer be deduced from humanly comprehensible motives'. In the process, anti-Semitism and other motivating factors disappeared behind the 'inherent logicality' of mass murder. Terror became an end in itself to 'stabilise' men and formed the essence of totalitarian domination.[30]

Arendt's thesis that the annihilation of the Jews followed some kind of inner logic broadened the scope of perpetrators to encompass all of German society, and influenced generations of historians. Hilberg's seminal work *The Destruction of the European Jews* from 1961 exploited a massive body of empirical evidence and interpreted the Shoah as a process of successive steps that were initiated by countless decision-makers inside a vast bureaucratic apparatus that was operating and coordinating on an unprecedented scale.[31] This bureaucratic machinery was driven by a shared comprehension, synchronisation and efficiency, and was not limited by any morals because the process was dehumanised (e.g. the commandant of Treblinka and Sobibor, Franz Stangel, described the Jews as 'cargo'). According to Christopher Browning, Hilberg's great contribution was to portray an extensive 'machinery of destruction' that 'was structurally no different from organized German society as a whole'. Indeed, 'the machinery of destruction *was* the organized community in one of its specialized roles'. Moreover, these bureaucrats 'were not merely passive recipients of orders from above' but 'innovators and problem solvers'.[32] However, Hilberg's overall focus on the bureaucratic process and the structure of extermination, emphasising the division of labour in the killing process, meant that there was still no detailed focus on the background and motivation of perpetrators. In other words, whilst Hilberg had put the perpetrator at the centre of his analysis and emphasised the involvement of a large number of groups in the killing process, his focus was on the role of perpetrators as members of an institution rather than as individuals.[33]

The 1961 trial of Adolf Eichmann boosted discussions on the Holocaust.[34] The trial is often associated with Hannah Arendt's famous book *Eichmann in Jerusalem: a Report on the Banality of Evil*. Arendt was clearly influenced by Hilberg's study and depicted the Shoah as a modern, bureaucratically organised and industrially driven extermination process in which Eichmann was merely a mechanical link. Her description of Eichmann's actions as 'banal' was meant to challenge the prevalent notion that the mass murder was carried out by a limited number of pathological killers and outsiders. To Arendt, Eichmann appeared very ordinary, but, like most other Germans, 'had succumbed to Hitler' and was therefore afflicted by an 'inability to think'. With this, 'the moral maxims which determine social behaviour and the religious commandments – *"Thou shalt not kill!"* – which guide conscience had virtually vanished'. Eichmann was not determined by 'fanaticism' or violent anti-Semitism, but by his 'extraordinary loyalty to Hitler and the Führer's order'.[35]

Gerhard Paul has argued that this paradigm of the 'mechanised' crime has been the central explanation for the Shoah until today.[36] Martin Broszat, who in 1958 published the autobiographical notes of Rudolf Höβ, commandant of Auschwitz, described an executioner who appeared to be a normal petit-bourgeois human who zealously and unemotionally obeyed orders from authorities and was part of a factory-like and anonymous mass murder. This new picture of perpetrators entailed that they were not particularly evil, but orderly, conscientious, and thus appeared extremely suitable to take part in the anonymous mechanism of modern mass murder. A flood of publications described

Eichmann's mediocre normality and depicted him as model example of the loyal bureaucrat – a cog in a machine that operated beyond his control – hence the description 'banal bureaucrat' and 'bureaucratic murderer'.

Authors from Israel in particular criticised Arendt's assessment that in the modern world all humans are potential Eichmanns and are not aware of the consequences of their actions. To some, this minimises the horrific crimes that were committed and gives them a universal character. To others, like Raul Hilberg, 'there was no "banality" in this "evil"' as Eichmann was not only a loyal bureaucrat but rather a trailblazer in continuously finding new ways of achieving the incredible dimension of his barbaric deed. Finally, Alf Lüdtke warned that by describing automatic processes without humans one reaffirms a widespread consensus amongst the perpetrator society that denied that each killing had to be carried out again and again by the will and action of the perpetrators.[37] Not surprisingly, Ulrich Herbert described this period as 'the second suppression of the past' in Germany.[38] Gerhard Paul argued that the Shoah turned into an 'automatism without people' that 'found its description in the metaphor of the "factory of death"': Auschwitz. This discourse did not deal with the activities of killers in shooting pits or the liquidations of ghettos, and enabled 'normal' Germans once more to distance themselves from the perpetrators.[39]

There was, to be true, a widespread trend to conceptualise the Holocaust. Marxist scholars in the GDR continued to describe fascism as the most imperialist element of finance capital. Theodor Adorno argued that the support for fascism, anti-democracy and anti-Semitism in the inter-war period was caused by the appearance of an 'authoritarian personality'. And the Jewish sociologist Zygmunt Bauman in his book *Modernity and the Holocaust* proposed 'to treat the Holocaust as a rare, yet significant and reliable, test of the hidden possibilities of modern society'.[40]

However, change was on the way and approaches and methodologies diversified especially in German historiography in the course of the 1980s (there is no room here to discuss the growing attention amongst the American public to the Holocaust from the mid-1970s[41]). Several factors help to explain this. The airing of the fictional television series *Holocaust* in 1979 had a significant impact in West Germany and, according to Judith Doneson, broke 'a thirty-five-year taboo on discussing Nazi atrocities', whilst Federal President Richard von Weizäcker's groundbreaking speech on 8 May 1985, which 'placed Jews, Poles and Russians higher up the list of victims than the Germans themselves', indicated change at the highest political level.[42] The turn towards local history and the history of everyday life meant that coming to terms with one's past took place in real terms, including a growing awareness of the places of crimes and the perspective of victims – albeit that the aspect of perpetrators continued to be neglected for a long time.[43] Furthermore, increasing research on the 'Third Reich' heightened the awareness about the enormous gaps in the knowledge about the Holocaust – and German scholarship rejoined an international debate on the topic. Moreover, critics who have attacked 'functionalists' in particular for depersonalising the Holocaust, have often not recognised that historians such as Hans Mommsen and Martin Broszat drew attention away from the Nazi leadership 'towards different functional elites in the bureaucracy, military and judiciary, their interaction and, ultimately, towards German society at large'.[44] Hence, the racial activities of institutes and social groups beyond the SS attracted some attention. The policies against the Jews appeared more and more as the core of a comprehensive policy of extermination that unleashed its destructive features during the war and that involved the participation of all key institutions of the 'Third Reich' and targeted a growing number of victims: Hans-Heinrich Wilhelm presented a detailed description of the murderous activities of *Einsatzgruppen* in Belarus and the Baltic nations in the context of early occupation policies; Ernst Klee, a social worker for the handicapped, produced a major study of the Nazi 'euthanasia' killing (in which around 250,000 people were murdered); the geneticist Benno Müller-Hill revealed the involvement of German geneticists and anthropologists in the selection of Jews, Gypsies, the mentally ill and the retarded, for sterilisation and genocide; Gisela Bock published an important study about forced sterilisation (between 320,000 and 350,000 people were sterilised in accordance with Nazi racial criteria); Hans-Walter Schmuhl explored the concept of racial hygiene and the euthanasia killing; Ulrich Herbert looked at the war economy, the exploitation of foreign slave workers (around 7.7 million foreign men and women were forced to work in Nazi Germany by autumn 1944), and the role of employers; and Burkhard Jellonek studied the treatment of homosexuals.[45] Many new impulses came from 'outside' the mainstream German scholarship, including non-historians, who turned to empirical studies of everyday life and mentalities, published sources about the actual killing process, and discovered the importance of letters from the front.[46]

These original studies on organisational, ideological, regional and biographical aspects of Nazism led to a much better understanding of the

Nazis' policies of extermination and the role and motivation of perpetrators. For instance, Michael Zimmermann demonstrated that the Nazi policy of persecution against the Romani 'drew on traditional anti-Gypsy prejudices, but managed to radicalize them at decisive points by representing them as scientifically sound with the aid of social and biological theories'. There was 'no evidence of a unified process of decision-making... nor of a corresponding chain of command for the murder of "Gypsies"' (more than 200,000 Gypsies were killed in the Holocaust).[47] Meanwhile, researchers abroad were also producing innovative studies.[48] One notable pioneer was the US-Israeli historian Omer Bartov with his investigation of the unprecedented brutalities committed by the German *Wehrmacht* in the East. Bartov challenged the post-1945 memories of loyal and self-sacrificing German soldiers who were victims first of the Nazi regime, then of partisan terror, and then of Stalin's military aggression and captivity. He explained the murderous activities of soldiers, from top-ranking officers to foot soldiers, with a combination of 'the terrible physical and mental hardship at the front', the draconian military system of repression and, most crucial, 'ideological conviction' and 'a general and widespread support [for], if not "belief", in Hitler'.[49]

'Perpetrator studies' since the 1990s

The 1990s proved to be the decade when mainstream scholarship and the public in Germany were ready to confront the National Socialist past head-on for the first time and debate it as never before. Bill Niven argued that 'the time was right' not only because of special anniversaries (e.g., the 50th anniversaries of Stauffenberg's attempt on Hitler's life and the end of the war) and spectacular media events (e.g. Steven Spielberg's film *Schindler's List* in 1993), but, more importantly, because German unification brought an awareness and acceptance of a common past. Furthermore, the crucial impact of generational shifts, particularly in the 1960s and again the 1980s, explained why 'the 1990s were a continuation and radicalization of a process of coming to terms with the past, rather than its first phase'.[50] Scholarship and the wider public realm were now ready to confront what stood at the heart of the Nazi dictatorship and the Holocaust: war, genocide, perpetrators and crime scenes, the precise implication of every group in society in mass murder, and, of course, the victims. One could argue that the opening of the massive Memorial to the Murdered Jews of Europe in the centre of Berlin in 2005 has finally shifted the fate of the victims of Nazism right into the heart of German society.

A real breakthrough in scholarship was Christopher Browning's exemplary micro-analysis from 1992 of around 500 members of Police Battalion 101, a unit comprising middle-aged reservists from a working-class or petit-bourgeois background in Hamburg.[51] Most of the men were not fanatical Nazis, but took part in the Holocaust in Poland and shot at least 38,000 Jews. Browning's focus on the murderous activities and motivation of these 'ordinary men' – the great majority of them became executioners although they had the opportunity of not participating in these mass shootings – put this key issue at the top of the scholarly agenda for the first time. The US scholar based his research on court proceedings from the 1960s and, favouring a multi-causal, anthropological approach, argued that the behaviour of these men was determined by a combination of factors: a willingness to obey orders and authority, group conformity and peer pressure, career-mindedness, the brutalising effects of a racist imperialist war, and the insidious effects of constant propaganda and indoctrination. Anti-Semitism, according to Browning, played only a minor role. Browning's complex conclusion was influenced by the Milgram and Stanford prison experiments and emphasised how social group processes create specific conditions which can have a de-inhibiting effect, potentially turning 'ordinary men' into brutal murderers.[52] To Browning, the genocide against the Jews was a unique consequence of the potential for destruction in the modern age. He also emphasised that the Shoah should not be seen as the execution of a central decision to exterminate but as a process in which local initiatives played a crucial role (pioneering work about the Holocaust in the occupied territories – e.g. in the Lublin district, Belarus and Galicia – have meanwhile confirmed this[53]). Furthermore, with reference to Primo Levi he asked scholars to pay more attention to complex and contradictory aspects of human behaviour, i.e. the 'Gray Zone' of victims (e.g. the corruption and collaboration that flourished in the camps) and perpetrators (e.g. 'the pathetic figure' of commander Trapp, 'who sent his men to slaughter Jews "weeping like a child" ').[54]

The controversy surrounding the 'Crimes of the *Wehrmacht*' exhibition and the 'Goldhagen debate' sparked off a massive public discussion about perpetrators. Suddenly the spotlight was on locating killers and their motives at the heart of society, and the brutal suffering of victims. The public was confronted with the accusation that 'ordinary' Germans participated in systematic mass murder (previously, similar findings had not received much public reaction). The breaking of the 'visual taboo' regarding the Shoah made this situation even more dramatic. Whilst Goldhagen described the barbaric killings in graphic detail and used photos as sources – e.g. how an 'ordinary' German soldier 'takes aim at a Jewish mother and child during the slaughter of the Jews of Ivangorod, Ukraine, in 1942' – the exhibition displayed photos, letters and documents of 'ordinary' soldiers taking part in the widespread mass murder of civilians and Soviet POWs.[55] Suddenly perpetrators and bystanders of the crimes were not anonymous any more but identifiable individuals, sometimes neighbours, relatives or even one's own father. The *'Wehrmacht'* exhibition in particular sparked off an unprecedented public response because it challenged a collective memory and 'one of the founding myths of the German Federal Republic – the legend of a "decent" army that had steered clear of atrocities perpetrated by the SS'.[56]

Whilst the *'Wehrmacht'* exhibition was largely concerned with setting the record straight, Goldhagen's aim was to explain the motivation of 'ordinary' killers. Like Browning, he dismissed the thesis that perpetrators were exceptional pathological killers and that the Shoah was an abstract industrial genocide. Instead, both emphasised that it was a mass murder carried out by a large number of individual perpetrators. In particular, Goldhagen stressed that each individual is an autonomous being and responsible for his/her actions, and also possesses freedom to make decisions about whether or not to participate in actions that violate human morals.[57] But whilst Goldhagen analysed the same sources as Browning (witness statements in the court case against members of Police Battalion 101), he came to strikingly different conclusions: he saw the Shoah rooted in Germany's specific political and cultural development and argued that 'ordinary' Germans became 'Hitler's willing executioners' because of a deep-seated 'eliminationist anti-Semitism'.

At a time when empirical research suggested the complex multicausal nature of the Holocaust, Goldhagen was turning the clock back to simplistic interpretations. However, the debate that was sparked off by Goldhagen's probing questions and provocative theses exposed serious deficiencies in our knowledge about key aspects of the Holocaust, and led to the acceptance that a change of paradigm, already started by Browning, was essential. This included shifting the focus from the Nazi elite to 'ordinary Germans' as killers; a cultural anthropological approach that incorporates a detailed analysis of the crimes and responsibilities of individual perpetrators; and an attempt to situate the crimes in the context of the wider society. Furthermore, it became clear how little was known about the precise extent, form and role of anti-Semitism and its link with the Holocaust, and how this virulent German anti-Semitism compared to other forms of this phenomenon.[58]

One final contributor who deserves singling out for making a whole range of original and challenging contributions to the then newly emerging subject of Perpetrator Studies (*Täterforschung*) was the Berlin historian Götz Aly. Aly, in tandem with Susanne Heim, argued in the early 1990s that there was a 'political economy of the Final Solution' – i.e. young planners identified overpopulation as the source of a deep-rooted structural problem of the region and aimed to spark off a revival and modernisation of the economy by destroying the socio-economic existence of Polish Jews.[59] Whilst this thesis did not convince many fellow experts – it is difficult to prove the impact of these ideas on policy, and one striking feature of the Holocaust seemed to be precisely the irrelevance of economic criteria – Aly and Heim challenged mainstream scholarship: they proved that those responsible for the extermination policy were not restricted to the SS and the Nazi party, and they insisted that the Holocaust was not motivated by irrational racial hatred but primarily 'utilitarian goals'. Aly, Heim and a whole group of like-minded scholars who published books on the role played by young, well-trained experts such as statisticians, economists, doctors and historians, saw Nazism as providing them with a unique opportunity to realise their shared visions of a rationalised social and economic utopia.

In the mid-1990s Aly's book *Final Solution* provided an empirical basis for the amended thesis that the policies against the Jews became radicalised due to the *failure* of plans for the deportation of the Jews.[60] However, as Herbert points out, whilst Nazi deportation plans 'also involved Poles, Russians, even entire populations of countries lying to Germany's east', their failure only led to the practice of genocide against the Jews. This raised fundamental questions:

> What role then did anti-Semitism play here? In what way did the dilemmas – real or contrived – arising in specific situations link up with long-standing attitudes and aims? What was the relationship between ideological factors, such as racism and hatred of Jews, to goal-oriented, 'rational' motives, such as economic modernization or dealing with food scarcity? How did the motives – both individual and situationally determined – of the murderers and those who bore responsibility for their actions relate to a general dynamic of violence directed against Jews?[61]

After Browning, Goldhagen and Aly had thrown down the gauntlet to their peers, Perpetrator Studies became a 'boom' subject amongst a new generation of historians who exploited the newly available documents in the former Eastern bloc states. The new interest in people and protagonists led to a turn towards the history of mentalities (*Mentalitätsgeschichte*) and biographical studies, an emphasis on detailed empirical research, a focus on comparative typologies and motivations of perpetrators, and the exploration of the decentralised perspective of the policies of extermination in the occupied territories.[62]

The core group of perpetrators near the top of the Nazi hierarchy, the men who bore responsibility for the organisation of the mass murders, emerged as an 'ideological elite'. For instance, the leadership of the Reich Security Head Office (RSHA; perhaps the most central group of planner-perpetrators) were born after the turn of the century in the middle and upper strata of German society, were radicalised by war and post-war crisis, and were influenced by *völkisch* racism, enthusiasm for technology and ideas of a 'heroic realism' (a term referring to murderous actions not being based on hatred but on rationality, i.e. killing did not spark off empathy as it served the interest of the *Volk*).[63] These educated members of the core group of perpetrators, like the key official in Heydrich's security police apparatus, Werner Best, or Götz Aly's 'ethnic planners', camp commandants, Gestapo chiefs, *Einsatzgruppen* commanders, Sipo and SD, SS and police leaders, 'Jewish experts', and T-4 killers, were technically efficient and well-trained professionals. But whilst each group had its own 'generational, social, and/or professional homogeneity', they were all willing and committed ideologues who exploited their considerable autonomy to pursue their vision of a racist world order ('ideological bureaucracy').[64] This ideal was worth any sacrifice and transcended any traditional limits. Ideological commitment, although it was complex and varied, played a crucial dual function amongst the core group of perpetrators: it served as motivation for individuals and provided a focus of orientation for a variety of competing interests. This helps to explain the smoothly functioning division of labour and the 'networks of Nazi persecution' that coordinated genocide in a polycratic environment.[65]

The more recent research has increasingly focused on the 'shooters' – the rank-and-file *Einsatzkommandos*, Reserve Police, Waffen-SS, and *Wehrmacht* – who were composed mainly of a cross-section of German-Austrian society. Members of these vast groups had no typology: 'no age, gender, social, educational, ethnic, or religious cohort proved immune to involvement'.[66] But whilst individuals had different biographical patterns and showed individual forms of behaviours, like members of *Einsatzgruppe D* who carried out mass killings in the south of the Soviet Union, their murderous impact was frighteningly homogeneous.[67] Two interpretations about the dramatic transformation from upright burgher to brutal killer seem worth mentioning. Klaus-Michael Mallmann dismisses the common explanation such as obedience to orders, the brutalisation of war and the impact of propaganda because these murderous shooters had volunteered and there was no time to get used to violence and to be affected by propaganda. Instead, he argues that the radicalisation of the anxiety and hatred of 'Jewish Bolshevism', a sentiment that had gradually grown since 1917, became virtual reality when confronted with 'alien' Jews in enemy territory and legitimised 'the removal of a collective security risk as necessary self-defence'.[68] Whilst there is a growing body of research on perpetrators from the *Wehrmacht*, Thomas Kühne has recently provided the first comprehensive explanation of what turned 'ordinary' soldiers into murderers, why these soldiers fought so long in a war that was lost, and what explains the way soldiers communicated their experiences after 1945.[69] At the heart of his explanation stands the concept of comradeship which was central to everyday social practices of the military community and its moral rules – and which entailed enormous pressures to conform. It included the shared experience of being away from home, being accomplice in murder and then belonging to the 'community of suffering' when the war turned against Germany. Soldierly comradeship was the epitome of everything 'good'. Kühne concludes: 'The "human" side of comradeship made the "inhumane" side of war bearable, morally as well as emotionally', but it simultaneously functioned as the motor of violence as peer pressure made an opt-out extremely difficult.

The growing interest in women and the Holocaust and in the social environment of perpetrators led to the scholarly 'discovery' of the female perpetrators – until then an almost completely neglected topic. The 'feminist' *Historikerstreit* (struggle amongst historians) over whether women were victims of an extreme male-dominated and sexist-racist Nazi dictatorship that reduced women to the status of mere 'objects' (Gisela Bock), or whether women played an active role in the regime and shared some responsibilities for the crimes (Claudia Koonz) constructed an over-simplistic perpetrator-versus-victim dichotomy.[70] It is only more recently that studies about the personnel of perpetrator groups, in particular research about the 'euthanasia' killing and concentration camps, made visible the important and varied functions women fulfilled as perpetrators and bystanders in mass murder.[71] Female doctors, nurses, midwives and administrative assistants directly or indirectly participated in the killing of innocent people in the Nazi 'euthanasia' programme.[72] Women worked as cooks, office personnel, nurses, laboratory assistants, doctors and camp guards in women's divisions in some of the best-known concentration camps, such as Auschwitz-Birkenau, Majdanek, Bergen-Belsen, Mauthausen, Dachau and Sachsenhausen, and in numerous women's concentration camps, such as Ravensbrück, Moringen and Lichenberg. In total, around 10 per cent of all camp guards, i.e. 3,500, were female. They participated in tormenting and torturing prisoners, and helped to select and murder victims. Female perpetrators pursued their work under no duress, regarded concentration camps as a normal place of work and the attached SS estate as a normal place to live in, and often perceived inmates as 'sub-humans' who had no right to live in the Nazi state. Gudrun Schwarz argued that SS wives (240,000 women were married to SS men) were directly involved in the system of terror by providing domestic and emotional stability at the place of crime for the husbands, and by actively participating in the system of exploitation and robbing. Some wives of members of the SS or the Gestapo even volunteered to take part in encroachments and shootings.[73] Overall, female perpetrators worked as efficiently and professionally as their male counterparts to ensure a smooth killing process. They were not passive tools in the apparatus of repression but used their freedom to pursue personal initiatives.

Very recently an expert stated bluntly that 'the full history of wartime collaboration in much of eastern Europe remains to be written'.[74] However, scholarship has made considerable progress since the discourse about societies in Nazi-occupied territories hardly went beyond the description of stigmatised collaboration and heroic resistance. A discussion about the motives of non-German perpetrators exemplifies the complexities of the subject. Michael MacQueen argued that there were six basic motivations for, or types of, Lithuanian perpetrators:

1. *Revenge*, by those who had suffered at the hands of the Soviets.
2. *Careerists*, who sought personal advancement under the new regime.
3. *Turncoats*, who attempted to expiate service to the Soviets by enthusiastic loyalty to their new masters.
4. *Greedy individuals*, seeking to gain booty.
5. *Anti-Semites*, who had baited the Jews before the war and participated in anti-Jewish violence under the Nazis.
6. So-called *accidental perpetrators*, who just happened to be recruited and went with the flow.[75]

Martin Dean, who studied the motivations of police volunteers in the killing in Belarus and the Ukraine, came independently to almost identical conclusions. He argued, however, that one could add the 'sadistic types' and 'those who lusted for power'. Dean also believed that 'usually a combination of several of these motivations played a role within each individual'. Furthermore, whilst anti-Semitism played an important motivation amongst some local policemen who participated in the killing, 'it was more a matter of personal animosity for political or economic reasons' and lacked the dehumanising racial basis of Nazi ideology. MacQueen and Dean also stress the 'gruesome intimacy of the killings'. Many of the perpetrators 'personally knew the victims and had lived together with them previously as schoolmates, co-workers, and neighbours'. Hence local economic and personal relations played an important role. Dean concluded: 'The active core was driven particularly by self-made careerists, the dynamic force of any society, who were particularly susceptible to the new opportunities and the disorientation of society's moral compass created by Nazi rule.'

Finally, sociologists, psychologists, anthropologists, political scientists and others, have shown sustained interest in topics dealing with violence, killing, mass murders, ethnic cleansing and genocide over the last two decades or so.[76] Their 'multifaceted approaches and different "models" of explanation' have stimulated and broadened the discourse in Perpetrator Studies of the Holocaust. Two main approaches have stood out amongst scholars who have tried to answer what motivates mass murder and genocide. Whilst one group insists that murderous events like genocide 'have occurred throughout history in all parts of the world', another group emphasises 'change over continuity', and, for instance, links modernity with genocide (those pursuing comparative genocide studies approach the Holocaust not as a 'unique' event but as an extreme form of genocide). Some social psychologists have offered particularly innovative analyses. James Waller has developed a complex theory that looks at the interaction among dispositional, situational and social factors.[77] He emphasises the importance of moral disengagement, a gradual process in which perpetrators distance themselves from the victims and become capable of producing extraordinary evil. This 'culture of cruelty' rewards individuals for violence against victims and is stimulated by professional socialisation, binding factors of the group, and the merging of role and person. Harald Welzer, in a study that bears great similarities to Waller's findings, investigated the social psychological parameters, i.e. the moral concepts of the majority group in society, combined with a micro-study of the crime and the killing.[78] He argued that most humans have the potential to turn into mass murderers. This happens through a process in which the majority group's feeling of solidarity towards a minority has vanished and systematic killing is not regarded as a crime but is desired.

Conclusions and future perspectives

Our knowledge and understanding of the Holocaust, the instruments of terror and their personnel, have made enormous progress over the last decade.[79] Perpetrator Studies has established itself as a new discipline within the broad topic of National Socialism and has contributed towards many innovative findings.[80] These studies aim to analyse the interaction between the structures of persecution, the bureaucracy of extermination, the (group) biography of perpetrators below the top Nazi leadership, the motivation of mass murderers beyond madness and racial hatred, the act of killing, and the time and place of killing. There were probably several hundred thousand Germans and Austrians who planned, organised, carried out and assisted persecution and murder. They were complemented by thousands of ethnic Germans (*Volksdeutsche*) who often pursued auxiliary functions, and hundreds of thousands of foreign auxiliaries.[81] The forms of persecution and murder, and the motivation behind them, were extremely broad. Typical, however, was the mixture of state-prescribed and individually initiated violence – forms of violence which were difficult to separate and mutually conditional – through which they received their particular power and dynamics. The latest research suggests that there were at least three periods of political socialisation that shaped a 'radicalising career': the violent *völkisch*-Nazi milieu in post-war Weimar (a climate of hate, racist prejudice and glorification of violence), the integration into Nazi organisations and an internalisation of violence during the Nazi dictatorship after 1933 (turning 'pre-war extremists' into 'full-time Nazis'), and the terrorist milieu in the occupied territories after 1939 (cumulative radicalisation and violence with a de-inhibiting effect; socialisation in violent comradeship). Overall, research suggests that whilst disposition is more important among the 'architects' of genocide, the behaviour of the 'shooters' is more determined by situational factors. It is likely that the largest group of perpetrators only radicalised after 1939 into 'wartime Nazis'. However, the social psychologist Leonard Newman reminds us of the enormous complexities involved at any level: personal and situational factors interact in complicated ways... Situations do not only interact with dispositional factors to affect behaviour, they also shape and change those dispositions: people do not just react to situations... and finally, 'situations' themselves do not even objectively exist but need to be cognitively constructed by the people they then go on to affect... While attitudes do indeed give rise to behavior, it is also the case that one's behavior affects one's attitudes and beliefs... The *cognitive dissonance* literature shows that when people are led to engage in behaviors that violate their normal standards, they will be motivated to change their attitudes and beliefs to reduce the discrepancy between their behavior and their cognitions.[82]

These and many other insights represent great achievements in Perpetrator Studies but cannot obscure the fact that the list of shortcomings, desiderata and methodological problems remains daunting.[83] The importance of racist ideology, and in particular anti-Semitism, in the mass murder has reoccupied centre stage but remains disputed. The core group of men who organised genocide were willing and committed ideologues. Furthermore, Christopher Browning now believes that the 'significant minority' of so-called 'eager killers' amongst low-level perpetrators were ideologically motivated to kill Jews and not overtly influenced by 'situational/organizational/institutional factors'.[84] However, among the majority of killers it is impossible to establish a direct causal relation between fanatical anti-Semitism and actually killing Jews. Even the most committed racist ideologues, including Wildt's 'generation of the unbound', required a process of 'cumulative radicalization' 'to the point where they could actually comprehend that the most extreme conclusions of their ideas were realizable.'[85] Also, how exactly did moral scruples and human ethics disintegrate: was it, for example, a mixture of escalating pragmatism and social-Darwinist racism during a radicalising war? Or did years of political and social indoctrination by the Nazis create a 'new moral conscience' that discarded universal human rights?[86] Why did the mentality in the occupied territories (endemic corruption and violent excess, particularly in the East) differ so much from that of the old Reich (bureaucratic inhumanity and measures of persecution)?[87] Furthermore, George Browder raises a number of crucial questions that remain unanswered:

> Were those who behave proactively at all levels 'normal' representatives of German society or a radicalized minority? Were all involved 'normal' representatives of Western industrial societies, individuals

whom extraordinary circumstances and pressures had turned into perpetrators?...What made the difference for those who withdrew or even resisted?[88]

And finally: how do humans live with murderous crimes? How do perpetrators reintegrate themselves into society?

There are also serious limitations and methodological problems. Whilst many experts see the most promising approach in biographical analyses (following Herbert's study of Best), the biographical source base is often very limited (particularly for members of the lower classes), long-term personal dispositions often appear of only limited importance for the situational behaviour of a person, and perpetrators often acted collectively, in an environment of bureaucracy or comradeship, where their individual character disappeared. More generally, shortages of primary sources and inherent problems with existing sources impose severe limits to our abilities to analyse the motivation of killers: e.g. the most prominent perpetrator analyses are based on witness statements and testaments from court trials (Browning, Goldhagen); most accounts on collaborators are based on oral testimonies from war crimes investigations; female camp guards hardly left any letters, diaries, personal notes or even post-war interrogations. Most perpetrator studies are based on predominantly German (Nazi) sources and do not take into consideration the perspectives of the victims of genocide and occupation.[89] Furthermore, Jürgen Matthäus has warned that whilst more and more researchers have studied (and at times have become obsessed with) the personalities of perpetrators, their crimes and the crime locations, 'the more we restrict our analysis to the incriminating act, the greater the risk of severing casual and chronological connections with other, no less relevant aspects of the past'.[90] Finally, the call by some historians for multi-causal interpretations based on multi-disciplinary approaches has only been partially attempted. However, social psychological explanations which concentrate on group dynamics (but are often ahistorical – i.e. they neglect specific historical conditions and cultural factors, including ideology – and have a tendency to down-play the responsibility of perpetrators) can provide essential additions to historical attempts to find answers as to why normal people became mass murderers under Nazism.[91]

Other serious challenges remain. There are still hardly any attempts at a systematic gender perspective in Perpetrator Studies, and it is necessary to reflect anew about the methodologies of how to write women's history under Nazism. It is not clear to what extent or whether at all the systematic investigations of their male counterparts are applicable to women. Susannah Heschel argues: 'there is a widely shared assumption that men's cruelty is, in part, an expression of masculinity, but no exploration into whether women's acts of cruelty are linked to expressions of their femininity, understanding both terms as social constructs.'[92] There are also difficult pedagogical tasks. In Germany, the gap between historical knowledge and the willingness to confront the past in one's own immediate environment has not changed since Anna Rosmus became the 'nasty girl' of Passau for exploring Nazism in her home town in the early 1980s. In fact, there is a widespread acceptance throughout Western European societies today that Nazism was evil and collaboration was often as deadly, but, according to private family discourses, there were never any Nazis or Nazi sympathisers in one's own family. On the contrary, according to family memories the whole of Europe was full of heroic resistance fighters.[93] The enormous reaction to the controversial book *Neighbours: the Destruction of the Jewish Community in Jedwabne* (Poland) from 2000/1 by the sociologist Jan Tomasz Gross exemplifies how difficult and sensitive the discussion of local collaboration in the Holocaust continues to be more than 60 years after the defeat of Nazism.[94] More generally, knowledge of the mass murder during the Nazi dictatorship has become so complex and multi-layered that it is hardly of any pedagogical use.

Finally, several leading experts have called for a more holistic approach in Holocaust studies. This questions the predominant historiographical focus on the perpetrators and promises to give Perpetrator Studies an innovative momentum.[95] Peter Longerich expressed the need for a more comprehensive and understandable explanation of the events, for integrating Perpetrator Studies into the whole period between 1933 and 1945. He argues that the structuring of the debates in the form of the now classic dichotomies (Was the decision to murder rooted in 'predisposition' or 'situation'? Were perpetrators driven by 'utilitarian' or 'ideological' motives? Was the murder driven locally or by the centre?) does not do justice to the complexities of the topic. Similarly, Saul Friedlander demands an 'integrated history of the Holocaust' that includes German activities; activities from authorities, institutes and various groups in societies in the occupied countries and satellite states; Jewish perceptions and reactions; and simultaneous description of events on all levels and at various places. This promises to enhance the perception of the scale, the complexity and mutual interweaving of the enormous number of components of the Holocaust.

Notes

1. *Germany 1944: the British Soldier's Pocketbook* (reprint, Kew, 2006), 26 (capital letters as in original).
2. Jürgen Matthäus, 'Historiography and the Perpetrators of the Holocaust', in Dan Stone (ed.), *The Historiography of the Holocaust* (Basingstoke, 2004), 197–215, here, 197.
3. H. L. Ansbacher, 'Attitudes of German Prisoners of War: a Study of the Dynamics of National-Socialist Followership', *Psychological Monographs. General and Applied*, 62(1) (1948), 38f.
4. For this see Thomas Kühne, 'Der nationalsozialistische Vernichtungskrieg und die "ganz normalen" Deutschen. Forschungsprobleme und Forschungstendenzen der Gesellschaftsgeschichte des Zweiten Weltkrieges. Erster Teil', *Archiv für Sozialgeschichte*, 39 (1999), 580–662, here 589.
5. For this see Thomas Kühne, 'Der nationalsozialistische Vernichtungskrieg im kulturellen Kontinuum des Zwanzigsten Jahrhunderts. Forschungsprobleme und Forschungstendenzen der Gesellschaftsgeschichte des Zweiten Weltkrieges. Zweiter Teil', *Archiv für Sozialgeschichte*, 40 (2000), 440–86, here 475f.
6. Klaus-Michael Mallmann and Gerhard Paul, 'Die Gestapo. Weltanschauungsexekutive mit gesellschaftlichem Rückhalt', in Klaus-Michael Mallmann and Gerhard Paul (eds), *Die Gestapo im Zweiten Weltkrieg "Heimatfront" und besetztes Europa* (Darmstadt, 2000), 599–650, esp. 633–7; Martin Dean, 'Where Did All the Collaborators Go?', *Slavic Review*, 64(4) (2005), 791–8.
7. Dieter Pohl, however, emphasises the important Polish work by Artur Eisenbach (*Hitlerowska polityka zaglady Żydów*, Warsaw, 1961) that explained the origins of the persecution of the Jews in racial biology. See Dieter Pohl, 'Die Holocaust-Forschung und Goldhagens Thesen', *Vierteljahreshefte für Zeitgeschichte*, 45 (1997), 1–48, here 2.
8. For the following see Gerhard Paul, 'Von Psychopathen, Technokraten des Terrors und ganz gewöhnlichen Deutschen. Die Täter der Shoah im Spiegel der Forschung', in Gerhard Paul (ed.), *Die Täter der Shoah. Fanatische Nationalsozialisten oder ganz normale Deutsche?* (2nd edn, Göttingen, 2003), 13–90, here 16ff.
9. Matthäus, 'Historiography', 199.
10. Eugen Kogon, *The Theory and Practice of Hell: the German Concentration Camps and the System Behind Them* (London, 1950), 289 (*Der SS-Staat: Das System der deutschen Konzentrationslager* (Düsseldorf, 1946)). Cf. Paul, 'Psychopathen', 19.
11. Der Nürnberger Prozess. CD-ROM. Digitale Bibliothek. Vol. 20 (Berlin, 2002). For the English translation see http://www.einsatzgruppenarchives.com/ohlendorf.html.
12. Joachim Perels, 'Wahrnehmung und Verdrängung von NS-Verbrechen durch die Justiz', in Peter Gleichmann and Thomas Kühne (eds), *Massenhaftes Töten. Kriege und Genozide im 20. Jahrhundert* (Essen, 2004), 361–71.
13. Paul, 'Psychopathen', 18.
14. See Anette Kretzer, ' "His or her spezial job". Die Repräsentation von NS-Verbrecherinnen im ersten Hamburger Ravensbrück-Prozess und im westdeutschen Täterschafts-Diskurs', in KZ-Gedenkstätte Neuengamme (ed.),

Entgrenzte Gewalt. Täterinnen und Täter im Nationalsozialismus (Bremen, 2002), 134–50.
15. Robert G. Moeller, *War Stories: the Search for a Usable Past in the Federal Republic of Germany* (Berkeley, 2003).
16. Ulrich Herbert, 'Extermination Policy: New Answers and Questions about the History of the "Holocaust" in German Historiography', in Ulrich Herbert (ed.), *National Socialist Extermination Policies: Contemporary German Perspectives and Controversies* (Oxford, 2000), 1–52, here 4.
17. Cf. Ian Kershaw, *Hitler, 1889–1936: Hubris* (London, 1998), xxi–xxiii.
18. See Eberhard Jäckel, *Hitlers Weltanschauung: Entwurf einer Herrschaft* (Tübingen, 1969); Rainer Zitelmann, *Hitler. Selbstverständnis eines Revolutionärs* (Hamburg, 1985); Kershaw, *Hubris*; Ian Kershaw, *Hitler, 1936–1945: Nemesis* (London, 2000).
19. Hans Buchheim, Martin Broszat, Hans-Adolf Jacobsen and Helmut Krausnick (eds), *Anatomie des SS-Staates* (Olten, 1965). See Herbert, 'Extermination', 5; Pohl, 'Holocaust-Forschung', 3.
20. Peter Longerich, 'Tendenzen und Perspektiven der Täterforschung', *Aus Politik und Zeitgeschichte*, 14–15 (2 April 2007), 3–7, here 3f.
21. For example, see Karl Dietrich Bracher, *Die deutsche Diktatur: Entstehung, Struktur, Folgen des Nationalsozialismus* (Cologne, 1969); Karl Dietrich Bracher, Manfred Funke and Hans-Adolf Jacobsen (eds), *Nationalsozialistische Diktatur 1933–1945. Eine Bilanz* (Bonn, 1983); Martin Broszat et al. (eds), *Bayern in der NS-Zeit*, 6 vols. (Munich, 1977ff.). Cf. Paul, 'Psychopathen', 28f.
22. Uwe Dietrich Adam, *Judenpolitik im Dritten Reich* (Düsseldorf, 1972); Christian Streit, *Keine Kameraden: Die Wehrmacht und die sowjetischen Kriegsgefangenen 1941–1945* (Stuttgart, 1978).
23. Cf. Pohl, 'Holocaust-Forschung', 4; Herbert, 'Extermination', 9.
24. Ingo Haar and Michael Fahlbusch (eds), *German Scholars and Ethnic Cleansing 1919–1945* (Oxford, 2005), xi; Matthäus, 'Historiography', 203.
25. Herbert Jäger, *Verbrechen unter totalitärer Herrschaft. Studien zur nationalsozialistischen Gewaltkriminalität* (Frankfurt/Main, 1967). See Pohl, 'Holocaust-Forschung', 12f.; Thomas Sandkühler, 'Die Täter des Holocaust. Neuere Überlegungen und Kontroversen', in Karl-Heinrich Pohl (ed.), *Wehrmacht und Vernichtungspolitik. Militär im nationalsozialistischen System* (Göttingen, 1999), 39–65, here 42f.; Kühne, 'Vernichtungskrieg – Erster Teil', 606f.
26. Cf. Matthäus, 'Historiography', 204.
27. Raul Hilberg, *The Politics of Memory: the Journey of a Holocaust Historian* (Chicago, 1996), 141ff.
28. Lucy S. Dawidowicz, *The War against the Jews 1933–1945* (New York, 1977); Nora Levin, *The Holocaust: the Destruction of European Jewry 1933–1945* (New York, 1968).
29. Hannah Arendt, *The Origins of Totalitarianism* (London, 1986), xiv. This largely follows Matthäus, 'Historiography', 201f.
30. Arendt, *Totalitarianism*, viii, 464f., 472.
31. Raul Hilberg, *The Destruction of the European Jews* (London, 1961).
32. Christopher R. Browning, 'German Killers: Orders from Above, Initiative from Below, and the Scope of Local Autonomy – The Case of Brest-Litovsk',

in Christopher R. Browning (ed.), *Nazi Policy, Jewish Workers, German Killers* (Cambridge, 2000), 116–42, here 116.
33. Paul, 'Psychopathen', 27f.; Kühne, 'Vernichtungskrieg – Erster Teil', 594.
34. Notable exceptions before 1961 are Léon Poliakov, *Breviaire de la Haine. Le Troisiéme Reich et les Juifs* (Paris, 1951); Gerald Reitlinger, *The Final Solution: the Attempt to Exterminate the Jews of Europe, 1939–1945* (London, 1953).
35. Hannah Arendt, *Eichmann in Jerusalem: a Report on the Banality of Evil* (rev. and enlarged edn, New York, 1994), 295, 49, 148–50.
36. For this and the following see Paul, 'Psychopathen', 21ff.
37. Hilberg, *Politics*, 150; Paul, 'Psychopathen', 26f.
38. Herbert, 'Extermination', 8.
39. Paul, 'Psychopathen', 20ff. Also see Herbert, 'Extermination', 8.
40. Zygmunt Bauman, *Modernity and the Holocaust* (Ithaca, NY, 1989), 12.
41. James E. Young, *The Texture of Memory: Holocaust Memorials and Memory* (New Haven, 1993). For a world-wide overview, see David S. Wyman (ed.), *The World Reacts to the Holocaust* (London, 1996).
42. http://www.museum.tv/archives/etv/H/htmlH/holocaust/holocaust.htm; Bill Niven, *Facing the Nazi Past: United Germany and the Legacy of the Third Reich* (London, 2002), 4.
43. Detlef Garbe, 'Die Täter. Kommentierende Bemerkungen', in Ulrich Herbert et al. (eds), *Die nationalsozialistischen Konzentrationslager. Entwicklung und Struktur*, vol. II (Göttingen, 1998), 822–38, here 823f.
44. Matthäus, 'Historiography', 205.
45. Helmut Krausnick and Hans-Heinrich Wilhelm, *Die Truppe des Weltanschaungskrieges. Die Einsatzgruppen der Sicherheitspolizei und des SD 1938–1942* (Stuttgart, 1981); Ernst Klee, *'Euthanasie' im NS-Staat: Die 'Vernichtung lebensunwerten Lebens'* (Frankfurt/Main, 1983); Benno-Müller-Hill, *Tödliche Wissenschaft: Die Aussonderung von Juden, Zigeunern und Geisteskranken, 1933–1945* (Reinbek, 1984); Gisela Bock, *Zwangsterilisation im Nationalsozialismus* (Opladen, 1986); Hans-Walter Schmuhl, *Rassenhygiene, Nationalsozialismus, Euthanasie. Von der Verhütung zur Vernichtung 'lebensunwerten Lebens' 1890–1945* (Göttingen, 1987); Ulrich Herbert, *Fremdarbeiter. Politik und Praxis des 'Ausländer-Einsatzes' in der Kriegswirtschaft des Dritten Reiches* (Berlin, 1985); Burkhard Jellonek, *Homosexuelle unter dem Hakenkreuz. Die Verfolgung der Homosexuellen im Dritten Reich* (Paderborn, 1990). Cf. Kühne, 'Vernichtungskrieg – Erster Teil', 596.
46. For example, see Ebbo Demant (ed.), *Auschwitz – 'Direkt von der Rampe weg...' Kaduk, Erberg, Klehr: drei Täter geben zu Protokoll* (Reinbek, 1979); Ernst Klee et al. (eds), *'Schöne Zeiten'. Judenmord aus der Sicht der Täter und Gaffer* (Frankfurt/Main, 1988); Ortwin Buchbender and Reinhold Sterz (eds), *Das andere Gesicht des Krieges. Deutsche Feldpostbriefe 1939–1945* (2nd edn, Munich, 1983). See Paul, 'Psychopathen', 33ff.; Kühne, 'Vernichtungskrieg – Erster Teil', 637.
47. Michael Zimmermann, *Verfolgt, vertrieben, vernichtet. Die nationalsozialistische Vernichtungspolitik gegen Sinti und Roma* (Essen, 1989); cit. Herbert, 'Extermination', 15.
48. Henry V. Dicks, *Licensed Mass Murder: a Social-psychological Study of Some SS Killers* (Edinburgh, 1972); Gitta Sereny, *Am Abgrund. Eine Gewissensforschung.*

Gespräche mit Franz Stangl, Kommandant von Treblinka, und anderen (Frankfurt/Main, 1979); Stein Ugelvik Larsen et al. (eds), *Who Were the Fascists? Social Roots of European Fascism* (Bergen, 1980); Tom Segev, *Soldiers of Evil: the Commandants of the Nazi Concentration Camps* (New York, 1988); Charles W. Sydnor, *Soldiers of Destruction: the SS-Death's Head Division, 1933–1945* (Princeton, 1977). See Paul, 'Psychopathen', 34ff.
49. Omer Bartov, *The Eastern Front, 1941–1945: German Troops and the Barbarisation of Warfare* (Basingstoke, 1985), 144, 152f.; Omer Bartov, *Hitler's Army: Soldiers, Nazis and War in the Third Reich* (New York, 1991), 182.
50. Niven, *Facing*, esp. 1–4.
51. Christopher Browning, *Ordinary Men: Reserve Police Battalion 101 and the Final Solution in Poland* (orig. New York, 1992; this edn London, 2001).
52. Stanley Milgram, *Obedience to Authority: an Experimental View* (New York, 1974); Craig Haney, Curtis Banks and Philip Zimbardo, 'Interpersonal Dynamics in a Simulated Prison', *International Journal of Criminology and Penology*, 1 (1973), 69–97.
53. Bogdan Musial, *Deutsche Zivilverwaltung und Judenverfolgung im Generalgouvernement. Eine Fallstudie zum Distrikt Lublin 1939–1944* (Wiesbaden, 1999); Christian Gerlach, *Kalkulierte Morde: die deutsche Wirtschafts- und Vernichtungspolitik in Weißrußland 1941 bis 1944* (Hamburg, 1999); Dieter Pohl, *Nationalsozialistische Judenverfolgung in Ostgalizien 1941–1944* (Munich, 1996).
54. Browning, *Ordinary Men*, 186–8. See Primo Levi, 'The Gray Zone', in Primo Levi, *The Drowned and the Saved* (New York, 1989), 36–9. Cf. Paul, 'Psychopathen', 38.
55. Daniel Jonah Goldhagen, *Hitler's Willing Executioners: Ordinary Germans and the Holocaust* (New York, 1997), 407; Hamburger Institut für Sozialforschung (ed.), *Vernichtungskrieg. Verbrechen der Wehrmacht 1941 bis 1944. Ausstellungskatalog* (Hamburg, 1996).
56. Matthäus, 'Historiography', 209; Kühne, 'Vernichtungskrieg – Erster Teil', 587, 590, 650.
57. Paul, 'Psychopathen', 41.
58. For this and the above see Kühne, 'Vernichtungskrieg – Erster Teil', 609. Meanwhile, see, for example, Frank Bajohr, *'Unser Hotel ist judenfrei': Bäder-Antisemitismus im 19. und 20. Jahrhundert* (Frankfurt/Main, 2003); Cornelia Hecht, *Deutsche Juden und Antisemitismus in der Weimarer Republik* (Bonn, 2003); Saul Friedländer, *Nazi Germany and the Jews: the Years of Persecution 1933–39* (London, 1997); Saul Friedländer, *Das Dritte Reich und die Juden. Die Jahre der Vernichtung, 1939–1945* (Munich, 2006); Peter Longerich, *'Davon haben wir nichts gewusst!' Die Deutschen und die Judenverfolgung 1933–1945* (Frankfurt/Main, 2006).
59. Götz Aly and Susanne Heim, *Vordenker der Vernichtung. Auschwitz und die deutschen Pläne für eine neue europäische Ordnung* (Hamburg, 1991).
60. Götz Aly, *'Endlösung'. Völkerverschiebung und der Mord an den europäischen Juden* (Frankfurt/Main, 1995).
61. Herbert, 'Extermination', 14.
62. Paul, 'Psychopathen', 43; Pohl, 'Holocaust-Forschung', 8; Hans Mommsen, 'Forschungskontroversen zum Nationalsozialismus', *Aus Politik und Zeitgeschichte*, 14–15 (2 April 2007), 14–21, here 16f.

63. Kühne, 'Vernichtungskrieg – Erster Teil', 615. Michael Wildt, *Generation des Unbedingten. Das Führungskorps des Reichssicherheitshauptamtes* (Hamburg, 2002). For this and the following also see Paul, 'Psychopathen', 43ff.; George C. Browder, 'Perpetrator Character and Motivation: an Emerging Consensus?', *Holocaust and Genocide Studies*, 17(3) (Winter 2003), 480–97, esp. 480ff.
64. Browder, 'Perpetrator', 495. For example, see Martin Cüppers, *Wegbereiter der Shoa. Die Waffen-SS, der Kommandostab Reichsführer-SS und die Judenvernichtung 1939–1945* (Darmstadt 2005); Mallmann and Paul, *Gestapo*; Michael Wildt (ed.), *Nachrichtendienst, politische Elite und Mordeinheit. Der Sicherheitsdienst des Reichsführers SS* (Hamburg, 2003); Karin Orth, *Die Konzentrationslager-SS: Sozialstrukturelle Analysen und biographische Studien* (Göttingen, 2000); Ulrich Herbert, *Best. Biographische Studien über Radikalismus, Weltanschauung und Vernunft, 1903–1989* (Bonn, 1996); Götz Aly et al. (eds), *Cleansing the Fatherland: Nazi Medicine and Racial Hygiene* (Baltimore and London, 1994).
65. Gerald D. Feldman and Wolfgang Seibel (eds), *Networks of Nazi Persecution: Bureaucracy, Business and the Organization of the Holocaust* (Oxford, 2005); Michael Thad Allen, *The Business of Genocide: the SS, Slave Labor, and the Concentration Camps* (London, 2002).
66. Browder, 'Perpetrator', 481. Also see Michael Mann, 'Were the Perpetrators of Genocide "Ordinary Men" or "Real Nazis"? Results from Fifteen Hundred Biographies', *Holocaust and Genocide Studies*, 14(3) (2000), 331–66.
67. Andrej Angrick, *Besatzungspolitik und Massenmord. Die Einsatzgruppe D in der südlichen Sowjetunion 1941–1943* (Hamburg, 2003), esp. 386–450.
68. Klaus-Michael Mallmann, 'Der Einstieg in den Genozid. Das Lübecker Polizeibataillon 307 und das Massaker in Brest-Litowsk Anfang Juli 1941', *Archiv für Polizeigeschichte*, 10(3) (1999), 82–8; cit. Paul, 'Psychopathen', 52f.
69. See Rolf-Dieter Müller and Gerd R. Ueberschär (eds), *Hitler's War in the East: a Critical Assessment* (Oxford, 2002); Thomas Kühne, *Kameradschaft. Die Soldaten des nationalsozialistischen Krieges und das 20. Jahrhundert* (Göttingen, 2006), 272.
70. Claudia Koonz, *Mothers in the Fatherland: Women, the Family and Nazi Politics* (New York, 1987); Gisela Bock, 'Die Frauen und der Nationalsozialismus: Bemerkungen zu einem Buch von Claudia Koonz', *Geschichte und Gesellschaft*, 15(4) (1989), 563–79. See Kirsten Heinsohn et al., 'Einleitung', in Kirsten Heinsohn et al. (eds), *Zwischen Karriere und Verfolgung. Handlungsräume von Frauen im nationalsozialistischen Deutschland* (Frankfurt/Main, 1997), 7–23.
71. For an overview see Susannah Heschel, 'Does Atrocity Have a Gender? Feminist Interpretations of Women in the SS', in J. M. Diefendorf (ed.), *Lessons and Legacies VI: New Currents in Holocaust Research* (Evanston, Illinois, 2004), 300–24.
72. For example, see Esther Lehnert, *Die Beteiligung von Fürsorgerinnen an der Bildung und Umsetzung der Kategorie 'minderwertig' im Nationalsozialismus. Öffentliche Fürsorgerinnen in Berlin und Hamburg im Spannungsfeld von Auslese und 'Ausmerze'* (Frankfurt/Main, 2003); Claudia Taake, *Angeklagt: SS-Frauen vor Gericht* (Oldenburg, 1998).
73. Gudrun Schwarz, *Eine Frau an seiner Seite. Ehefrauen in der 'SS-Sippengemeinschaft'* (Hamburg, 1997); Gudrun Schwarz, 'Frauen in Konzentrationslagern – Täterinnen und Zuschauerinnen', in Herbert, *Konzentrationslager*, 800–21.

74. Dean, 'Where Did All the Collaborators Go?', 798.
75. For this and the following see Martin Dean, 'Schutzmannschaften in Ukraine and Belarus: Profiles of Local Police Collaboration', in Dagmar Herzog (ed.), *Lessons and Legacies: the Holocaust in International Perspective* (vol. VII; Evanston, Illinois, 2006), 219–32, esp. 226–9. Also see Ruth B. Birn, *Die Sicherheitspolizei in Estland 1941–1944. Eine Studie zur Kollaboration im Osten* (Paderborn, 2006); Bernd Chiari, *Alltag hinter der Front. Besatzung, Kollaboration und Widerstand in Weißrußland 1941–1944* (Düsseldorf, 1998).
76. For the following see Robert Gelatelly and Ben Kiernan, 'The Study of Mass Murder and Genocide', in Robert Gelatelly and Ben Kiernan (eds), *The Specter of Genocide: Mass Murder in Historical Perspective* (Cambridge, 2003), 3–26.
77. James Waller, *Becoming Evil: How Ordinary People Commit Genocide and Mass Killing* (Oxford, 2002).
78. Harald Welzer, *Täter. Wie aus ganz normalen Menschen Massenmörder werden* (Frankfurt/Main, 2005).
79. Peter Longerich, *Politik der Vernichtung. Eine Gesamtdarstellung der nationalsozialistischen Judenverfolgung* (Munich, 1998); Christopher R. Browning, *The Origins of the Final Solution: the Evolution of Nazi Jewish Policy, September 1939–March 1942*. With contributions by Jürgen Matthäus (Lincoln, 2004).
80. For this and the following see Klaus-Michael Mallmann and Gerhard Paul, 'Sozialisation, Milieu und Gewalt. Fortschritte und Probleme der neueren Täterforschung', in Klaus-Michael Mallmann and Gerhard Paul (eds), *Karrieren der Gewalt. Nationalsozialistische Täterbiographien* (Darmstadt, 2005), 1–32, esp. 1f., 5, 9–16. For a recent discussion also see Mark Roseman, 'Beyond Conviction? Perpetrators, Ideas and Action in the Holocaust in Historiographical Perspective', in Frank Biess et al. (eds), *Conflict, Catastrophe and Continuity: Essays on Modern German History* (Oxford, 2007), 83–103.
81. Dieter Pohl, *Verfolgung und Massenmord in der NS-Zeit 1933–1945* (Darmstadt, 2003), 154f.
82. Leonard S. Newman and Ralph Erber (eds), *Understanding Genocide: the Social Psychology of the Holocaust* (New York, 2002), 50–3, cit. Browder, 'Perpetrator', 493f.
83. For research desiderata about Nazi occupied territories of the Soviet Union, see Dieter Pohl, 'Die einheimische Forschung und der Mord an den Juden in den besetzten sowjetischen Gebieten', in Wolf Kaiser (ed.), *Täter im Vernichtungskrieg. Der Überfall auf die Sowjetunion und der Völkermord an den Juden* (Berlin, 2002), 204–16.
84. Christopher R. Browning, 'Postscript', in Browning, *Nazi Policy*, 170–5, here 175.
85. Browder, 'Perpetrator', 495.
86. Claudia Koonz, *The Nazi Conscience* (Cambridge, MA, 2003).
87. Pohl, 'Holocaust-Forschung', 11.
88. Browder, 'Perpetrator', 481.
89. For a recent exception, see Christoph Dieckmann, *Deutsche Besatzungs- und Vernichtungspolitik in Litauen 1941 bis 1944* (Hamburg, 2004).
90. Matthäus, 'Historiography', 209.
91. Harvey Asher, 'Ganz normale Täter. Variablen sozialpsychologischer Analysen', *Zeitschrift für Genozidforschung*, 3(1/2) (2001), 81–115.

92. Heschel, 'Gender?', 314. More recently, see Elizabeth Harvey, *Women and the Nazi East: Agents and Witnesses of Germanization* (New Haven, 2003).
93. Anna E. Sosmus, *Widerstand und Verfolgung am Beispiel Passaus 1933–1939* (Passau, 1983); also see Michael Verhoeven's film *Das schreckliche Mädchen* (The Nasty Girl) from 1990. Harald Welzer (ed.), *Der Krieg der Erinnerung. Holocaust, Kollaboration und Widerstand im europäischen Gedächtnis* (Frankfurt/Main, 2007).
94. Antony Polonsky and Joanna B. Michlic (eds), *The Neighbors Respond: the Controversy over the Jedwabne Massacre in Poland* (Oxford, 2004).
95. Longerich, 'Tendenzen', 4; Saul Friedländer, 'Eine integrierte Geschichte des Holocaust', *Aus Politik und Zeitgeschichte*, 14–15 (2 April 2007), 7–14, here 9ff.; Ulrich Herbert, 'The Holocaust in German Historiography: Some Introductory Remarks', in Moshe Zimmermann (ed.), *On Germans and Jews under the Nazi Regime: Essays by Three Generations of Historians* (Jerusalem, 2006), 67–84, here 82f.

2
Male Bonding and Shame Culture: Hitler's Soldiers and the Moral Basis of Genocidal Warfare*

Thomas Kühne

Early in October 1941 Captain Friedrich Nöll was given an assignment which caused him grave disquiet. His battalion commander, Major Commichau, ordered him to shoot the entire Jewish population of the village of Krutscha in Russia – men, women and children. In this village to the west of Smolensk, to the rear of the German army, Nöll was in command of the 3rd company of the 1st battalion of the 691st infantry regiment. All three companies of the battalion received similar killing orders. But their leaders reacted in different ways. Lieutenant Kuhls, a member of the Nazi party and the SS, carried out the order with his company without hesitation. The opposite reaction came from Lieutenant Sibille, a teacher aged 47. Alluding to the systematic killing campaigns of the *Einsatzgruppen*, he told his superior officer that he 'could not expect decent German soldiers to soil their hands with such things'. He said that his company would only shoot Jews if they were partisans. He had, however, been unable to establish any connection between the Jews and the partisans. The old men, women and children amongst the Jews were, he maintained, no danger to his men, so that there was no military necessity for such a measure. Asked by his superior, when would he finally get tough, he answered: in such cases, never.[1]

After initial evasiveness Nöll in the end reacted as ordered. He too was in no doubt that carrying out such shootings was no part of the duties of the *Wehrmacht*, and that according to paragraph 47 of the military penal code he could and should reject an order which he recognised to be criminal.[2] But Nöll did not refuse to carry out the order. He was afraid of making himself unpopular with the battalion commander and of being considered soft. All the same, he did not wish to burden his own conscience with the deed. He gave the task of carrying out the executions to his company sergeant-major. The sergeant-major was outraged that he had been landed with it, or so he said to comrades and subordinates, but he defused the indignation articulated amongst the soldiers by remarking that 'orders is orders' and organised the shooting of between one and two hundred Jews before the evening.[3]

Doubtless most of the soldiers only obeyed the order with reluctance. Many of them declined to pursue escaping Jews and grumbled later about the 'dirty business' demanded of them, especially since 'pregnant women' had been amongst the victims.[4] Some of the soldiers were 'totally shocked and close to nervous breakdown'.[5] After the executions a theology student gave vent in conversation with a comrade to his 'spiritual distress' over 'being compelled as a theologian to have to take part in such terrible measures'.[6] Another soldier asked on the way to the place of execution to be relieved of this duty. The request was granted, but only after the executions had begun and after he himself had started shooting, albeit deliberately missing, as he stated later. On the other hand there were also soldiers who regarded the matter as necessary in view of the danger from partisans.[7] Some even showed 'enthusiasm for the executions'.[8] But they represented a minority – just like the objectors.

The *Wehrmacht* and the Holocaust

This story throws a glaring light on the participation of the *Wehrmacht* in the Holocaust, but also on the soldiers' freedom of action (thus resembling the story told by Christopher Browning about Reserve Police Battalion 101), and it raises the question: why? Why did soldiers murder defenceless civilians instead of doing what soldiers everywhere have always done and still do, namely fight armed adversaries?

That the *Wehrmacht* played a crucial role in the murder of the European Jews and not only supported the genocidal prosecution of the war between 1939 and 1945, but also initiated it, has become amply clear since the end of the 1970s through historical research and then since 1995 thanks to the exhibition 'Crimes of the *Wehrmacht*' mounted by the Institute for Social Research in Hamburg. Leaders of the *Wehrmacht* were decisively involved from 1941 in the planning of the war of annihilation against 'Bolshevism and Jewry', and with the so-called 'criminal orders' they laid the basis for unprovoked attacks on civilians, especially Jews and Communists. They allowed more than half of their 5.7 million Soviet prisoners of war to be shot, to die of starvation or be condemned to forced labour and its fatal consequences. The great majority of soldiers in the *Wehrmacht*, of whatever rank, paid homage (like the rest of the Germans) to an anti-Semitic ideology. In many occupied areas such as Serbia the *Wehrmacht* organised the Holocaust largely independently of the SS. Individual *Wehrmacht* units and soldiers participated voluntarily in the mass shootings of Jews in the East. Countless units gave the *Einsatzgruppen* logistical support by tracking down the local Jewish population, rounding it up, cordoning off places of execution and instigating deportations. In the context of the escalating partisan war in the Soviet Union, but also in other theatres of war after 1942 the *Wehrmacht* was responsible, as well as the SS but by no means any less than them, for innumerable massacres amongst Jews and other sections of the population.[9]

Surveying the research over the last thirty years, two tendencies are notable. First, the independent genocidal conduct of ever larger sections and in particular of lower ranks of the *Wehrmacht* has come under scrutiny. In other words, soldiers in the *Wehrmacht* were not simply victims of hierarchies of command and of indoctrination but were independently operating perpetrators.[10] Secondly, it has been established that the war of annihilation did not begin in 1941 but instead went back to the invasion of Poland in 1939 and of France in 1940.[11]

At the same time, however, there is no doubt that the *Wehrmacht*, unlike the SS, was not only ideologically heterogeneous, but also manifested different patterns of behaviour in carrying out the Holocaust and in terrorising the subjugated civilian population.

Why did so many join in? What was it that made 'ordinary men' into mass murderers? And why did so many look on and thus condone the genocide? In answering these questions research on the perpetrators of the Holocaust has so far concentrated on the mass shootings in the East and therefore on the *Einsatzgruppen* and associated units, for example the police troops. Two competing models of explanation have become popular. Based on the Milgram experiment, Christopher Browning argues from the perspective of social psychology and stresses the group conformity and the authority structures operating in small face-to-face groups. Daniel Goldhagen, on the other hand, has laid emphasis pointedly on what is in his view a specifically German and historically particular disposition, 'eliminatory anti-Semitism', i.e. on the role of ideology.[12]

The dualism of the two approaches, which has not really been overcome in research since the middle of the 1990s, has a long tradition reaching back to the Second World War, as allied opponents of Germany tried to understand why the Germans were fighting so doggedly when their defeat was long since predictable. Whilst the American public presumed that the Germans were suffering from a mass psychosis rooted in racism, a group of American military sociologists interrogated German prisoners of war and demonstrated that it was not hatred of the Jews which led German soldiers to fight on, but group sociology: primary group ties, strong personal bonds, familial in character and based on trust, in the smaller military units. Such compulsive ties, reinforced by the paternalistic authority of the non-commissioned officer (NCO) and subaltern officers, represented the putty which held the *Wehrmacht* together, according to Edward Shils and Morris Janowitz.[13] This recourse to the supposedly timeless soldierly virtue of comradeship was then challenged around 1990 in an influential study by Omer Bartov; in his assessment the anti-Semitism of the soldiers combined with the draconian military discipline to which they were subject and with the catastrophic living conditions on the Eastern Front to produce legalised brutalisation and 'barbarisation'.[14] The most recent research into partisan warfare involving the *Wehrmacht* also employs categories such as brutalisation.[15]

The present chapter suggests an integrating answer to these problems, and does so in two respects. On the one hand it combines the two practical questions about the 'joining in' of the soldiers during genocidal violence and their capacity for endurance in the face of defeat. On the other, it relates cultural and ideological factors to elements of social psychology and anthropology. To put it another way: it is not comradeship (sociology) or anti-Semitism (ideology) which explains the genocidal violence and the combat stamina of the soldiers, but the two together. More accurately, a specific and historically localised symbolic order, combining stereotypes of the enemy with the experience of community, formed the basis of the mass involvement in the Holocaust and total war. My thesis is: after the First World War the ethical code revolving around individual responsibility, which is characteristic of modern Western societies, was displaced by a moral system in which the only thing counting as 'good' is that which appears good for one's own community, whilst everything figures as 'bad' which is detrimental to it. This group morality was inculcated in the Nazi state in camps for youth, for training and for the military. In the war after 1939 it operated as the motor for involvement of the soldiers, by instigating and sanctioning group pressure, group life and group honour.[16]

The comradeship myth

At the end of August 1925 some 5,000 World War veterans and 6,000 further visitors assembled on one day in Constance for a veterans' meeting of the Baden infantry regiment 'Kaiser Friedrich III' No.114. The 'day of the 114th' was intended to indicate to 'the whole fatherland' the path out of the 'unspeakable hardship' into which it had descended as a result of the recent war. The old soldiers seemed destined to show the way. The typical soldier had been, as the town's Protestant vicar put it, 'sneered at by the horror of all the mass deaths, despised, degraded'. But he had been pulled from this hell by 'the supporting, compensating, alleviating counterweight of his comrades'. 'It was they who had loyally shared with him all the suffering and the meagre joys as well. [...] That was comradeship – that is comradeship.' The 'secret of comradeship', so the Catholic vicar added, lay in the 'enduring awareness of what is human'. Returning from the firing line, 'soldiers were able in the company of dear comrades properly to recover their sense of what it means to be a human being'.[17]

It was thought necessary to revive this comradeship if the hardship of the present was to be overcome. 'We need', demanded Schaack, the Catholic vicar, 'to steep and cleanse our whole public life in the spirit of comradeship', so that the Germans could again attain national greatness. At the same time the new nation, unlike German society in the war and afterwards, should be united, free from class and other internal splits. The 'day of the 114th' represented precisely this ideal. It was a comradely 'people's community in miniature'. Even the deepest political gulf dividing Germany – that between supporters and opponents of the Weimar Republic as a democratic state – seemed to be bridged. Other public gatherings often saw disputes over which flag to hoist – the black, red and gold of the Republic, or the black, white and red of the former Empire. But on 'the day of the 114th' both flags were flying 'peacefully together'.[18]

However, this picture of peaceful togetherness was deceptive. The people's community in miniature, which 'the day of the 114th' boasted to be, did not fully reflect the nation. The two Christian denominations were represented on the regimental day along with all the non-socialist parties – the conservatives, the Catholic Centre Party, the Liberals and the nationalist veterans' associations – but not the Social Democrat workers' movement and their veterans' association, the Black, Red and Gold *Reichsbanner*, nor the Jews. The festival committee had denied the Jews' former field rabbi the honour of giving an address to the fallen.[19]

The Social Democrats took a dim view of the whole event anyway. As they saw it, the 'fine title of "comrade"' was only employed by the 'so-called comrades' who as officers had found ways of tormenting their subordinates and treating them like 'pigs' on the parade ground, and often 'financially exploiting' them too.[20]

The events in Constance were not peculiar to this locality; they followed a pattern of public remembrance of the First World War prevalent everywhere in Germany. In the war the German nation had been more split than ever before. In the end the revolution on the Left had installed the Republic and swept away the monarchy and with it the rule of the Right. Whilst the Left celebrated this outcome of the war and condemned the monarchy and the military as the instigators of vast mountains of corpses and of economic disasters, the Right used the stab in the back legend to castigate the Left for its alleged responsibility for the military defeat, for the political chaos and the economic misery.

The categories Right and Left are not entirely adequate to describe the political and social fragmentation of Germany. But the dispute over the collective remembrance of the 'Great War' did have the character of a dichotomy. Around 1920 the pacifist 'No more war' movement was confronted by the 'everlasting' soldiers in the *Freikorps* groups. Around 1930 the conflict was revived in the mass media and in parliament when Erich Maria Remarque's anti-war novel *All Quiet on the Western Front* gained the hearts and minds of young people and the nationalist camp anathematised the pacifist 'infestation' of the younger generation.

The crux of this dispute was, however, that beneath the surface a consensus was developing. Militarists and pacifists were working on a myth of comradeship which, whilst not glorifying war, at least made it bearable. Those on the Left were not satisfied merely with repudiating the comradeship myth of the Right. They were constructing a counter-myth. Of course you had to keep alive, as the *Reichsbanner* saw it, the memory of the 'breach of comradeship' by the officers, who did not keep to 'the unwritten laws of comradeship', but filled their bellies at the expense of their 'hungry comrades'. But that 'type of person' did not deserve 'to be called comrade'. By contrast there were the 'real comrades' and real comradeship.[21] The comradeship of those below was directed against military authority. Comradeship thus denoted standing shoulder to shoulder against your superiors. The 'four infantrymen' in Ernst Johannsen's novel of the same name about life at the front take revenge on a sergeant who 'threatened to shoot a man who didn't want to go over the top' by shooting at him from behind. This deed had been carried out by a new member of the group, who precisely because of this subversive act 'was found to be worthy of their comradeship'.[22]

But in this as in other anti-war novels comradeship on the battlefield had the effect which the officers wanted. In all such cases comradeship operates as the motor of military violence, by carrying the individual soldier along and thus relieving him of personal responsibility. Nobody mutinies, nobody deserts. And after 1918 comradeship was invoked as the essence of humanity, altruism and solicitude. Even immediately after the end of the war the National Association of Disabled Soldiers, Veterans, and War Dependants (*Reichsbund der Kriegsbeschädigten, Kriegsteilnehmer und Kriegshinterbliebenen*), a Social Democrat organisation, had tightened the 'old bonds of comradeship' and exhorted every disabled veteran to remember the comrade 'who had once borne him out of the fire, when he himself was lying there helpless and with broken limbs'.[23] Those who had proved themselves as comrades in the war could not be inhuman.

Killing was presented, in both revanchist and pacifist remembrance of the war, as a collective act determined by fate. Comradeship produced, in the accounts of veterans on both Right and Left, a pull from which the individual could not escape.[24] Remarque's anti-heroes act outside of individual responsibility. 'Beside me a lance-corporal has his head torn off. [...] If we were not automata at that moment we would continue lying there, exhausted, and without will. But we are swept forward again, powerless, madly savage and raging; we will kill, for they are still our mortal enemies... and if we don't destroy them, they will destroy us.'[25]

The myth of comradeship transformed individual dismay into group conformity in warfare. The myth of comradeship thus responded to an onus placed on the Germans, namely the moral burden engendered by the piles of corpses the First World War had left behind. That burden had been intensified by the guilty verdict implied in the Versailles Treaty. After 1918, the experience of the horror of an industrialised war and personal participation in the immense violence of the war could no longer be 'categorised' as individual guilt and responsibility. The collective memory of these orgies of destruction concealed the 'I' in the 'we'. Individual responsibility was dissolved in that 'we'. Communities of comrades, resigned to their fate, neutralised their aggression towards those outside of the community through altruism and harmony within it.

What happened around 1930 in Germany might best be understood as a change of ethics. Ethics are the framework for ideas about our ways of living. We are accustomed to timeless definitions of moral behaviour. Historians, however, know that morals are a social construct. They depend on time, culture and society. For longer than historians, cultural anthropologists have been examining different moral settings. In a broad range of research they have dealt with the opposites of shame culture and guilt culture.[26] Guilt culture is seen as the moral paradigm of Western modernity. A society shaped by guilt culture trains its citizens to be responsible for their own actions. The question of morals is here a case for introspection. Guilt is experienced individually. It is dealt with in dialogue with God or with the superego. In shame culture, on the other hand, the controlling gaze of the community sets itself up as the highest moral authority. Shame is grounded in the fear of exclusion, exposure and disgrace, which the community allots to the individual who does not submit to its rules. Shame culture trains one to be inconspicuous, to conform, to participate – and to be happy through doing so, through being in good hands with the group, through enjoying security and relief within the community. Both moral paradigms arise, in variable proportions, in every society. The point is: in what ratio do they do so? In the military, shame culture is always more important than in the civilian areas of modern societies. That distinction evaporated in Germany after 1918 and even more during the Nazi era. At that time shame culture attained broad societal significance, which is otherwise most unusual in industrial societies.

Cultivating shame culture

By 1930 at the latest the conformist set of values had ceased to be the prerogative of the nationalists and militarists. It had become part of the common culture of the Germans. The youth movement had also prepared the ground for it. Arising out of disaffection with the rigid world of their elders of the Wilhelmine generation, this movement initially wallowed in the pathos of individualism. Friendship, not comradeship, was the idea which guided it in the period of the leagues of youth.[27] But the youth movement did not work on an individualistic counter-model to comradeship; it sought instead to merge it with friendship. This semantic syncretism reflects the indecision of a movement which tried to combine individualistic development of personality with the security of the community. Franz Matzke wrote in his widely read *Jugend bekennt* (Confessions of Youth) in 1930 that young people obeyed 'even when we know better and feel otherwise. But it is an obedience in the outer regions of the soul, not in its nucleus, which is always individual and foreign to the community, albeit longing for community.'[28] This 'Confession' is another indicator that the shift from guilt culture to shame culture was by no means total. But Matzke summed up what occurred: the morality and way of life revolving around the 'ego' became more shut away than ever. It was not allowed to break out into the external world. It could not be exhibited. It became less and less possible to speak about it. Beside the many egos united around the campfire a collective 'we' held sway in the 'hordes' and leagues of youth. You could expect suspicious looks if during a meal you withdrew from 'brotherly sharing' or if you gave in to an inclination to 'go your own way'.[29] The community – this was the threat implied in the youth movement or in the military – 'spots the outsider and knows how to defend itself'.[30] For 'the comrades themselves are the most vigilant when it comes to shirkers'.[31]

Before 1933 nobody was forced to participate in this community life. But young people from all political and social backgrounds wanted to be 'pressed into' a comradeship which compels a 'mother's boy' to 'curtail his private demands'.[32] It was left to the Nazi state to fulfil the longing for community and to place obstacles in the way of almost every alternative. The agencies engineering this were the Hitler Youth, the National Labour Service (*Reichsarbeitsdienst*), and the military service and various other paramilitary or military camps. It was there that young and older Germans alike learned how to give up a value system revolving around an individual perspective on life and on personal responsibility. Sebastian Haffner found himself confronted with this in 1933 in a camp he had to attend for candidates for the German civil service. 'If someone committed a sin against comradeship, or "acted superior" or "showed off" and exhibited more individuality than was permissible, a nighttime court would judge and condemn him to corporal punishment. Being dragged under the water pump was the punishment for minor misdemeanors. However, when one of us was proved to have favored himself in distributing butter rations – which were still quite adequate at that time – he suffered a terrible fate. [...] Before much could be said the unfortunate man had been dragged from his bed and spread-eagled on a table.' As Haffner saw it, comradeship 'actively decomposed' both 'individuality and civilization'. One of the highlights of such decomposition was the 'boyish' custom 'of attacking a neighboring dormitory at night with "water bombs", drinking mugs filled with water to be poured over the beds of the defenders... A battle would ensue, with merry ho's and ha's and screaming and cheering. You were a bad comrade if you did not take part. [...] It was taken for granted that comradeship prevented those who had been attacked from telling tales.'[33]

There could be no community without the others, the 'egoists' and outsiders. Military service was the drilling square for shame culture. There were many possible ways in which comrades educated deviants into comradeship and assimilated themselves into the community. A tank gunner received a symbolic burial for his failures in formal drill. On the command of a sergeant he was made to lie in a hole and pull his steel helmet over his face. His comrades covered him over with a sheet of corrugated iron, and the sergeant shot three blank cartridges over the 'grave'. When he made mistakes in shooting, he had to stand with a cigarette which the sergeant pretended to shoot out of his hand. Only later did the unfortunate gunner find out that blanks had been loaded. Once he fell in on parade with a dirty neck and his superior told him to wash, which his comrades took as an encouragement to drag the bawling young man into the washroom and 'scrub him down'. Some time later, with the sergeant to the fore, they poured two buckets of water into his bed in the night. A legal prosecution of the harsh but popular sergeant was stopped. In their evidence his comrades showed little sympathy for the 'sniveller', who at the slightest reprimand started 'trembling and howling' and 'wouldn't join in any more'. And the military judges took the view that such 'rough practical jokes' were entirely appropriate for the 'uncompromising demands of modern warfare' which were made on 'useful soldier material'.[34]

Anybody could find himself back in the outsider role who failed to adapt to the mood of his group and resisted demands to sacrifice his self on the altar of the 'we'. In the military your superior was at hand not only as the teacher of this virtue but also as its catalyst, in torturing the recruits with mud baths, locker room and dormitory roll calls, masquerades and confinement to barracks. For hatred for the tormentors had a conciliatory note. It ensured a certain harmony within the group. Thus in 1942 a *Wehrmacht* recruit wrote to his friend in the Hitler Youth that 'we' had 'imperceptibly grown together into firm comradeship' through the harassment suffered in the first three weeks of serving together – following the slogan 'nobody can get to us' and the motto 'and should our arses turn to leather, never mind, we'll stick together'.[35]

Military comradeship developed amongst recruits through defending themselves against the terrors inflicted on them by their superiors. Defensive comradeship provided power, security and a safe haven during the impotence, insecurity and loneliness of soldiers trapped in the workings of the military obedience and subjugation machine. It often issued in little 'conspiracies'. Dieter Wellershoff's comrade Edi had 'gone to the equipment vehicle in accordance with regulations and with official permission in order to have his boots soled, but had not come back, although it was only some four kilometers away. [...] That was an unauthorized absence from the unit.' Wellershoff and his comrades knew that they were liable to punishment if they did not report Edi. But they did not see him as a traitor and 'believed in Edi's nonchalance and his fantasies', which did not really endanger his ties to his comrades. 'And a secret solidarity with this crazy guy prevented us from reporting the incident.' Instead they hushed up Edi's absence for a day and even during the night, when there was trench digging to be done. Edi did indeed return after a day and turned out to be a 'good comrade', who had gone AWOL, not for himself, but for the sake of the group, to 'purloin things'. As 'booty' he brought a side of bacon which 'he shared out amongst us'.[36]

A comrade was someone with whom 'you could get up to something now and then'. So Lieutenant Gerhard Modersen put it in his diary in 1943.[37] For countless soldiers, getting up to something together meant one thing above all: adventures with women. Modersen was married. But it was precisely adultery, which along with his comrades he constantly practised, which for him represented the attraction of life as a soldier. It was *not only* a matter of sexual needs. At least as important was the ability to boast of sexual adventures to your circle of comrades. Showing off about sex was as much a part of assimilation into a community of male buddies as affectionate homo-eroticism. Both demonstrated the social sovereignty of the leagues of males, their independence from real women, their superiority over the family and home – over civilian society and civilian morality. The moral grammar of comradeship always obeyed the same rule: anything was allowed which the group liked, i.e. anything which enriched and intensified its social life.

Assimilation into the community through crime

Comradeship lived off collective breaches of the norm. All absorption into a community is based on demarcations and the construction of opposites. The radical form of these processes is the suspension of generally valid norms by sub-cultural groups, in other words entering a community by means of the illicit and the criminal. This acculturation via the illicit meant different things to men and to women. For men it was a privilege and a must. In order to be acknowledged as a man 'amongst men', they had to be prepared to do the illicit or at least the disreputable, and to do so in the company of other men and under their scrutiny. The comradely league of men was constituted by the infringement, the transgression or suspension of the norm. What norm it was, was not without a certain arbitrariness. The crucial thing was to breach the norm, which gave the league of men the illusion of being above morality and thus above the cultural foundations of society, in fact of being able to determine these foundations itself.

Leagues of men forming themselves into communities through the illicit and the criminal were not peculiar to the military or to Germany in the Nazi period. As shown by many historians, sociologists and cultural anthropologists in studies of male initiation rites, of criminal fraternities and street gangs, not least of other military organisations and other wars, such mechanisms seem to have almost universal importance. So what was specifically German or Nazi about it? What connection exists between the exceptional genocide orchestrated by the Nazi state and carried out in Europe by the Germans and the breach of norms in small, usually face to face relationships by restricted groups of males?

In Nazi Germany assimilation into the community via criminality was arranged by the state. Hitler himself was well aware of the sociology of crime and presented it as a political prescription. In 1923 he declared that there were 'two things which can unite human beings; shared ideals and shared roguery'.[38] This maxim was put into practice before 1933 as well as afterwards. An early high point in its state application was the brutal elimination of internal party opponents and other adversaries in the course of the so-called Röhm putsch in the summer of 1934. As is well known, the murders were carried out jointly by members of the SS and the Reichswehr. The two pillars of the Nazi state, the new and the old, thus combined in such a way as to leave no 'way back'.

Of fundamental significance in the present context, looking at the mass of soldiers in the Nazi war, are the criminal orders which were issued under the seal of secrecy during the preparations for the attack on the Soviet Union in the spring of 1941, but which could not remain secret and were not intended to do so. According to these orders, what were called 'political commissars' of the Red Army, although they were not more closely defined, were not to be treated as prisoners of war according to international law, but were to be 'seen to' either at once or after further 'checking over'. The war jurisdiction decree suspended 'obligatory prosecution' for offences against members of the subjugated civilian population by *Wehrmacht* personnel, even if it was a case of 'military crime'. *De facto*, the two commands together declared open season on both prisoners of war and the civilian population of the occupied areas.[39]

These orders, crassly contrary to international law as they were, were not carried out in all *Wehrmacht* units with equal consistency. They did, however, provide the basis on which the *Wehrmacht* was drawn into the Holocaust and thus into a social and cultural process which can best be understood as a comprehensive absorption into a community by means of criminality. That is not to say that all soldiers became criminals to the same extent. Some refused to take part or stood aside. But the wholly diverse attitudes and variations in conduct in themselves oiled the machinery of genocidal warfare. The functioning of this social mechanism has been well described by Primo Levi, with reference to concentration camp society and to the role of uncertain individuals and collaborators who wavered between refusal and participation. The collaborators 'betrayed once and they can betray again. It is not enough to relegate them to marginal tasks; the best way to bind them is to burden them with guilt, cover them with blood, compromise them as much as possible, thus establishing a bond of complicity so that they can no longer turn back. This way of proceeding has been well known to criminal associations of all times and places. The Mafia has always practised it.'[40] It was precisely this Mafia principle which operated in the German *Wehrmacht* too.

Lieutenant Fritz Farnbacher, a Protestant, although he took part in the Russian campaign from day one and served at the front, was probably never involved personally in the murder of Jews or other defenceless persons. Instead he tried to keep his distance. But three days after the attack on the Soviet Union the fact that the troops were feeding 'off the land' was already giving him a headache, for 'all manner of things are being "pinched"'.[41] In the middle of July 1941 his unit picked up a string of deserters – not partisans or such like – amongst whom there was a Jew 'who is supposed to be suspicious, a commissar or some such [...] And now it is decided that the Jew shall be shot. According to higher orders, commissars are to be shot. That is extended to Jews', he notes in his diary. First, though, the suspect is interrogated under the guidance of a 'very dashing' major who by means of his 'Jew comforter', a sturdy stick, tries to beat the whereabouts of other commissars out of him. Farnbacher finds it 'terribly spine-chilling'. After innumerable kinds of mistreatment the Jew is 'bumped off'.[42] So it goes on. Deserters are shoved into prison camps with catastrophic conditions – 'these people will maybe feel cheated'.[43] The villages and houses of civilians are set alight, their tearful inhabitants may well arouse pity, but nothing can be done, Farnbacher records. And again and again commissars turn up who have to be 'shot on the spot'; but 'nobody wants to do it', not Farnbacher either. 'People shrink from the responsibility.'[44] They were well aware of international law. Those who didn't want to infringe it, chose like Farnbacher to keep silent.

There was silence at the beginning. But in the threatening scenarios of the partisan war, dramatised by rumours and propaganda, the scruples about criminal warfare gradually dissolve. Farnbacher had heard 'in what bestial ways the Russians have handled our men, smashing their skulls and using bayonets on them', and so he was fully in agreement that 'no more prisoners should be taken' and that 'no more false moderation' should prevail.[45] Such rumours and experiences confirmed Nazi propaganda and the 'criminal orders' which insinuated that 'the political commissars' are guilty of 'hateful, cruel and inhuman treatment of our prisoners'.

What Farnbacher heard and saw was nevertheless not entirely based on imagination and insinuation. He experienced 'dirty tricks' perpetrated on his own troops by hostile 'civilians' and began by overcoming his inhibitions in 'requisitioning' food for his men. A gunner trying to requisition a pig drove his vehicle over a mine: 'three dead, one severely wounded, one lightly wounded. I'd sooner deprive these people here of their last cow!'[46] Soon afterwards his scruples about the 'bumped off' civilians begin to evaporate. 'What we've come to!', he remarked at the end of 1941 on hearing that some thirty Russian prisoners had been simply 'bumped off' because it was so far to the assembly point: 'Five months ago we wouldn't have even said that, let alone dared do it! And today it's a matter of course, of which every one of us approves on reflection. No mercy for these predators and beasts!'[47]

That the prisoners who were not shot at once starved to death, that one comrade set up a 'game hunt', in other words he decided to 'bump off' the next Russian (amongst the prisoners) wearing the kind of boots he wanted for himself, all of this soon merited only a mention in passing.[48] At the same time enthusiasm grew for shared experiences and adventures which reminded the troops of trips with boys' leagues and which occurred during the requisitioning forays and campaigns against partisans in the locality in spring 1942. You didn't run into partisans, but the booty in a village was all the more sumptuous: potatoes, greens, fifty chickens, grain, three sucking pigs, 'and above all a cow', were loaded on to thirty sledges. 'Then I put myself at the head of my forces, once I have assured myself again that they're all present [...] and march off homewards. The evening is as beautiful as the morning before it. The wind is at our backs and we race along.' The mood is one of elation, not least due to the ordinary soldiers' sense of humour: 'On our expedition, when I asked whether the cow had been paid for, they just said "Yessir!" To my question, how had they paid, came the answer "With cigarette cards!"'[49]

Another *Wehrmacht* lieutenant, Werner Groß, drove 'around the area' in a cart and horses with his men in the spring of 1943. They had, he proudly wrote: 'searched villages, combed woods and cleared the area of gangs [...] We lived like gypsies and tramps.'[50] The magic potion which enlivened these cleansing campaigns and plundering trips came from the awareness of being above civilian society. Soldiers like Farnbacher or Groß may not have entirely abandoned this morality. The regular troops of the *Wehrmacht* and the Waffen-SS did not murder defenceless opponents. That reflected the traditional understanding which the military had of themselves. In practice things looked different. The 'gangs' which Groß fought were a synonym for partisans, and Nazi propaganda equated partisans with Jews. 'Where there are partisans, there are Jews, and where there are Jews, there are partisans.' This was the succinct conclusion of a course which had been given in Mogilew at the end of September 1941 on the initiative of the commander of the forces at the rear of the middle sector on the front, General Max von Schenckendorff. The course was conducted by the head of *Einsatzgruppe B*, SS Brigade Commander Arthur Nebe, and the Senior Commander of the SS and Police in Russia Central, SS Gruppenführer Erich von dem Bach-Zelewski. At the end of the course the participants observed an action against partisans carried out especially for their benefit. Thirty-two Jews of both sexes were murdered. Infantry Regiment 691 was represented on this course by the head of the 2nd company of the 1st battalion, Lieutenant Kuhls, who two weeks later unhesitatingly carried out the order mentioned at the start of this essay. Major Commichau and Captain Nöll as well as Lieutenant Sibille were notified in a report of the result of the course.[51]

In the East they were not faced by normal adversaries, this was the message that propaganda and orders again and again sought to implant in the minds of German soldiers, in order to encourage commitment to a kind of warfare which was contrary to international law. This propaganda always followed the same principle. It was insinuated that the enemy was guilty of brutality and criminality, in order to justify brutality and criminality on the German side as merely a reaction to ensure physical survival or the preservation of honour. The former was used as an argument by Hitler in his notorious speech to the top leaders of the

Wehrmacht on 30 March 1941, a record of which has been preserved in the form of notes made by Fritz Halder. 'A communist is no comrade, before or after the battle. This is a war of extermination. If we do not grasp this, we shall beat the enemy, but thirty years later we shall have to fight the communist foe [...] The troops must fight back with the methods with which they are attacked. Commissars are criminals and must be dealt with as such. [...] In the East, harshness today means lenience in the future. Commanders must make the sacrifice of overcoming their personal scruples.'[52]

As well as anxiety about the physical security of your own unit and your own people's community, there was also the appeal to collective honour, which was tarnished by alleged earlier atrocities committed by an inhuman and thus inferior adversary. 'Soldiers on the Eastern front are not only fighters according to the rules of war, they are also the bearers of an inexorable folk concept and the avengers of all the bestialities inflicted on the German nation and its kindred peoples. So soldiers must show understanding for the necessity of tough but just atonement to be extracted from the sub-human Jewish race', declared Field Marshall von Reichenau on 12 October 1941.[53] Honour challenged in this way demanded vengeance, retaliation, atonement and abandonment of the morality of conscience, of sympathy and scruples. Retaliation, like other forms of terror and thus the brutalisation of warfare by the *Wehrmacht*, was justified by reference to its deterrent purpose, in other words to the future. But retaliation has a genuine moral dimension as well as this psychological one. The honour code of vengeance demanded the visitation of communal force on those who had done wrong to members of your own group, or on their relatives, and it legitimised this force against the background of a collective morality which was not interested in the personal responsibility of the victims or in your personal conscience – shame culture. On both sides there were no individual responsibilities, only collective ones. It was this morality which was appealed to by the atonement commands, a morality which instead of murdering the real instigators of partisan attacks permitted and required the killing of random members of their 'group'. Both sides, the group which was being avenged, and the other which was the target of the vengeance, could be defined arbitrarily, as could the number of victims. In order to combat the 'communist insurgent movement in the occupied areas', 50–100 Communists should be killed henceforth as 'atonement for one German soldier's life' and as a deterrent, the Chief of Staff Keitel laid down in a decree dated 16 September 1941.[54] That the proportions were jacked up from 1:5 or 1:10 to 1:100 was a result of the politics of toughness and deterrence, which regarded lenience as retreat and knew no better than to answer every destructive act suffered with ever greater destruction, in order to demonstrate the strength and the identity of your own group.[55]

From the information we possess about the perpetrators of these massacres it is possible in almost all cases to deduce that by no means all of them behaved unscrupulously. As much as mythical remembrance of the First World War and the secondary socialisation in the youth camps and in the *Wehrmacht* had prepared the ground for internalisation of shame culture, the scruples of many soldiers seem to confirm Theodor W. Adorno's hope that human beings are 'always better than their culture'.[56] Culture nevertheless was stronger than individual motives. The same is true of the 1st battalion of the 691st infantry regiment as of the Police Battalion 101 investigated by Browning. Many members of these units were afraid of being shown up in front of comrades, of being considered cowardly, feeble or not a man. Those who refused to join in were leaving the unpleasant duty of killing to the others, they were stared at by comrades and felt ashamed, knowing that they would be 'cut' and isolated. But their abstention was not absolute. Although they declined to be directly involved in the killing, they at the same time confirmed the morality which legitimised it. This morality made the 'we' of the in-group, which was committed to 'toughness', into an absolute, and suspended sympathy with the defenceless adversary, which was stigmatised as 'soft'. In abstaining, Sibille accepted that he was not 'tough'. And the policemen who stood aside in Poland not only had to swallow being labelled 'weaklings' or 'kids'. Talking to comrades who did join in, or to their superiors, they assessed themselves in the same light. In fact they did not claim to be 'too good' to kill, but 'too weak'. They thus went out of their way to stop their conduct appearing to be criticism of their comrades. They did not question the morality of the community, but instead interpreted their own psychological constitution as pathological.[57] In opting out, these individuals presented themselves as exceptions to the rule of the symbolic order of the male community, which they were tied into and on which they themselves were still dependent. Such was the division of labour in doing daily business, ensuring that those who refused to participate did keep a marginal position and at least alleviated their social isolation. In fact they performed an important function in the internal structure of the group. In a culture of dominant 'tough' masculinity they represented the other and thus helped to make it properly visible. In this way the non-participants contributed to the hierarchical internal integration of the group and reinforced the very criminal morality from which they were trying to withdraw.

The people's community as brotherhood in crime

Contrary to the legend created after the war, which would have us believe that the *Wehrmacht* acted decently, it must be assumed that very large numbers of *Wehrmacht* soldiers knew that the war they were waging was criminal in character, even if only a minority was directly involved in murdering Jews or in other massacres. The majority was well aware of their role as part of a great community of criminality. Even during the advance in the East in 1941 many a soldier couldn't help thinking 'what things would be like if we were ever to be defeated' and 'had to shudder'.[58] It was to such anxieties that propaganda appealed after 1942, painting a picture for the German population of the vengeance the Jews would take in the event of defeat. 'What would be the lot of the German people', so Göring asked in October 1942, if we were not to win this battle...*If the war is lost, you face annihilation.*' Nobody should delude themselves that afterwards they could disown 'these nasty Nazis'. 'The Jews' would treat everybody the same, for 'their thirst for vengeance is directed at the German people'.[59] Propaganda yoked the population into a community with a common fate, united by crime, from which there was no escape. The crimes of the Holocaust were treated as a secret, although as an open secret. That they were talked about, was not only something which could not be prevented, there was actually a method in it. Things that could not be talked about were morally dubious.[60] The message of fearful crimes reached its targets. 'It's true, we must win the war if we don't want to be helpless victims of the Jews and their revenge', a soldier remarked in June 1943.[61] Another soldier stated: 'We Germans are a nation which has gone for this war really actively and will have to bear the consequences.' This insight did not, however, shake the soldiers' conviction of the legitimacy of the war. On the contrary, fear of the vengeance of the Jews or the 'beasts' from the East only intensified the impression of the fateful nature of the war. 'We could have done without the war', the same soldier went on, 'but who would have wanted to answer to the coming generation for the consequences [...] The truth was that Russia was an enemy country and a shithole.'[62] A strong sense of the justice of their own cause was deeply rooted in the soldiers' ideological world. Faced with Italy's 'treachery' in 1943, one of them stated: 'You can honestly say, when a nation is deceived and faces a world of enemies [and] stands firm in spite of everything, that it is a chosen people. Should we still lose, then I don't know what you can call a just cause.'[63] That was the morality of shame culture. Nothing was more important to it than social cohesion. The good and morally right person was the one who, regardless of personal scruples, uncertainties or anxieties, unswervingly did what the community did and kept 'faith' with it. Those who broke ranks were morally reprehensible: 'We have no time for traitors.' Especially amongst small groups the rule was: 'if you won't join in, you're a rogue'.[64] Only those who joined in had a right to survive. Those who pulled out were outlaws.

Those who did join in and comply, though, even if only in the 'outer regions' of their personality, as Frank Matzke had said in 1930, enjoyed the easy life of comradeship, which both exonerated them of guilt and gave them solace. For the dispensation from the need to show humanity towards your adversary was legitimised not only by the dehumanised image of the enemy but also by the humanity which the group cultivated within its own confines. 'Humanity', selflessness, mutual solicitude, security, even affection, were not foreign to it. They just remained confined in general to one's own group. The longer the war went on, the more the soldiers were confronted not only with participation in the murder of the opposing population but also with the deaths of masses of their own comrades. But the experience of physical destruction did not lead the soldiers in any way to doubt its social productivity. They knew in the final years of the war better than at the outset how to produce social cohesion in the small combat units, over and over again and with constant new personnel. When Corporal Kurt Kreissler, in civilian life a high-ranking leader of the Hitler Youth, returned to his company in January 1945 after convalescent leave, it was clear: 'I shan't meet any more old comrades.' The question 'how few of us are left?' could not be suppressed. But it only made him redouble his efforts to ensure that 'the men and their leaders get to know each other as soon as possible, so that they'll be warmed up ready for the battles to come and for difficult missions'.[65] If the *memory* of the great crimes committed together remained alive through fear of the revenge of the adversary, the *expectations* of the soldiers were narrowed down to the radius of the action involving their own company. 'We chucked the Russkies out of some German villages. With barely 150 men we put over 1000 Russians to flight [...] Everybody is in a brilliant mood [...] In particular my small unit, the small section of the company which I lead, is of one heart and one soul [...] The spirit in our unit has never been better than at this time. To stick together and to fight side by side and be wounded side by side, that's our wish.' At the end of the war cohesion was no longer, as envisaged in the professional duties of the soldiers, the foundation of their fighting spirit. The battle, the destruction of physical life, formed the precondition for social experience.

Conclusion

Why did Hitler's soldiers hold out for so long? And why did they join in at all – in a war which amounted to mass murder and thus went beyond anything which war had previously meant? The answer does not lie only in the soldiers' anti-Semitism or anti-Communism, in their belief in Hitler or in the draconian machinery of repression with which military justice and the Gestapo terrorised them. These factors only become significant when related to the social grammar of absorption into the military community and to its moral rules. The 'human' side of comradeship made the 'inhuman' face of war and of their own conduct in it bearable, morally and emotionally. Over and above this compensating function, comradeship operated as the motor for violence, both regular and criminal. It was the basis of the group pressure which the soldiers sensed from their entry into the forces onwards and which to a large extent they had already encountered before, mainly in the training camps of the Nazi state. But group pressure is only one side of the phenomenon. At the same time comradeship was the symbol of social cohesion, which had a more intense effect the more acutely a social group managed to mark itself off from the outside world, however understood – best of all, by deliberate and definite infringement of the norms of this external world. Comradeship meant: joining in whatever the group deemed to be good, right and appropriate. The apotheosis of this group morality operated as the lubricant of the machinery for annihilation and war. Not only a gallantly fought battle, but also attacks on the subjugated civilian population generated collective feelings of omnipotence. The group celebrated itself and the social sovereignty of the league of men, the awareness that they were above civilian morality (and the international laws of war). It defined the rules of social life anew – or it liked to give itself up to this illusion. That individual members of the group, or many of them, had scruples about the communally committed deeds or abstained from them, did not in principle call the life of the group into question, but instead acted more as the catalyst for a process of assimilation into the community which did not bother with individual lives or responsibilities, and aiming rather at their continual destruction, but otherwise put up with external, though not necessarily internal conformity.

Cultural anthropologists have coined the term 'shame culture' for this group morality and contrasted it to conscience culture. That the paradigm of shame culture in Germany was able to trigger conduct and establish norms to an extent otherwise uncommon in industrialised societies, is not only to be explained by reference to the totalitarian regime of the National Socialists, but has older roots, above all in German coming to terms mentally with the First World War. Society was overstretched in dealing with the consequences of the war, both emotional and moral. On account of the defeat and the humiliation by the Versailles Treaty this burden hit Germany harder than all the other nations involved in the First World War. The socio-cultural fragmentation of Germany as a 'latecomer' amongst the European nation-states propelled it in the same direction. From around the turn of the century growing unease was stirring over the division into classes, denominations, regions and not least over gender conflict. In the First World War the split in the nation escalated and caused the longing for a great 'people's community' healed of all inner conflicts to grow all the more. In a certain sense this longing was fulfilled in the Second World War – in the shape of a great 'people's community', which could indeed put aside inner conflicts, because it felt bound together by means of a unique and communally committed crime.

Notes

Translated by Richard Littlejohns

1. According to statements made by Sibille and other witnesses interrogated at the beginning of the 1950s. See letter Sibille, 2.2.1953, Hauptstaatsarchiv Darmstadt, H 13 Darmstadt, 979, Ks 2/54. Nöll, Zimber and Magel, 207–10, and verdict from 10.3.1956, here 756f.
2. Erich Schwinge, *Militärstrafgesetzbuch nebst Kriegssonderstrafrechtsverordnung* (2nd edn, Berlin, 1944), 100–9.
3. The verdict of the appeal court assumed a minimum number of 15 men and women. See note 1, verdict from 10.3.1956, here 756. Numbers of between 50 and 250 victims were given in witness statements.
4. Statement by Adolf Z. 24.09.1953, ibid., 360; similar Karl B. 5.12.1953, here 379.
5. Statement by Hans W. 28.8.1953, ibid., here 337.
6. Statement Hans W. 28.8.1953, ibid., here 336.
7. Statement Hans W. 28.8.1953, ibid., here 337.
8. Wilhelm W., 11.12.1953, ibid., here 386.
9. On the state of research see most recently Christian Hartmann, Johannes Hürter and Ulrike Jureit (eds), *Verbrechen der Wehrmacht* (Munich, 2005).
10. Thomas Kühne, 'Die Viktimisierungsfalle', in Michael Th. Greven and Oliver von Wrochem (eds), *Der Krieg in der Nachkriegszeit* (Opladen, 2000), 183–96.

11. Jochen Böhler, *Auftakt zum Vernichtungskrieg. Die Wehrmacht in Polen 1939* (Frankfurt/Main, 2006); Raffael Scheck, *Hitler's African Victims* (Cambridge, 2006).
12. Christopher Browning, *Ordinary Men* (New York, 1992); Daniel Goldhagen, *Hitler's Willing Executioners* (New York, 1997).
13. Edward Shils and Morris Janowitz, 'Cohesion and Disintegration in the Wehrmacht in World War II', *Public Opinion Quarterly*, 12 (1948), 280–315.
14. Omer Bartov, *Hitler's Army, Soldiers, Nazis, and War in the Third Reich* (New York, 1992).
15. Benjamin Shepherd, *War in the Wild East: the German Army and Soviet Partisans* (Cambridge, 2004).
16. For more details see Thomas Kühne, *Kameradschaft. Die Soldaten des nationalsozialistischen Krieges und das 20. Jahrhundert* (Göttingen, 2006).
17. Special page of the *Konstanzer Zeitung* marking the 1925 regimental day, and *Deutsche Bodensee-Zeitung*, celebratory supplement on 'the day of the 114th'. Both 31.8.1925.
18. *Konstanzer Zeitung*, 31.8.1925.
19. Ibid., 28.8.25.
20. *Konstanzer Volksblatt*, 12.5.1921.
21. *Das Reichsbanner*, 26.9.1931, 310.
22. Ernst Johannsen, *Vier von der Infanterie* (Hamburg-Bergedorf, 1929), 11, 13f., 48f.
23. *Mitteilungen des Reichsbundes der Kriegsopfer und Kriegsbeschädigten*, 6.12.1918, 5.
24. See, for example, Joseph M. Wehner, *Sieben vor Verdun* (Munich, 1935), 40f.
25. Erich Maria Remarque, *All Quiet on the Western Front* (New York, 1982), 115.
26. Ruth Benedict, *The Chrysanthemum and the Sword* (Boston, 1946). On Benedict's shortcomings see M. R. Creighton, 'Revisiting Shame and Guilt Cultures', *Ethos*, 18 (1990), 279–307.
27. Matthias von Hellfeld, *Bündische Jugend und Hitlerjugend* (Cologne, 1987), 33f.
28. Frank Matzke, *Jugend bekennt* (Leipzig, 1930), 57.
29. *Das junge Deutschland* (1930), 599.
30. *Das Reichsbanner*, 17.10.1931, 336f.
31. *Das junge Deutschland* (1931), 303.
32. *Arbeiterjugend* (1926), 108.
33. Sebastian Haffner, *Defying Hitler* (New York, 2002), 288–91.
34. Criminal case against Feldwebel (Staff Sergeant) Wilhelm J., 18.5.1944 a.o., Bundesarchiv-Zentralnachweisstelle Aachen-Kornelimünster, W 11/M 59.
35. Hermann Melcher, *Die Gefolgschaft* (Berg a.S., 1990), 112f.
36. Dieter Wellershoff, *Der Ernstfall* (Cologne, 1995), 188.
37. Gerhard Modersen (pseudonym), Diary 1935–49, copy owned by the author of this chapter.
38. Adolf Hitler, *Reden* (Munich, 1925), 89.
39. *Verbrechen der Wehrmacht. Dimensionen des Vernichtungskrieges 1941–1944. Ausstellungskatalog* (Hamburg, 2002), 43ff.
40. Primo Levi, *The Drowned and the Saved* (New York, 1988), 43. Compare Letizia Paoli, *Mafia Brotherhoods: Organized Crime, Italian Style* (New York, 2003).
41. Fritz Farnbacher, Diary, 1941–48, typescript in the possession of the author of this chapter, 23.6.1941.
42. Ibid., 20.7.1941.

43. Ibid., 21.7.1941.
44. Ibid., 3.8.1941.
45. Ibid., 2.7.1941.
46. Ibid., 27.10.1941.
47. Ibid., 30.12.1941.
48. Ibid., 5.1.1942.
49. Ibid., 27.3.1942.
50. Werner Gross (pseudonym), letters to his parents from his time in school, in the Hitler Youth, and in the war, 1930–45. Landeshauptarchiv Koblenz, Best. 700,153, Nr. 286–291, 4.4.1943.
51. *Verbrechen der Wehrmacht*, 462–8, 580–5.
52. Charles Burdick and Hans-Adolf Jacobsen (eds), *The Halder War Diary 1939–1942* (Novato, CA, 1988), 346.
53. *Verbrechen der Wehrmacht*, 89.
54. Facsimile in ibid., 515.
55. See esp. Michael Geyer, 'Civitella della Chiana on 29 June 1944: the Reconstruction of German "Measure"', in Hannes Heer and Klaus Naumann (eds), *War of Extermination: the German Military in World War II* (New York, 2000), 175–216.
56. Theodor Adorno, *Minima Moralia* (Frankfurt/Main, 1987), 51.
57. Browning, *Ordinary Men*, 185f.
58. Farnbacher's diary, 25.9.41. Cf. Ernst Klee et al. (eds), *'The Good Old Days'* (New York, 1991), 43.
59. Speech by Göring, 4.10.1942, quoted in David Bankier, *Die öffentliche Meinung im Hitler-Staat* (Berlin, 1995), 225.
60. Peter Longerich, *'Davon haben wir nichts gewusst!' Die Deutschen und die Judenverfolgung* (Berlin, 2006); Jeffrey Herf, *The Jewish Enemy: Nazi Propaganda during World War II and the Holocaust* (New York 2006).
61. Ortwin Buchbender and Reinhold Sterz (eds), *Das andere Gesicht des Krieges* (Munich, 1982), 117f.
62. Correspondence between Franz and Hilde Wieschenberg, 1940–5, Kempowski-Archiv Nartum, Best. Nr. 3386, here Franz Wieschenberg, 28.8.1944.
63. Correspondence between Helmut and Edith Wißmann (née Wulf), 1940–5, privately owned, here Helmut Wißmann, 9.8.1943. Compare with Buchbender and Sterz, *Gesicht des Krieges*, 141ff.
64. Joachim Dollwet, 'Menschen im Krieg, Bejahung – und Widerstand?', *Jahrbuch für Westdeutsche Landesgeschichte*, 13 (1987), 279–322, here 318.
65. Kurt Kreißler, Memoirs (a type of diary in manuscript, around 1943/44, copy in the possession of the author of the present chapter), 149, 153–8.

3

The Men of *Einsatzgruppe D*: an Inside View of a State-Sanctioned Killing Unit in the 'Third Reich'*

Andrej Angrick

In the eyes of the state, of Himmler, but also of the army, the *Einsatzgruppen* of the security police and of the *Sicherheitsdienst* (SD) were an instrument that, since the first annexations by the nascent Greater Germany, delivered the desired results when combating political opponents. Consequently, at the height of its power in the world war, the regime was more than ever reluctant to dispense with them.[1] Already during the assault on Poland the mobile units of uniformed SD members, Gestapo, and police officers from the criminal branch, as well as ordinary policemen, followed the troops immediately after the capture of a town or locality. Their task was to seize opponents' files and compile lists of suspects and of individuals and organisations assessed as hostile; but they were also empowered to remove, that is to kill, what in the jargon of the time were called 'uncongenial elements'. These were not isolated cases. Even during the Polish campaign the number of victims ran into thousands. This resulted from the elimination of 'Polish identity' (*Polentum*) within the framework of 'reprisal measures', or from shooting hostages, but also from the targeted murder of Jews in the course of the fighting.[2] So 'successful' were the *Einsatzgruppen* that – as Michael Wildt has rightly stressed more than once – their operations in the field accelerated the formation in September 1939 of the headquarters of terror, that is: the Reich Security Head Office (RSHA), and assisted the process by which violence by party and state was concentrated in one authority.[3]

During the campaigns in the west or north the *Einsatzgruppen* were allowed to carry out their murderous activities only to a limited extent, since, from the outset, they were only scantily equipped with both men and material.[4] However, their employment in the south-east of Europe gave bloody notice of what was to come.[5] Confronted during the war of competing philosophies with the Soviet Union on 22 June 1941 by the ideological mortal enemy, that is 'Jewish Bolshevism', they abandoned all civilised reservations in regard to the genocide they were planning and they were also eventually to carry through.[6] This gives rise to a complex set of questions. What group of persons was selected to carry out this task and why? Was National Socialist ideology or a certain socio-cultural profile of the perpetrators essential for their later activity? Conversely, were there radicalising elements, such as the ever-expanding brutalisation of the war or situational options, which affected the comprehensive scope of the annihilation measures? In order to form a judgement on these issues, it is imperative to reveal the structure and the original establishment of the *Einsatzgruppen* – and that of *Einsatzgruppe D* in particular – and their mission, as well as to sketch their murderous trail to the East.

The establishment of *Einsatzgruppe D* and its advance to the Caucasus as mirrored in the mass executions it carried out

The establishment of the *Einsatzgruppen* and, therefore, at least the search for its prospective leaders extends back to spring 1941, once it had emerged that the leadership had rejected the conquest of Great Britain[7] and that Hitler's longed-for Russian campaign was to become a reality instead.[8] Originally there were three *Einsatzgruppen* – distinguished by the designations A to C – planned for the projected attack with its cover name 'Operation Barbarossa'. In agreement with the General Quartermaster of the High Command of the army,[9] these groups were to advance in the wake of the German armies towards Leningrad in the northern sector, in the direction of Moscow in the central sector, and through the Ukraine in the southern sector.[10] After a short period it became clear that Romania would enter the war as an ally of Germany, since under the rule of Marshal Ion Antonescu its programmatic aim was the hope of recovering north Bukovina and Bessarabia which it had ceded to the Soviet Union.[11] As a result it was decided ad hoc in the middle of June 1941 to set up *Einsatzgruppe D*.[12]

Otto Ohlendorf was named as the leader of the unit. Ohlendorf was a long-standing supporter of the movement and a member of the SD since its earliest days. He differed from the majority of functionaries in that he was an unconventional intellectual: an economic expert oriented towards the middle class, typical of an awkward exception rarely encountered in dictatorships and even more rarely in an executive capacity. Ohlendorf, however, a graduate in economics, rose in the course of his career to be Head III (Inland SD) of the RSHA, making him subordinate in the SS hierarchy only to Heydrich and Himmler. At the same time, he held the office of a Deputy State Secretary in the Reich Ministry of Economics, though rumour had it that, in secret, he was the Minister. There was a distinctively acute and pointed quality to his thinking, which encouraged him – in spite of the pragmatism of his office – to develop a quintessentially modern-looking variant of National Socialist philosophy, so that at times he seemed to form a contrast to Himmler with his vulgar romanticism. Ohlendorf was an internal critic of the party whom Himmler, in a mixture of respect and mockery, called the 'keeper of the holy grail' of the movement. There should, however, be no delusions about the relationship between these two powerful figures, especially after the assassination of Heydrich and the gap which it left in the overall structure of the SS. The two remained loyal to each other and to the regime until the end, despite their differing position and characteristics. In other words, Himmler and Ohlendorf represented two sides of the same coin.[13] The appointment of Ohlendorf meant that one of the most high-profile RSHA functionaries had taken charge of an *Einsatzgruppe*. He saw to it that further SD intellectuals from circles around him were assigned to its leadership, along with tried and trusted pragmatists from the Gestapo and the criminal branch, since he knew full well that there was a need for men to do the 'rough and ready'. Due to the shortage of manpower, a further body was recruited to the *Einsatzgruppen*: the 90 students of the active year cohort of the Berlin-Charlottenburg Führer School, designated as 'Candidates for Leadership Service', in practice the future avant-garde of the RSHA. These individuals were intended to form the real backbone of the *Einsatzgruppen* and to act as commanders in dealing with lower service personnel whilst the higher leaders stayed hierarchically remote from the other ranks.[14] These lower ranks represented the bulk of the personnel, consisting of the 4th company of the 9th Police Battalion from Berlin Spandau, recruited as a block; members of the Waffen-SS, seconded individually;[15] and, above all, 'those eligible for emergency service', i.e civilians who were 'called up' and put in uniform. Those in this last category – including, for example, the very necessary lorry drivers and radio operators – were in general not selected arbitrarily but on account of their qualifications. Most of them had also already had some contact with the Gestapo or the SD: so, for instance, the baker who had supplied bread to the police station in his home locality was sent for on grounds of trustworthiness. As far as is known, amongst the group 'eligible for emergency service' having an ideologically entrenched philosophy was not a criterion for selection. In fact, selection on that basis would probably not have been possible during the few days available for getting *Einsatzgruppe D* ready before the start of the offensive.[16] Another group who should not be forgotten, and whose influence should certainly not be underestimated, are the translators and exiles from the USSR. They were needed for their knowledge of places and facts and they provided the nucleus for the volunteer units formed as the advance proceeded, especially since *Einsatzgruppe D* consisted of barely 600 men at the start of hostilities and was thus badly understaffed.[17] Each of the *Einsatzgruppen* was divided up like a compressed version of the structure of offices in the RSHA. That is, there was an SD department as an intelligence service; the Gestapo and criminal branch acted as the executive; and the staff department held the whole organisation together. Ohlendorf's staff formed the executive headquarters. It was also responsible for contact with the leadership of the army as well as functioning as a pivot for reports to be sent back to Berlin and as the recipient of basic orders arriving from the leadership of the RSHA, from Himmler or from his deputies in the occupied areas, the so-called Higher SS and Police Leaders (HSSPF). At the same time, the subordinate special or task commandos (*Sk* or *Ek*) were to have a decisive effect on the ground.[18] From its own complement *Einsatzgruppe D* formed *Sk 10a* and *10b* as well as *Ek 11a, 11b* and *12*. *Sk*'s were deployed closer to the front, *Ek*'s further to the rear of the armies. Heinz Seetzen from the Hamburg Gestapo was appointed leader of *Sk 10a*, and *Sk 10b* was put under the command of an old fighter from the 'Ostmark', the leader of the Salzburg section of the SD, Alois Persterer. *Ek 11a* was commanded by Paul Zapp, the *volk* essayist and leader of the Kassel section of the SD; *Ek 11b* by Bruno Müller who had already gained 'experience' in other assignments abroad; while *Ek 12* received as its commander the Aachen Gestapo chief Gustav Nosske.[19]

This was a motley crew of some 600 men. It should be remembered that, despite being uniformed, *Einsatzgruppe D* did not all wear identical military outfits, since their uniforms reflected instead their allegiance to a regional unity or an authority in their home area. Consequently, ordinary constables in their green uniforms operated alongside grey Waffen-SS personnel or members of the SD.[20] Like the staff of the other *Einsatzgruppen*, they had been assembled in the town of Pretzsch, there to be sworn in for the campaign by Heydrich and Bruno Streckenbach, the staff chief of the RSHA. The real task ahead, on the other hand, was known only to the leadership of the groups. They had been apprised of it either in Pretzsch or at first hand during a staff meeting for this purpose in Berlin at the RSHA.[21] The Berlin headquarters had compiled a list of citizens of the USSR in whom the various departments of the RSHA had a particular interest, because they were regarded either as especially dangerous adversaries or as potential collaborators.[22] Collecting information to profitable effect and making use of it in economic policy or in forming alliances, intelligence activities had a significance which should not be underestimated.[23] However, the task of murdering people was clearly in the foreground, although – contrary to what researchers once assumed[24] – it in no way amounted to an authorisation to implement the 'Final Solution', the liquidation of all Jewish inhabitants of the USSR irrespective of age and gender. That was more to do with Heydrich. He had formulated the killing guidelines precisely, drawing careful distinctions and, within the framework of Nazi philosophy, had let himself be guided by the pressures of *realpolitik* – as can be deduced from a key document which has been preserved and is, therefore, quoted here extensively. In regard to executions:

> The following are to be executed: all Comintern functionaries (as well as communist professional politicians as a group, in general); the higher, middle, and radical lower functionaries of the party, of the central committee, of district and regional committees, people's commissars; Jews in party and state positions; other radical elements (saboteurs, propagandists, snipers, assassins, agitators, etc.) *so far as* in individual cases they are not, or are no longer, needed to provide information in a political or economic regard which is particularly important for further security measures or for the economic reconstruction of the occupied areas. Particular care must be taken not to liquidate economic, trades union, and trade committees entirely, lest suitable persons are no longer available as sources of information. No obstacle is to be placed in the way of attempts by anti-communist or anti-Jewish circles to carry out their own cleansing processes in the areas to be occupied. On the contrary, they are to be encouraged, albeit without leaving any traces, so that these local 'self-protection' circles will be unable later on to point to orders or to political assurances given to them [...] Particularly careful procedures are to be followed when shooting doctors or other persons involved in medical occupations. Since in the countryside there may be only one doctor to 10,000 population, shooting doctors would cause a vacuum which could hardly be filled, if epidemics were to occur. If in an

individual case an execution is required, it is of course to be carried out, but it must be preceded by an exact examination of the circumstances.[25]

The *Einsatzgruppen* leaders entrusted with the liquidation order regarded themselves as insufficiently informed in respect of the systematic murder of the Jewish population and found the order in need of interpretation. To some extent they did not know what Heydrich expected and how radical they had to be. The two leaders of *Einsatzgruppe A* consulted each other as to how to proceed and decided to await the further course of events, but did not want to draw attention to themselves.[26] This attitude may also have been typical of the leaders of *Einsatzgruppe D*. At the end of June 1941 it had moved to Piatra Neamt in Romania to take part in the invasion in the lee of the 11th German and 3rd and 4th Romanian armies and to instigate the first security measures in Bukowina and Bessarabia.[27] Unlike *Einsatzgruppen A* to *C*, Ohlendorf's unit had in these areas to take account of the interests of their independently minded ally (who in traditional fashion prohibited interventions by the SS and the SD). For its part, reclaiming the territory for Romania, which culminated in attacking the Ukrainian inhabitants and suppressing them, was more important than the liquidation of the Jewish population.[28] In spite of these adversities the commandos were able to demonstrate 'impressive results'. Thus *Sk 10b* which had entered Czernowitz with troops of the 3rd Romanian army, began at the start of July by murdering 100 Jewish academics, then shortly afterwards, on 9 July, went on in conjunction with Romanian troops to execute a further 500 men, amongst them the chief rabbi and other dignitaries. In addition, there were numerous individual killings in the course of the chaos of war. In similar fashion *Sk 10b* 'worked' the surrounding areas and killed 150 men in Chotin. *Sk 10a* was active in Belzy where it entered into a kind of competition with Romanian killing units which shot several hundred Jews, whilst Seetzen's commando in the middle of July 'only' managed various hostage shootings: on repeated occasions Jewish men were executed in atonement for alleged offences by the population against the occupying troops. *Sk 11a* marched on Kischinew, the capital of Bessarabia, with the Romanian 4th army. Although the commando was reined in by Romanian troops, it took the opportunity of its stay in the locality of Barlad to compel Jewish men to do forced labour and to torment them sadistically.[29] On the capture of Kischinew *Sk 11a* became active at once. In agreement with the Romanian local command under Colonel Dumitru Tudosse (listed in German files as Tuodossi) a 'hostage reservoir' was set up and called a concentration camp. In addition, the Jewish population was ordered to move into a ghetto – estimates of the number of Jews in the city vary from a good 9,000 to 11,000. This command was in accordance with latest instructions sent from Berlin. Moreover, a Führer command was conveyed to *Sk 11a* requiring the inclusion of women and children in the killing measures. Paul Zapp set his unit to work in compliance with this command and in agreement with the Romanian military. On 1 August 1941, 351 Jewish men and 250 women were shot 'in retaliation' for the setting on fire of a coal dump by saboteurs.[30] *Sk 11b* under Müller's command did not let itself be outdone by the other commandos: it arrested, tortured and murdered Jews and Communists in Akkerman (Cetatea-Alba), Bolgrad and Tighina (Bendery), and there is evidence that at this point an infant and its mother were shot. This execution was deliberately staged for the men of *Sk 11b* by Bruno Müller: he himself shot the mother and child in order to give particular emphasis to the Führer order that, henceforth, the *Einsatzgruppen* should proceed ruthlessly. Only *Ek 12* had not yet gone into action, having been retained by the 11th army which wanted to keep the specialists at its own disposal. All the other commandos had fully met the expectations placed in them, which only served to give a dynamic impetus to the radicalisation of further executions.[31]

All the commandos were able to act freely only once they had left the territory claimed by Romania which, following the agreement of 30 August 1941 in Tighina, was designated Transnistria with Odessa as its capital.[32] Until this point conflicts with their allies had kept on recurring. The view of the *Einsatzgruppen* was that their police and soldiers sometimes murdered too excessively and sadistically and sometimes were too kind to Jews, simply getting them out of the way without regard to military considerations.[33] Only *Sk 11b* worked in unison with the Romanians when, after the capture of the city on 16 October 1941, the Jewish population of Odessa was murdered. It remained behind in Odessa and, in the vicinity of its own accommodation, shot at least 1,000 people placed in its charge, while the number of Jewish victims after the capture of the city may in total have amounted to as many as 25,000 persons.[34] In September 1941 in Dubossary the first mass execution organised by *Ek 12* took place – some 4,000 victims were executed in two days.[35]

Once the river Bug on the border had been crossed and the town of Nikolajew occupied, the *Einsatzgruppe* could act with scant regard to Romanian military and government leaders, since it was now on the soil of the future Reich commissariat of the Ukraine. The commandos seized this opportunity to shoot their way uncompromisingly through to the East and from now on to liquidate Jewish communities in their entirety. In exceptional cases, a few families of Jewish craftsmen or doctors were left alive if the German authorities were in desperate need of them. A steam-roller of annihilation now traversed the whole country. In Nikolajew the victims numbered around 5,000, and in the neighbouring town of Cherson a campaign lasting several days produced an equally high figure. There was now no quarter given to the mentally and physically handicapped, to soldiers of the Red Army, or to Gypsies, who were included in the mass executions as part of the 'ethnic [*völkisch*] territory cleansing'.[36] An entirely identical procedure is documented for, amongst other places, Melitopol (2,000 victims), Berdjansk (1,000 victims), Mariupol (8,000 victims), Taganrog (1,800 victims),[37] the smaller townships of the Noga steppe as well as for all the Crimean towns. In wiping out the Jewish community of Simferopol around the turn of the year 1941/2 *Einsatzgruppe D* achieved a clear record of 11,000 victims shot, even though this figure leaves out the resident local Gypsies and the Krimtschaken whom the SS leaders also regarded as 'racial Jews' and who were included in the death sentence.[38]

At the start of the summer offensive in 1942 commandos of the *Einsatzgruppe* advanced from Crimea across the straits at Kertsch to the Taman peninsula or marched via Rostov on the Don into Southern Russia and pushed on to the Caucasus. For the Jewish population of the captured cities this meant the completion of the 'Final Solution': in Rostov, Stavropol, Maykop, Kislowodsk, Minerlynie, Wodie, Pjatigorsk, Budjennowsk, Georgijewsk, Elista, Krasnodar, and many other towns and places, thousands were shot or gassed by means of the new killing tool, the gas car. The killing commandos also found time to comb the prisoner of war camps for Jews and Communists or to eliminate the inmates of sanatoriums, even children.[39] During the retreat the commandos were split up and further utilised in various regions of Europe under German occupation. In the course of combating gangs – often a synonym for the ruthless destruction and suppression of the civilian population in those areas frequented by or controlled by partisan groups – they exported their brutal procedures to White Russia which was already suffering badly, to the General Government, the Balkans, Italy and Greece.[40] Some of the contingents in the *Einsatzgruppe* were pressed into actual combat as the front lines collapsed and, consequently, they took casualties: for instance, the 3rd Reserve Police Battalion from Berlin Pankow had joined the *Einsatzgruppe* in December 1941 to relieve the Spandau police. But the functionaries of *Einsatzgruppe D* continued to occupy important positions in police offices of the Reich itself or in the remaining rump of occupied territories, even during the terminal agonies of the Reich. From this unit which, during its existence, was responsible for the murder of some 130,000 people, only a few members stood trial after the war, and fewer still were convicted.[41]

A death squad viewed from the inside

It is indisputable that the leading personnel of the *Einsatzgruppen* held positions of influence in the RSHA and belonged to the up-and-coming elite of the regime. Consequently, it can be assumed that they identified both with Hitler's ideology and with the anti-Semitism which it encompassed and the concept of 'combative administration'. Unlike their higher ranking older rival, the HSSPF, this 'generation of the absolute', as Michael Wildt called them, were for the most part far more flexible and were sober and pragmatic in their approach. Convinced as they were of the intrinsic necessity of what they were being ordered to do and of the need to demonstrate a record of active service – gained abroad, and significant in their own perception and that of society – which would benefit them in the progress of their careers, it was perfectly self-evident for them to think that they had done 'the right thing'. Nor was the regime backward in handing out favours, such as promotions and decorations, including medals for valour. They gave them a status on a par with 'war heroes' and might elicit official recognition for those ordered back home when their secondment to the unit ended. Bound up with this was a professionalism which demanded a distanced, academic attitude towards the victims, prescribed and intended by Himmler, that was supposed to prevent indiscipline and sadism but also 'wet sentimentality'. Although the staff officers of the *Einsatzgruppen* and the leaders of the commandos had to be models, they operated in a hierarchical and remote fashion. There is no evidence that either Otto Ohlendorf or others themselves fired a shot during the executions: they monitored, gave commands, consoled 'weaker' subordinates, and praised more robust personalities. As established leaders they were also under no pressure to prove anything to themselves and to others. Having certainly internalised the doctrine of protecting the state, but not feeling a need to operate with others on a collective basis, they may well in addition have viewed themselves as individuals singled out for high office. After all, had they not been individually seconded? Only the head of *Sk 11b*, Bruno Müller, a brutal man and a heavy drinker, who was all for practical action, was led by his make-up and nature to behave otherwise. As their brief to kill was extended, he insisted on giving the NCOs an example of what the leadership expected. In carrying out previously the execution in Tighina he murdered first the infant and then the mother, saying 'you have to die for us to live'. However, there are no other reports that during the campaign he was any more active than the other leaders.

Leaders at the lower level, on the other hand, those linking the real leadership with the other ranks, were for the most part assigned on repeated occasions to join in the executions directly. It was they who had to organise the executions and their smooth running for the perpetrators, and who at a larger execution were allocated individual trenches for which they were responsible. It was their job to issue the order to shoot and to order themselves to fire what in their jargon were called *Fangschüsse* ('coup de grâce' shots – coming from the hunting term, used when a wild animal is still alive and has to be put out of its misery). Put the other way round, this meant: the more inefficiently the lower ranks under their command worked, the more frequently they merely wounded their victims, and so the more the junior commanders had to rectify their men's incompetence by firing 'coup de grâce shots'. They were supposed to shoot them in a well-drilled way, according to the prescribed pattern of the 'regulated course' of an execution: assembling the victims; removing their valuables and garments; lining them up or making them lie down beside each other in front of the firing squad; finally, execution by a salvo or by walking along the rows and killing them by a shot to the back of the neck. The 'failure' of the lower ranks and the 'cowardice' of individuals who disgraced the group were thus visited on their commanders in the form of a bloody necessity to act.[42]

The division of labour in these procedures, with its various areas of responsibility, can be explained not only in terms of the conceptual guidelines as to how an execution should be properly carried out, but also by reference to the ritual of military executions that was deliberately chosen to be transferred onto them. Consequently, reports from the *Einsatzgruppe* constantly made fun of the Romanian troops who in the reporters' eyes performed their bloody handwork too sadistically, inefficiently, and above all for their own gain. It should not be forgotten that all the members of the *Einsatzgruppen* were uniformed, even if they belonged to various organisations, and, lacking any self-awareness, they viewed themselves more as a combat group than as a police or party unit. Consequently, in the self-perception of their leaders, they also had to carry out the execution of criminals or 'ethnic [*volk*] pests' in accordance with military traditions and norms. The aim was to stage their own self-legitimation and thus to offer reassurance to the lower ranks, that is, those who pointed the rifles. In order to induce this group of marksmen to commit mass murder, it was necessary to acquaint them with killing. It should be pointed out here that many reserve police officers or those 'eligible for emergency service' might well have never used a weapon before, not even in self-defence. The first executions were performed as if by a military firing squad. The victims – men of an age suitable for army service – had to line up, and the execution squad took up their position. Two marksmen were selected to fire on each victim, one at the head, one at the heart. Firing took place in salvos: orchestrating the shooting effectively contained any feeling of individual responsibility. With everybody shooting and not just one person on his own, the perpetrators turn into a collective acting on higher orders.[43]

However, this method could succeed only if the number of executions remained manageable, the victims were in accordance with the norms of the military system, and there were no doubts in the minds of the lower ranks of the *Einsatzgruppe* about the guilt of those condemned. The desire to annihilate and the task of annihilating with their intensifying dynamic and increasing scope saw to it that this illusory means of relieving guilt could only work in the short run. Even in Czernowitz members of the *Einsatzgruppe* wondered why German-speaking and educated Jewish exiles were amongst those persecuted, as they did not fit the stereotype of the coarse Bolshevik Jew. Once the number of victims rose and women and children were also subject to the measures, none of them could fail to see that these could not be cases of military executions according to a code of guilt and punishment under the extreme conditions of war service. The squads continued to function, however, murdering people in more extreme ways, and accepting the changed situation. It is tempting to explain this in terms of their long-standing and highly developed duty of loyalty and obedience which really cannot be underestimated.[44] But other factors were at work too. Thus the brutalisation of war, of this ruthless ideological war in which the rules of 'civilised' warfare were suspended, may have played a part. Reports of the corpses abandoned in NKWD prisons which were exploited for propaganda purposes, the brutal maimings, and, not least, the apparently uncontrolled aggression of the Romanians, could not fail to have a radicalising effect on the character of this Eastern campaign.[45]

For those actively involved, the concept of vengeance propagated by Müller and Ohlendorf came into play. Children could of course turn into avengers, and in this connection individual members of the *Einsatzgruppe* – so I believe – may well have viewed the campaign, in their own recollection but also as part of collective memory, as a continuation of the First World War and the activities of the *Freikorps*, so that for them this 'argument' proved really convincing. Thus, according to their interpretation, the systematic murder of Jewish Bolsheviks and their offspring was regarded as protection of their own family and of the fatherland, that is, as a prophylactic act of national self-defence in the face of future menace. This was, incidentally, a line of argument which Otto Ohlendorf continued to maintain at the Nuremberg trials for the clear reason that he found it intelligible and self-evident.[46] This aspect of the monstrousness of the Stalinist reign of terror was emphasised in particular by interpreters and exiles who had often undergone painful experiences in the Soviet state and considered their part in the war on the Eastern Front as a personal campaign of revenge for wrongs suffered at the hands of a hostile regime which should never gain power over Germany.[47] A member of another mobile killing unit stressed to his colleagues the need for self-imposed discipline during an execution by referring to the need to protect his own family, in the hope that this war would be the last required to attain the expansion which was Germany's target. His appeal went as follows: 'Good god! Damn it! A generation has to go through this for our children to have some peace.'[48]

It is also the case that the internal organisation of the *Einsatzgruppe D* encouraged the instrumentalisation of the lower ranks. They had been taken out of their previous command structure, thereby forming a separate detachment within the forces, but they could no longer make use of the classic channels for orders and complaints. Companies were separated off and split into platoons (some twenty men strong), and in practice they were drilled by a sergeant-major. Any possible 'complaints' did not end up at the staff office of the company or the battalion, but at that of the *Einsatzgruppe*, where decisions were taken, not by members of the homogeneous community of the police, but by those belonging to the 'others'. To ask such people to understand their own doubts about the legality and appropriateness of the executions was beyond the mental horizons of many lower ranks. Yet the leadership did show sensitivity and understanding in the face of possible scruples or misgivings, so that it was possible to give notice of one's reluctance to take part (today) in the shooting. In considering such situations we should not underestimate the group pressure that was aimed at removing such inhibitions. If more timid characters were not to find themselves excluded from the community, they were urged, even forced, to join in the shooting after all.[49] Even if consideration was shown to individuals when their scruples related to particular victims – do I really have to shoot a baby? – they were still locked into the overall operation by, for instance, 'only' stocking up the ammunition. Many of them may not have recognised that a role such as that, or such as standing guard over the victims, collecting up clothes and valuables, or filling in the burial trenches, was in fact essential for the successful conduct of an execution.[50] The main thing for them was that they had not fired a shot, or at least not on this occasion, which at a superficial level allowed them to salve their conscience, since it was the others who had killed, and they could claim that they had objected to taking part. In the long run a refusal would inevitably encounter only severe opposition, particularly because the leadership of the *Einsatzgruppen* did not want only ambitious 'shooters' as executioners, as they feared the brutalisation of these comrades with their critical attitudes and their tendency to regard the executions as a stimulant and thus to run the risk of infringing 'manly discipline'. They thought that it ought rather to be normal serving men who should do the deed, since in this way its significance could be emphasised. If an armed man who was emotionally controlled had an insight into the necessity of taking this action and functioned, then the wishes of the leadership could not be wrong. For some the killing, seen thus, may also have become a kind of catharsis, in which the Jews had to die in order for Germany to arise as providence had planned it and for the long-awaited Thousand Year Reich to begin. It thus amounted to the ancient or medieval form of human sacrifice, transferred to enlightened modernity with its apparently so different values. This is the context in which we should perhaps interpret the vulgar humiliations inflicted on individual victims who were forced to scorn their own faith or were subject to derision because they were religious Jews.[51]

It is a known fact, however, that the commanders of *Einsatzgruppe D* – like those of all other killing units – gradually lost the ability to control events. Such explanations of motives, the ballast of arguments deposited in the memory by self-manipulated historical understanding, may have been used up in the days and nights of military duty over all those months. Inevitably, the individual perpetrator found himself acting in a more uncontrolled and reflexive way when faced with the increasing level of performance demanded. During the mass killing in Nikolajew a member of the leadership by the name of Zöllner got into a rage when during a pause in the shootings – the killers were having a break for lunch – the executioners were given blood sausage (black pudding) to fortify them when close by there were victims awaiting imminent death. This 'insensitivity' by the unit leadership and the cook, ruining their lunch with food like this which physically reminded them whilst eating of what they had just been doing and what they still had to do and so made it impossible for them to 'switch off', was 'one hell of a disgrace', the infuriated Zöllner insisted. He asked if they had been 'trying to push things to the limit' and stated that 'in this situation' such provisions should have been left off the menu. It is clear from this example how one of those in authority amongst the perpetrators had evolved in his view of himself and in his psychology. No doubt was expressed about carrying out their murderous assignment, nor was there any show of sympathy for the victims, who were probably regarded more as creatures without individual personalities, perhaps even as things. It was more that Zöllner saw himself and his comrades as victims, as this incident made it only too clear to them that their superiors lacked any concern for their interests when they were doing this 'filthy work'. Ohlendorf soon arrived on the scene and agreed with the criticisms Zöllner had made, but thought that he should behave like an officer. If Zöllner protested and was ticked off, one of his fellow commanders had a totally different reaction during the events in Nikolajew. He suffered a nervous breakdown, because he couldn't stand the killing any more, particularly his own part in the shootings, and he requested a transfer back home, so that he didn't have to serve as a constant bad example to his comrades. After some resistance – it was doubtless feared that others might follow his lead – the request was granted.[52] Others again were comfortable with the additional power they had gained during the campaign, a freedom of action which they themselves saw as total power. They requisitioned things, held parties which they termed 'comradeship evenings', and contravened the laws of the SS by raping women, forcing Jewish women to sleep with them or torturing them in other ways. Himmler was quick to recognise the trend to an uninhibited sexual drive and to general brutalisation and, a pedagogue through and through, tried to combat it. He instructed the commando leadership and other SS functionaries involved that in gatherings of comrades they – by 'introducing our men to the beauties of German intellectual and spiritual life' – had personally to resist not only the brutalisation he feared but also their 'melancholia'.[53] Himmler was not so naïve as to believe that such instructions would in reality achieve the desired effects. It therefore seemed more important to him to unburden perpetrators of their heavy task by using mobile machines – gas cars – which could do the work for them. It was also appreciated that serving on the Eastern Front should normally be kept within bounds, both for units and for individuals, and so care was taken to bring in other units to relieve those on duty. In addition the leadership of the *Einsatzgruppen* and other mobile units had taken to employing more volunteers during the executions, since they were valued for their unscrupulousness and their motivation, thereby at least spreading the load over several shoulders if it could not be delegated altogether.[54] None of this, however, changed the fundamental organisation of the *Einsatzgruppen*. Until they were disbanded they remained heterogeneous units of uniformed individuals who for the most part departed from the characteristic patterns of behaviour of the SS leadership. Even if many of them tended to suppress their guilt, perhaps for tactical reasons during criminal proceedings, and successfully reconstructed their biographies for themselves and others in the post-war period, their collective activities remain indissolubly lodged in the memory of the human race as one of the greatest mass killings in modern times.

Notes

* Translated by Richard Littlejohns

1. On recent research and its deficiencies see above all: Klaus-Michael Mallmann, 'Menschenjagd und Massenmord. Das neue Instrument der Einsatzgruppen und- kommandos 1938–1945', in Gerhard Paul and Klaus-Michael Mallmann (eds), *Die Gestapo im Zweiten Weltkrieg*. *'Heimatfront' und besetztes Europa* (Darmstadt, 2000), 291–316; Helmut Krausnick and Hans-Heinrich Wilhelm, *Die Truppe des Weltanschauungskrieges. Die Einsatzgruppen der Sicherheitspolizei und des SD 1938–1942* (Stuttgart, 1981), esp. 19–106.
2. Alexander B. Rossino, *Hitler Strikes Poland: Blitzkrieg, Ideology, and Atrocity* (Kansas, 2003); Dorothee Weitbrecht, *Der Exekutionsauftrag der Einsatzgruppen in Polen* (Filderstadt, 2001), esp. 39–57; Jochen Böhler, *Auftakt zum Vernichtungskrieg. Die Wehrmacht in Polen 1939* (Frankfurt/Main, 2006), 201–21.
3. Michael Wildt, *Generation des Unbedingten. Das Führungskorps des Reichssicherheitshauptamtes* (Hamburg, 2002), 276–82, 419–85; Michael Wildt, 'Radikalisierung und Selbstradikalisierung 1939. Die Geburt des Reichssicherheitshauptamtes aus dem Geist des völkischen Massenmordes', in Paul and Mallmann (eds), *Gestapo*, 11–41.
4. Robert Bohn, *Reichskommissariat Norwegen. 'Nationalsozialistische Neuordnung' und Kriegswirtschaft* (Munich, 2000), 74–9; Erich Thomsen, *Deutsche Besatzungspolitik in Dänemark 1940–1945* (Düsseldorf, 1971), 11–21; Helmut Krausnick, 'Hitler und die Morde in Polen', *Vierteljahrshefte für Zeitgeschichte*, 11 (1963), 196–209, here 200–2.
5. Christopher R. Browning, *Fateful Months: Essays on the Emergence of the Final Solution* (London, 1985), 39–41, 68–85; Walter Manoschek, '*Serbien ist judenfrei*'. *Militärische Besatzungspolitik und Judenvernichtung in Serbien 1941/42* (Munich, 1993), 29, 35–49, 169–84; Tomislav Dilic, *Utopias of Nation: Local Mass Killing in Bosnia and Herzegovina, 1941–42* (Uppsala, 2005), 165–8; Heinz A. Richter, *Griechenland im Zweiten Weltkrieg* (Mannheim, 1997), 470.

6. Ralf Ogorreck, *Die Einsatzgruppen und die 'Genesis der Endlösung'* (Berlin, 1996); Klaus-Michael Mallmann, 'Die Türöffner der "Endlösung". Zur Genesis des Genozids', in Paul and Mallmann (eds), *Gestapo*, 437–63.
7. Ronald Wheatley, *Operation Sea Lion: German Plans for the Invasion of England 1939–1942* (Oxford, 1958), 122–4.
8. Andrej Angrick, *Besatzungspolitik und Massenmord. Die Einsatzgruppe D in der südlichen Sowjetunion 1941–1943* (Hamburg, 2003), 74–9.
9. Ibid., 43–68. Andrej Angrick, 'Zur Rolle der Militärverwaltung bei der Ermordung der sowjetischen Juden', in Babette Quinkert (ed.), *'Wir sind die Herren dieses Landes'. Ursachen, Verlauf und Folgen des deutschen Überfalls auf die Sowjetunion* (Hamburg, 2002), 104–23; Johannes Hürter, *Hitlers Heerführer. Die deutschen Oberbefehlshaber im Krieg gegen die Sowjetunion 1941/42* (Munich, 2006), 517–35; Dieter Pohl, 'Die Kooperation zwischen Heer, SS und Polizei in den besetzten sowjetischen Gebieten', in Christian Hartmann, Johannes Hürter and Ulrike Jureit (eds), *Verbrechen der Wehrmacht. Bilanz einer Debatte* (Munich, 2005), 107–16; Christian Gerlach, 'Militärische "Versorgungszwänge", Besatzungspolitik und Massenverbrechen: Die Rolle des Generalquartiermeisters des Heeres und seiner Dienststellen im Krieg gegen die Sowjetunion', in Norbert Frei et al. (eds), *Ausbeutung, Vernichtung, Öffentlichkeit. Neue Studien zur nationalsozialistischen Lagerpolitik* (Munich, 2000), 175–208.
10. Peter Klein (ed.), *Die Einsatzgruppen in der besetzten Sowjetunion 1941/42. Die Tätigkeits- und Lageberichte des Chefs der Sicherheitspolizei und des SD* (Berlin, 1997), particularly the contributions by Peter Klein, Wolfgang Scheffler, Christian Gerlach and Dieter Pohl that provide an introduction to *Einsatzgruppen A, B* and *C*, 9–87; Andrej Angrick and Peter Klein, *Die 'Endlösung' in Riga'. Ausbeutung und Vernichtung 1941–1944* (Darmstadt, 2006), 40–62; Angrick, *Besatzungspolitik*, 80–104; Wildt, *Generation*, 538–61; Krausnick and Wilhelm, *Truppe*, 141–72. Christian Gerlach, 'Kontextualisierung und Aktionen eines Mordkommandos – die Einsatzgruppe B', in Wolf Kaiser (ed.), *Täter im Vernichtungskrieg. Der Überfall auf die Sowjetunion und der Völkermord an den Juden* (Berlin, 2002), 85–95; Dieter Pohl, 'Schauplatz Ukraine: Der Massenmord an den Juden im Militärverwaltungsgebiet und im Reichskommissariat Ukraine 1941–1943', in Frei, *Ausbeutung*, 135–73.
11. Sebastian Balta, *Rumänien und die Großmächte in der Ära Antonescu (1940–1944)* (Stuttgart, 2005), 122–135, 183–93; Dennis Deletant, *Hitler's Forgotten Ally: Ion Antonescu and his Regime, Romania 1940–1944* (Basingstoke, 2006), 69–88; Mariana Hausleitner, *Die Rumänisierung der Bukowina: Die Durchsetzung des nationalstaatlichen Anspruchs Grossrumäniens 1918–1944* (Munich, 2001), 374–8.
12. Angrick, *Besatzungspolitik*, 90f.
13. Ibid., 91–3, 408–13; Wildt, *Generation*, 378–85. Ludolf Herbst, *Der Totale Krieg und die Ordnung der Wirtschaft. Die Kriegswirtschaft im Spannungsfeld von Politik, Ideologie und Propaganda 1939–1945* (Stuttgart, 1982), 182–8.
14. Angrick, *Besatzungspolitik*, 81–3, 95f; Wildt, *Generation*, 550.
15. This is one of the striking differences from the other *Einsatzgruppen, A* to *C*, to which complete companies of the special battalion of the Waffen-SS were allocated. See Martin Cüppers, *Wegbereiter der Shoah: Die Waffen-SS,*

der Kommandostab Reichsführer-SS und die Judenvernichtung 1939–1945 (Darmstadt, 2005), 271f.
16. Angrick, *Besatzungspolitik*, 399f.
17. Angrick, 'Die Einsatzgruppe D und die Kollaboration', in Kaiser, *Täter*, 71–84.
18. Angrick, *Besatzungspolitik*, 87, 107, 145–7.
19. On the make-up of *Einsatzgruppe D* and on the biographies of individual commando leaders, see Angrick, *Besatzungspolitik*, 94–6, 415–21; Wildt, *Generation*, 482, 551–2; Lawrence D. Stokes, 'Heinz Seetzen – Chef des Sonderkommandos 10a', in Klaus-Michael Mallmann and Gerhard Paul (eds), *Karrieren der Gewalt. Nationalsozialistische Täterbiographien* (Darmstadt, 2004), 196–206; Konrad Kwiet, 'Paul Zapp – Vordenker und Vollstrecker der Judenvernichtung', in ibid., 252–63. See also: French L. MacLean, *The Field Men: the SS Officers Who Led the Einsatzkommandos – the Nazi Mobile Killing Units* (Atglen, 1999), 90, 95, 113, 123, 129, though the detailed information on the officers' career-paths is partially incomplete.
20. Heinz Artzt, *Mörder in Uniform. Organisationen, die zu Vollsteckern nationalsozialistischer Verbrechen wurden* (Munich, 1979), 58-59. See also the essay by Scheffler, in Klein, *Einsatzgruppen*, 29.
21. Angrick, *Besatzungspolitik*, 108–12.
22. For a facsimile of the list, see Werner Röder (ed.), *Sonderfahndungsliste UdSSR* (Erlangen, 1978).
23. Andrej Angrick, 'Otto Ohlendorf und die SD-Tätigkeit der Einsatzgruppe D', in Michael Wildt (ed.), *Nachrichtendienst, politische Elite und Mordeinheit. Der Sicherheitsdienst des Reichsführers SS* (Hamburg, 2003), 267–302.
24. Krausnick and Wilhelm, *Truppe*, 156–67. Helmut Krausnick, 'Hitler und die Befehle an die Einsatzgruppen im Sommer 1941', in Eberhard Jäckel and Jürgen Rohwer (eds), *Der Mord an den Juden im Zweiten Weltkrieg. Entschlußbildung und Verwirklichung* (Frankfurt/Main, 1987), 88–106; Jürgen Förster, 'Das Unternehmen "Barbarossa" als Eroberungs- und Vernichtungskrieg', in Horst Boog (ed.), *Das Deutsche Reich und der Zweite Weltkrieg. Vol. 4, Der Angriff auf die Sowjetunion* (Stuttgart, 1983), 413–47, here 426.
25. Bundesarchiv Berlin-Lichterfelde, R 58/241, Head of the Security Police and the SD, B. Nr. IV-1100/geh.Rs of 2 July 1941. Letter to all four HSSPF who were to be sent into action in the Soviet Union from 1941. For them Heydrich recapitulated his basic instructions to the four *Einsatzgruppen* in composite form. This document is reproduced complete in Klein, *Einsatzgruppen*, 323–8. Idiosyncrasies are reprinted as in the original.
26. Angrick and Klein, '*Endlösung*', S. 61f.
27. Angrick, *Besatzungspolitik*, S. 139–40.
28. Andrej Angrick, 'Rumänien, die SS und die Vernichtung der Juden', in Mariana Hausleitner et al. (eds), *Rumänien und der Holocaust. Zu den Massenverbrechen in Transnistrien 1941–1944* (Berlin, 2001), 113–38, here 121–30; Andrej Angrick, 'Im Wechselspiel der Kräfte. Impressionen zur deutschen Einflußnahme bei der Volkstumspolitik in Czernowitz vor "Barbarossa" und nach Beginn des Überfalls auf die Sowjetunion', in Alfred Gottwaldt et al. (eds), *NS-Gewaltherrschaft. Beiträge zur historischen Forschung und juristischen Aufarbeitung* (Berlin, 2005), 318–55; Viorel Achim, 'The Romanian Population Exchange Project Elaborated by Sabin Manuila in October 1941', *Jahrbuch des italienisch-deutschen historischen Instituts in Triest*, 27 (2001), 593–617; Hausleitner, *Rumänisierung*, 399–404.

29. Angrick, *Besatzungspolitik*, 146–72; Angrick, 'Wechselspiel', 337–44.
30. Angrick, *Besatzungspolitik*, 177–85; Radu Ioanid, *The Holocaust in Romania: the Destruction of Jews and Gypsies under the Antonescu Regime, 1940–1944* (Chicago, 2000), 124–6, 139–42; Paul A. Shapiro, 'The Jews of Chisinau (Kishinev): Romanian Reoccupation, Ghettoization, Deportation', in Randolph L. Braham (ed.), *The Destruction of Romanian and Ukrainian Jews during the Antonescu Era* (New York, 1997), 135–93, here 138–55; Jean Ancel, *Transnistria, 1941–1942: the Romanian Mass Murder Campaigns*, vol. 1 (Tel Aviv, 2003), 95, 435.
31. Angrick, *Besatzungspolitik*, 186–90.
32. Andreas Hillgruber, *Hitler, König Carol und Marschall Antonescu. Die deutsch-rumänischen Beziehungen 1938–1944* (Wiesbaden, 1965), 139–42.
33. Angrick, *Besatzungspolitik*, 190–203.
34. Ibid., 204–5 and 298–302; Ancel, *Transnistria*, 182–203; Ioanid, *Holocaust*, 177–82; Alex Mihai Stoenescu, *Armata, Maresalul si Evreii* (Bucharest, 1998), 347–73.
35. Angrick, *Besatzungspolitik*, 239–41.
36. Ibid., 244–52.
37. Ibid., 307–23.
38. Ibid., 323–61; Manfred Oldenburg, *Ideologie und militärisches Kalkül. Die Besatzungspolitik der Wehrmacht in der Sowjetunion 1942* (Cologne, 2004), 159–209; Norbert Kunz, *Die Krim unter deutscher Herrschaft 1941–1944. Germanisierungsutopie und Besatzungsrealität* (Darmstadt, 2005), 179–204; Marcel Stein, *Die 11. Armee und die 'Endlösung' 1941/42. Eine Dokumentensammlung mit Kommentaren* (Bissendorf, 2006), 143–78.
39. Angrick, *Besatzungspolitik*, 560–90, 612–25 and 644–51; Oldenburg, *Ideologie*, 297–306.
40. Angrick, *Besatzungspolitik*, 687–712; Christian Gerlach, *Kalkulierte Morde. Die deutsche Wirtschafts- und Vernichtungspolitik in Weißrußland 1941 bis 1944* (Hamburg, 1999), 902, 959–63; Carlo Gentile and Lutz Klinkhammer, 'Gegen den Verbündeten von einst. Die Gestapo in Italien', in Paul and Mallmann, *Gestapo*, 521–40, here 525f.
41. Angrick, *Besatzungspolitik*, 711, 716–28.
42. On this point see the generally correct analyses by reference to other killing commandos in Harald Welzer, *Täter. Wie aus normalen Menschen Massenmörder werden* (Frankfurt/Main, 2005), 150–60.
43. Angrick, *Besatzungspolitik*, 152–3; Welzer, *Täter*, 105–32; Rolf Pohl, 'Normalität und Pathologie – Sozialpsychologische Anmerkungen zur Psychogenese von Massenmördern', in Peter Gleichmann and Thomas Kühne (eds), *Massenhaftes Töten. Kriege und Genozide im 20. Jahrhundert* (Hamburg, 2004), 158–79, here 175–7. For a comparison, see also: Dorothee Frank, *Menschen töten* (Düsseldorf, 2006), 178–83.
44. Welzer, *Täter*, 151–3; Herbert Jäger, *Verbrechen unter totalitärer Herrschaft. Studien zur nationalsozialistischen Gewaltkriminalität* (Frankfurt/Main, 1982), 64–7, 139–41, 152–5.
45. Klaus Jochen Arnold has pointed to the atmosphere of violence which led to the suspension of moral values and norms. Unfortunately he uses this argument as a means of comprehending crimes in a mechanistic way, i.e. of making them understandable (terming them 'reciprocal embitterment' or 'reciprocal radicalisation' or 'reciprocal brutalisation'), which can end up

in an exculpation of those responsible, barely according them the possibility of acting on their own, but rather making them appear to be driven by events. Klaus Jochen Arnold, *Die Wehrmacht und die Besatzungspolitik in den besetzten Gebieten der Sowjetunion. Kriegführung und Radikalisierung im 'Unternehmen Barbarossa'* (Berlin, 2005), 177–90, 503–28. See also the comments by Herbert Jäger, *Makrokriminalität. Studien zur Kriminologie kollektiver Gewalt* (Frankfurt/Main, 1989), 48f.

46. For an assessment of the court proceedings, see Kazimierz Leszczynski (ed.), *Fall 9: Das Urteil im SS-Einsatzgruppenprozeß* (East Berlin, 1963), 88–96.
47. These individuals were, incidentally, perpetrators as well, and they themselves frequently had a tendency to commit excesses.
48. Angrick, *Besatzungspolitik*, 362.
49. Jäger, *Verbrechen*, 147f.
50. Christopher Browning has already emphasised the typical ways in which the perpetrators justified and deceived themselves: Christopher Browning, *Ganz normale Männer. Das Reserve-Polizeibataillon 101 und die 'Endlösung' in Polen* (Hamburg, 1993), 105–13. What he discovered is clearly applicable to the personnel of *Einsatzgruppe D*.
51. Hyam Maccoby, *Der Heilige Henker. Menschenopfer und das Vermächtnis der Schuld* (Stuttgart, 1999), 278–80. On what went on in Barlad, see Angrick, *Besatzungspolitik*, 171.
52. Angrick, *Besatzungspolitik*, 246–9, here 248.
53. Hans-Heinrich Wilhelm, 'Die Verfolgung der sowjetischen Juden', in Klaus Meyer and Wolfgang Wippermann (eds), *Gegen das Vergessen. Der Vernichtungskrieg gegen die Sowjetunion 1941–1945* (Frankfurt/Main, 1992), 59–74, here 63–4.
54. Angrick, *Einsatzgruppe D*, 378–82; Dieter Pohl, 'Ukrainische Hilfskräfte beim Mord an den Juden', in Paul, *Täter*, 205–34, here esp. 213–16, 220–2; Ruth Bettina Birn, *Die Sicherheitspolizei in Estland 1941–1944. Eine Studie zu Kollaboration im Osten* (Paderborn, 2006), 28–31; Martin Dean, *Collaboration in the Holocaust: Crimes of the Local Police in Belorussia and Ukraine, 1941–1944* (New York, 2000), esp. 78–104.

Part II

Female Perpetrators of the Holocaust

4
Women under National Socialism: Women's Scope for Action and the Issue of Gender*

Christina Herkommer

Immediately after the termination of National Socialist rule, historians in the Federal Republic made a start on the academic assessment of it. Explanations were sought as to how such a violent, expansionist regime had been able to come to power, and attempts were made to slot the National Socialist system of government into the overall context of German history.[1]

This period saw the history of the events and political history being written, questions about the continuity between the German nation-state and National Socialism being raised, theories of totalitarianism, fascism and modernisation being discussed, incorporating analyses from the social sciences. Until well into the 1970s, however, only a few of the attempts at a historiographical treatment of National Socialism contained any reference to the role of women in building and maintaining the criminal system of government. Women did not count as 'great personalities' in the history of political events; they had not been primarily involved in the formulation of National Socialist policies. Least of all were they involved in the planning of the war. But it was precisely these topics which post-war historiography regarded as central. The long tradition of ignoring women as part of history, in fact as the subject of history, was thus further extended.

It was only in the 1970s, when a new Federal German women's movement started to form, that women's studies began, not only to expose, to analyse and to criticise the repressive ruling structures which existed, but also to focus on the role of women in history. In doing so women's studies also looked at National Socialism. Women social scientists and historians were faced with the challenge of tracing the contribution of women to the construction and maintenance of the criminal National Socialist system of government.

A contentiously conducted exchange of views arose, centred on the issue of the role taken by women in National Socialism. This will be outlined below and, at the same time, embedded in the adjacent discussion about feminist theorising. The conclusion will discuss the way in which the topic of women under National Socialism has been dealt with and what possibilities present themselves for its treatment in the future.

The 'victim thesis'

In early historiographical attempts to analyse National Socialism women occupied either no position or merely a marginalised one. An exception to this is Joachim C. Fest who in his work on the leading personalities of National Socialism analysed the role of women in the National Socialist system of government. Fest notes that 'the National Socialist movement, from the beginning a militant community of like-minded men, had almost no place in its ranks for women'.[2] He refers to National Socialist ideology which allotted women merely reproductive tasks in the family and reduced them to their functions as wives and mothers. Thus he starts by constructing the thesis that women were in the first place victims of a misogynist system in which they had no say at all. In spite of this alleged (political) impotence of women, Fest argues that women 'discovered, chose and idolized' Hitler.[3]

Fest starts from the premise that National Socialism made targeted use of particular female traits, such as 'capacity for self-surrender or demand for authority and order',[4] and that in these traits women are 'more susceptible to psychological manipulation'.[5] Fest criticises this treatment of women as objects, the exploitation of their supposedly weak position, without subjecting these disparaging assumptions in themselves to question. Instead he himself reverts in his analyses to images of women which originate in patriarchal interpretations of femininity and female sexuality.[6]

This view of women as hysterical adulators of Hitler, voting for him on that basis, was opposed in the early stages of women's studies which had evolved out of the new women's movement in the 1970s and saw itself as counteracting the dominant trend in scholarship which was perceived as androcentric. Women's studies was characterised above all by the need to make women and their repressed position visible, both in the present and in the past.[7] The intention was that in this way women should no longer be considered, as was the norm in traditional research, as 'appendages' of the male subject to be 'included' with the male, but should receive subject status themselves.

Women's studies clung in the Federal Republic to the assumption that there was a fundamental difference between the sexes and for a time stylised women as the 'better' part of the human race. In such research in the 1970s and up until the end of the 1980s (and in part beyond) women thus appeared as victims of the historical development of society. They were considered to be dealt with by men, prepared to male recipes, domesticated and trained by men, in short as the victims of oppressive patriarchal social structures.

The priority was to raise the visibility of women under National Socialism and to repudiate the thesis, articulated prominently by Fest but also widespread in some quarters of the workers' movement, that it was women's support which had brought Hitler to power.[8] In the mid-1980s various publications appeared in which the role of women under National Socialism was explicitly the centre of attention. These investigations placed National Socialist women's and gender policies in the foreground.[9] National Socialism was interpreted as an extreme manifestation of patriarchy and all women in National Socialist Germany were accordingly declared to be victims of the repressive conditions.

This debate in women's studies about the thesis of women as victims did not proceed in a homogeneous way at all. Two central perspectives can be recognised. The first perspective starts from the 'real life' of women under National Socialism which was determined by an ideologically shaped National Socialist women's policy but also, at the latest from 1939, by the demands of a society at war. The economic and employment policies of the National Socialists, driven by preparations for war, also affected the everyday life of women.[10] This approach was taken at the beginning of the 1980s and it was concluded that the National Socialist labour policy was in part in direct contradiction to its ideological propaganda. What predominated in the ruling interests of the National Socialists was not the reduction in gainful work by women heralded in propaganda but the reconstruction of the gender-specific division of labour: women were to be forced back into household work or underpaid work in the economy.[11] The 'real life' of women under National Socialism was shaped not only by Nazi employment policy, but also by other elements of Nazi women's policies, such as for instance the sterilisation policy of the National Socialist system of government. Gisela Bock argues in a study on compulsory sterilisation under National Socialism, that it was anti-natal and thus a counter-model to the pro-natal stance of National Socialism, which was primarily characterised by the encouragement to give birth to 'racially pure' children. Bock does not assess this anti-natal policy as a preliminary stage of National Socialist mass murder and genocide, but as an integral component of National Socialist murder policy. It was, as she sees it, shaped above all by a bipolar relationship between sexes, with mainly male actors and female victims. She regards the treatment of the victims of compulsory sterilisation as an indicator of the overall situation of women under National Socialism. She sees the sterilisation policy as part of National Socialist women's policy and also as a form of racism.[12] In addition, she asserts, it was almost exclusively men as legislators, medical officers and experts, judges and surgeons who decided on the implementation of Nazi sterilisation policies.[13]

Bearing in mind that women were involved in racism and anti-Semitism as well as in the 'racial hygiene' of the National Socialist system of government, Bock qualifies this fact by pointing out that it was usually childless female assistants in the euthanasia programme and female camp guards who pursued racist strategies. According to Bock their racism had not, however, derived from their own motivation, but had been more of a female way of conforming to the racism of men. Bock was highly criticised for that by Atina Grossmann because 'she comes [...] close to implying that non-mothers are not really women'.[14]

The assumption that there could have been a female species of racism/anti-Semitism conforming to the racism/anti-Semitism of men is visible in another line of women's studies. This seeks to explain the involvement of women in National Socialist crimes and enquires into the actual participation of women in National Socialism. However, this participation is traced back exclusively to the oppressed status of women within patriarchal structures, thus ultimately making women appear yet again as victims. This is the line taken for example by Margarete Mitscherlich. From a psychoanalytical angle she refers to psychic dispositions in women which cause them to participate, not from their own motives, but in conformity with male strategies.[15]

Mitscherlich's starting point is the anti-Semitism which in the National Socialist system of government determined all aspects of policy. In psychoanalysis anti-Semitism is usually understood as a consequence of unresolved Oedipal conflicts. The development of the super-ego is central to this conception. According to Freud it represents an internalisation of the father's authority and is fully generated only by the male, due to his fear of castration. Aggression towards the father is turned against his own ego. Seeking to escape this psychological pressure, the man looks for scapegoats (e.g. Jews) on to which he can project his aggression.[16]

Mitscherlich shows that in previous psychoanalytical investigations there has been hardly any consideration of the question as to why women become anti-Semites.[17] She argues that the male anti-Semitic super-ego (*Über-Ich*) diverges clearly from the typical female super-ego. Going back to Freud, Mitscherlich takes it that the super-ego of women is only incompletely formed and is also directed more at retaining the love of people close to them than at projecting aggressive tendencies on to other persons. In Mitscherlich's view it is, therefore, not so much their aggressions and projections which predispose women to anti-Semitism but rather their fear of losing love. This fear led also, she says, to women accepting and carrying out, largely without resistance, the often contradictory roles assigned to them.[18]

As we see, Mitscherlich does focus on women as anti-Semites and thus as participants in the criminal National Socialist system. Nevertheless, she takes the view that women were themselves victims who shared the anti-Semitic and racist views only out of an urge to conform and had no motives of their own for taking part in the criminal system.

The 'perpetrator thesis'

In the middle of the 1980s a change took place in the debate in the Federal Republic amongst those involved in women's studies, and this change continued beyond reunification and was only slightly influenced by it. The assumption of a difference between the sexes, which had previously been the basis of women's studies in the Federal Republic, was called into question and confronted by the conception of equality between the sexes.

This was particularly true of women's studies in relation to National Socialism. However, in this area too from the middle of the 1980s the increasing tendency was to examine women more intensively as perpetrators in the National Socialist system. Three approaches can be identified which discuss women as perpetrators in National Socialism, – albeit from varying theoretical angles and in very different fashions. First, there is the theory of women as joint perpetrators. A second approach is based on the assumption that women were perpetrators in the role of housewife and mother which society assigned to them. Over and above this, there are the first investigations registering a direct involvement of women in the implementation of the National Socialist killing policy and not evaluating it merely as an act of conforming to male strategies, but seeking instead to discern independent motivations on the part of women.

Women as joint perpetrators

The thesis of women as joint perpetrators in the construction and maintenance of oppressive patriarchal structures was introduced into the debate in women's studies in the middle of the 1980s by Christina Thürmer-Rohr.[19] She criticises previous women's studies for its view of women as mere victims of patriarchal ruling structures. In her opinion this passive understanding of female behaviour ultimately discriminates against women themselves and contributes to the perpetuation of female impotence.[20] She remarks that both the complementarity of man and woman (difference) and conformity by women to male strategies (equality) ultimately form the basis of joint perpetration. Thus, on the one hand, women become joint perpetrators in those instances where they have accommodated themselves to the idea of supplementing the male by the female and have developed their own female repertoire of behaviour which forms a counterweight to the world of the men and which is supposed to support the man in his deeds, indeed even to make his deeds possible for him. Women can also, on the other hand, turn into joint perpetrators when they have fitted into the idea of equality and have begun to see 'general human' logic in patriarchal logic, since in this way they represent no threat to the preservation of patriarchal social structures.[21]

Related to National Socialism and the extreme patriarchal structures which it is perceived to manifest, this thesis means that women, although not themselves responsible for the formulation of the racist policies of persecution and extermination, nevertheless made implementation of these policies possible in two ways. Either women fitted in with concepts of the complementarity of man and woman in line with the theory of difference, thus withdrawing into their own female sphere, within which they kept house as faithfully caring wives and mothers and ensured 'racially pure' progeny. Or they committed themselves to the idea of the equality of man and woman and in this way allowed themselves to be drawn into the patriarchal system of government, e.g. as concentration camp guards.

Thürmer-Rohr repeatedly emphasises that her analysis of women as joint perpetrators does not exonerate men from their deeds, but is intended to expose women's persistent self-deception. She nevertheless excludes any perpetration oriented by women's own motives and (power) interests. Rather, she concludes that women have so far remained stuck in their passivity, which ultimately led them to become joint perpetrators, and demands that they abandon this victim posture, since only in this way is opposition possible against the oppressive structures.

Women as perpetrators: housewives, wives and mothers

Besides the concept of joint perpetration, other analyses introduced into the debate considered perpetration by women in their own right within the National Socialist system and, in so doing, foregrounded women's own interests. The first investigations into activities women had undertaken on their own account were not, however, produced by women in the Federal Republic, but from 'outside'. A contribution by the American Claudia Koonz had a particular influence on the course of the debate on the role of women in National Socialism.[22]

Koonz starts by assuming that women have their own power interest. She sees women as perpetrators within the role as caring housewife, mother and wife which society allots to them. Koonz places the National Socialist social order in the centre of her analysis. She sees National Socialism as shaped by the notion of separate spheres of life and spheres of operation for men and women. For her this social order, which assigned the private and domestic part of social life to women, whilst men occupied the public and political area, holds the key which made it possible for the National Socialists to implement their killing policy. Koonz places particular emphasis on the role of National Socialist women's organisations (and especially the role of the *Frauenschaft* leader Gertrud Scholtz-Klink) which took up and spread the notion of the separate spheres of operation. Their main interest was to use this separation to give women their own power sphere which was intended not only to encompass housework but also to produce specifically female professional perspectives (e.g. in the areas of education and health care).

Even if the creation of an autonomous female sphere of operation with its own claims to power was no more than an illusion, Koonz nevertheless sees in the traditional roles assigned to women in the family or as workers in caring and educational occupations the origin of women as perpetrators. Through their caring activities in the household, the family and their job women contributed, so Koonz believes, to preserving the appearance of decency in the National Socialist system of government and thus to concealing the murderous nature of the state.[23] Thus women provided their men, who were directly involved in the implementation of the National Socialist policies of extermination, with emotional support and ensured the spiritual equilibrium of the murderers. According to Koonz, women remained in what they regarded as their 'natural' place and kept the world of the family separate from the male world of politics and violence.

The direct participation of women in the National Socialist killing policies, e.g. as nurses or as concentration camp guards, is mentioned by Koonz only as a marginal phenomenon and not further analysed. She sees the real guilt and responsibility of women in the implementation of genocide more in the willingness of women to let themselves be forced back into the traditional role of housewife and mother and in its corollary of a demand for their own autonomous sphere of operation. For it was only by this conception of separate spheres of operation, so Koonz agues, that the appearance of normality and legitimacy in the 'Third Reich' could be maintained and thus the policies of extermination could be carried out.

Perpetration by women thus consists for Koonz primarily in the preservation of 'beautiful appearances', in masking crimes and emotionally supporting the killers. In doing so she refers to women's own power interests and their expectation that through National Socialism they could obtain space for translating these power interests into reality. Thus all women (in so far as they were not persecuted) count as potential perpetrators. However, this approach disregards other forms of perpetration by women it cannot accommodate, along with anti-Semitism and racism on the part of women which it has difficulty in explaining.[24]

Women as perpetrators: involvement in the policies of extermination

Besides the focus on the traditional female sphere in their role as housewife, wife and mother, there have also been investigations of women's direct participation in the implementation of National Socialist killing policies. Angelika Ebbinghaus was one of the first researchers in the Federal Republic of Germany who explicitly took issue with the prevailing tendency to see the majority of women as the victims of previous and continuing social conditions, and who also dealt with the topic of women as perpetrators in the implementation of National Socialist extermination policy.[25] By compiling biographies of women Ebbinghaus allows them to appear as perpetrators on their own account and so counteracts the myth of the 'good' woman as a means of generating identity.

She shows too that women did not only have to suffer under National Socialist policies, but definitely profited from them and were involved in implementing them in all spheres. In this way women no longer appear as a homogeneous group which, as an entity, is seen either as victim or as perpetrator. Ebbinghaus tried instead to bring out the multiplicity of the roles of women and their opportunities for action.

Going beyond the period of the National Socialist system of government, Ebbinghaus shows that the few women who were called to account for their actions defended themselves again and again by reverting to stereotyped notions of female behaviour which seemed to exclude cruelty by definition. As an example, Ebbinghaus cites the defence offered by nurses indicted after the end of the war. They attempted to excuse themselves and their involvement in murdering patients partly by arguing that they had acted under orders, but partly too by stating that their actions had been motivated by compassion and by presenting the deaths they induced as relieving the patients' suffering.[26] She demonstrates that these women remained fixed in the role of victim shaped by self-pity, although they were in reality perpetrators, and she pleads that (self-) critical women's studies help to end the encouragement of such denial of responsibility.[27]

Ebbinghaus thus takes a position at odds with previous lines of argument in women's studies, which assumed that 'women' were a homogeneous group. She was the first to present women as perpetrators responsible for their own actions. In this way she counteracts the myth which seeks to generate an identity for the 'good' woman who remained 'decent' even under National Socialism, and she introduces a new angle on the role of women in National Socialism.[28]

Victims or perpetrators: a '*Historikerinnenstreit*'

The thesis of women as perpetrators within National Socialist structures of rule was to some extent welcomed in women's studies, but it also became the object of fierce controversies which Gisela Bock called a '*Historikerinnenstreit*' (dispute amongst women historians).[29] The main focus of criticism was the thesis that women became perpetrators by adhering to their own female sphere.

The controversy reached a climax with the publication of the book by Claudia Koonz. Her theses were the object of annihilating criticism by Gisela Bock, even before the publication of the German translation, on the grounds of inadequacy of method and argument.[30] The main thrust of Bock's criticism was rejection of the thesis that women had become perpetrators due to their adherence to their own female sphere and their associated claims to power within the National Socialist system of government. She criticises Koonz for investigating the past with one eye on its usefulness in the present. Koonz had argued, Bock says, within one particular feminist line of thought, namely equal rights feminism. She had wanted to show that women, when thrown back into a specifically female sphere, help to prop up violent patriarchal structures even in this area, in fact especially in it.

The criticism of the thesis of women as perpetrators thus emerged as criticism by researchers in women's studies working from a theory of *difference* directed at arguments based on a theory of *equality* and the associated thesis of specifically female perpetration. This is also apparent from the fact that very little criticism was levelled at the work of Ebbinghaus.[31] By concentrating on women's biographies she had looked mainly at women as individual perpetrators. These perpetrators could be regarded in women's studies in the Federal Republic, still working very much from a theory of difference, as women who had adapted to male strategies and moved far away from their traditional gender role. The fact that the work of Ebbinghaus was far better suited to attack the basic presumptions of German women's studies, based on the theory of difference, was concealed by the wish to confine perpetration by women to a small number of 'extreme perpetrators'. For in Ebbinghaus's view it is no longer primarily men or women with their gender roles who are the centre of attention, but human deeds themselves. For Ebbinghaus, gender remains significant as a category of analysis, but no longer as a form of categorising which determines from the outset who counts as a perpetrator or as a victim.

Certainly, the thesis of women as perpetrators within the National Socialist regime did represent a tendency running counter to the first phase, based on the assumption that women in general had victim status, so that a controversy developed over the role of women in National Socialism. However, this alone did not (yet) lead on to a more discriminating consideration of the contribution of women to the construction and maintenance of National Socialist rule. Women were usually still regarded as a homogeneous group which through the performance of specifically female activities had contributed to the preservation of a social mechanism of oppression. Thus, although the content of the debate changed, the frame of reference of a fundamental division into two genders with all its attributes continued to be taken as given in considering the role of women in National Socialism.

The discourse on 'multiplicity of roles'

Nevertheless, from the mid-1980s the perspective in women's studies in West Germany began to change. The previously prevailing consensus of a fundamental difference between genders was abandoned as the division into two genders came to be seen as a construct. This tendency, to no longer see only the gender-specific social role expectations of women and men (gender) as a social construction but also to question physicality (sex) and thus the division into (two) genders itself as a biological fact, was continued in the 1990s.[32] Construction of gender and the opportunities for the deconstruction of it claimed the academic interest of those working in women's studies and led clearly to questioning the search for a 'female principle', an 'essential femininity', in German women's studies which previously had largely adhered to the 'paradigm of difference'.

With the new direction in women's studies in general there was also a change in women's studies in relation to National Socialism, which began to draw a more differentiated picture of women under the National Socialist system of government. Attention centred less and less on the portrayal of women as a homogeneous group with the same problems and experiences, and reference was made instead to the multiple life circumstances of women, their scope for action, and the gender arrangements within which they moved.

Spectators, fellow-travellers and perpetrators

Even researchers who, like Gisela Bock, had formerly argued strongly on the basis of the theory of difference and in doing so had stressed the victim status of women, could not elude this new perspective. Thus in her more recent work Bock emphasises the multiplicity of the positions of women under the National Socialist system of government. She asserts that, in relation to women in National Socialism, it was not all the same story but rather that precisely during National Socialist rule the distinctions between various groups of women could decide whether they lived or died. She thus does not (any longer) stress a basic commonality of all women, but rather the diversity of roles which led women to become perpetrators, victims, bystanders and fellow-travellers, seeing a similarity in this respect to the multiple roles of men in National Socialism.[33]

Bock uses examples to show what roles women occupied in the various phases of National Socialist rule and how diverse the actions and impacts of women could be in this connection. She reaches the conclusion that most German women, in so far as they were not persecuted, at least approved of the National Socialist system of government and were thus passive spectators. Many were involved in the implementation of the policies of persecution and extermination, and only a few offered resistance. She equates the convictions, motives and actions of women with those of 'ordinary men'.[34]

Bock does conclude that women were subject to the domination of men, but believes that this alone would not have sufficed as a reason for seeing women *per se* as victims of National Socialism, since this would render the real victims invisible. For Bock the singularity and novelty of National Socialism lie not in its patriarchal character, but in its consistent implementation of race policies. In arguing in this way she does not maintain that the difference between genders and the hierarchy of gender disappeared in the National Socialist system; but she does claim that the actions of women who helped implement racist policies were not primarily determined by gender differences but more by racism and thus by a similarity between genders.[35]

The issue of women as victims *or* perpetrators under National Socialism, previously so fiercely discussed, is largely resolved by emphasising the multiple roles of women. Analyses no longer aim at conveying an overall impression of the situation of *the* woman by investigating some partial aspect of the lives of women in National Socialism. Instead efforts are made to avoid generalisations.

The acceptance of the multiplicity of roles of women in the National Socialist system led in women's studies mainly to a widespread search for a theoretical position outside the previously so important victim–perpetrator duality. There were demands to abandon the concepts which had previously posited an unambiguous positioning of women under National Socialism. Thus Carola Sachse, for instance, states that binary concepts like victims/perpetrators, men/women etc. are 'probably indispensable political tools of modern societies', but that they are inadequate 'as heuristic tools for analysing totalitarian rule, which doesn't give a toss about language games and their rules'.[36]

This is contradicted by Annette Kuhn, who considers it premature 'to take up a position beyond the problematical issue of victims and perpetrators'.[37] Without binary concepts Kuhn sees a threat to the perception of women as perpetrators and thus to recognition of the victims.

This objection is certainly justified and the danger does exist that, if the concept of the perpetrator or the victim is not applied to women as a social group, women will no longer appear as active subjects, as participants in the National Socialist extermination policies. The fact does nevertheless remain that even with employment of the victim–perpetrator duality in women's studies in relation to National Socialism new insights into the conduct of women in Nazi Germany are hardly to be expected. As Heinsohn et al. remark, the binary concept has led primarily to tendentious or polemical discussions which have only proved fruitful in part.[38] It is also doubtful that the role of women in complex systems of government can in fact be grasped simply by enquiring as to their status as victims or perpetrators.[39]

There is still the question of whether emphasising the multiplicity of women's roles in National Socialism goes far enough in order to adopt the position beyond the victim–perpetrator duality as has been demanded. Some new publications with a predominantly popularising background give every cause to fear that the absence of a clear and theoretically based position 'beyond the victim–perpetrator duality' is allowing the multiple roles of women in National Socialism to be reduced to an 'anything goes' category. In these publications women are yet again not the focus of interest as individuals acting on their account but merely as decorative accessories or faithful lovers, indeed as 'The Nazis' Women'.[40] In this way racism and anti-Semitism as motives for women's behaviour are again marginalised and little attention is paid to the 'ordinary women' mentioned by Bock and to their scope for action.

Scope for action and images of gender

It may have appeared at first sight that the debate on women under National Socialism was losing not only in acuity but also in interpretive insight and, after the acceptance of the multiple roles of women, into a state of 'anything goes'. However, at the end of the 1990s new research emerged. These publications focused on women and gender to expose as a construct – and to deconstruct – the binary division of the human race, the division into two genders, which was previously understood as universal and fundamental. This research appears to be shaped above all by enquiries into National Socialist gender arrangements, into women's scope for action under National Socialism, and into images of gender, operative during and after the period of National Socialism and which affected the assessment of women's deeds. Let's have a look at some of these approaches.

National Socialist gender arrangements: women in the SS-Sippengemeinschaft

One of the most important recent contributions to research about women in National Socialism was that made by Gudrun Schwarz with her studies on women in the SS.[41] She too starts in her analyses from the assumption that people of both genders were involved in the implementation of National Socialist extermination policies, and she stresses the need to consider the history of female perpetrators, to expose their involvement in National Socialism, and to pursue the question of women's responsibility for National Socialist crimes. In doing so Schwarz takes a particular interest in women who joined the SS-Sippengemeinschaft (SS-kinship community) and in this organisation participated in the maintenance of the National Socialist system of government during their professional activities or as wives of SS men.

The SS does not at first appear to be a suitable group in which to look out for women as persons acting on their account, since it officially took the form almost exclusively of a band of men.[42] Schwarz shows, however, that women were not only involved as concentration camp guards in the implementation of the National Socialist extermination policies but were also, for example, employed in the administrative machinery of the SS and thus shared the responsibility amongst other things for the smooth running of deportations, or collaborated as SS doctors and nurses in the murder of patients and in human experiments.[43]

Schwarz takes up the thesis already put forward by Koonz that women made the killing possible by the emotional support which they gave their husbands, who were directly involved in the policy of extermination, and thus themselves became perpetrators. However, she gives this thesis a new accent. Not only does she emphasise women's own interest in the annihilation of European Jews, she also refers primarily to the relationship between genders or to the arrangement of genders in National Socialism, which ultimately permitted the implementation of the National Socialist extermination policy.[44] Schwarz finds that SS wives who, like their husbands, were subject to racist selection criteria for entry to the SS-Sippengemeinschaft, willingly adopted the standard line that the SS were to be counted as an elite group in the German nation. Belonging to this 'elite' strengthened them in the conviction that as 'Aryan' women they were superior to every Jewish man and also that through their function as mothers they were equal to men in importance in founding a new 'race'.[45]

This notion of an elite became part of the way in which SS wives viewed themselves and led, according to Schwarz, to a situation where these women not only condoned the extermination policy of National Socialism and supported their husbands in implementing it, but also were involved in the crimes themselves. Thus SS wives profited in no small measure, for example, from thefts from the Jewish population; they employed prisoners from the concentration camps in their households, where they treated and mistreated them as they saw fit; and they not only knew about the killings of Jewish people but took part in them when opportunities arose.

Schwarz covers a broad spectrum of the activities of SS women and their involvement in the National Socialist process of persecution and extermination, seeing them as active on their own account and showing that as perpetrators they had an eye above all on their own careers, on social climbing, and on the economic benefits.

Scope for action

In recent research on the role of women in National Socialism the focus has been more and more clearly on women and their scope for action. Even the relatively small group of women who acted as concentration camp guards and were directly involved in violence in the National Socialist system, and who again and again attracted public interest in the post-war period, are now more clearly the object of attention. Thus Johannes Schwartz, for example, is concerned with the scope for action of female concentration camp guards and analyses the biography of the Senior Guard Johanna Langefeld.[46]

Irmtraud Heike, who was the first to examine the biography of Langefeld, used this example to demonstrate that a woman of the rank of Senior Guard could exploit her position not only to put the brutal Nazi policy of extermination into practice, but also to intervene on behalf of prisoners.[47] Schwartz builds on this study and reveals Johanna Langefeld as a woman who had volunteered as a guard and who carried out her duties in various women's concentration camps using her own ideas of education and order.[48] He refers to Langefeld's gender-specific view of herself and her definition of women as lovers of peace and order and thus as particularly capable of running a women's concentration camp. Schwartz points out that Langefeld was particularly proud of the fact that under her control roll-calls and selection for extermination activities took place without 'screaming and shouting'.[49] In the framework of Langefeld's work as Senior Guard she enjoyed a scope for action which she was able to use, and did use, for the benefit of individual prisoners or groups of prisoners, orienting herself when 'helping' like this according to the general hierarchy of prisoners. Thus, although she helped mainly Polish women, by giving them various responsibilities,[50] she took part unreservedly in the extermination of Jewish prisoners at the lower end of the camp hierarchy.

Images of gender in post-war trials

Many of the most interesting recent publications on women in National Socialism are concerned with the perception in public debates in the post-war period of women who had been demonstrably involved in National Socialist injustice and violence, and also with the images of gender conveyed in this debate and with the function of these images. They show that National Socialist crimes committed by women are usually explained as deviant femininity and in this context are frequently sexualised.[51] This gender-specific evaluation of involvement in National Socialist crimes is especially apparent in criminal proceedings against female concentration camp guards. Julia Duesterberg examines the case of the former concentration camp guard Dorothea Binz who, during her trial, was described by the prosecution not only as 'a beast' but also as 'a sadistic slut', and shows that the violent actions of such concentration camp guards appear particularly brutal because they run counter to traditional images of femininity. In the case of women, brutality was and is regarded as deviant behaviour and demonised, with the consequence that the woman acting on her account is pushed into the background and at the same time the 'normal human being' is relieved of the responsibility.[52]

A similar conclusion is reached by Alexandra Przyrembel in her investigation of Ilse Koch, the wife of the concentration camp commandant and SS officer Karl Koch. Ilse Koch was not a camp guard but she did intervene in violent fashion in the everyday life of the camp.[53] Even before the liberation of the Buchenwald camp she had a reputation for cruelty, mainly because of the supposition that she had had a handbag made for her out of tattooed pieces of skin from prisoners. Subsequently she was repeatedly connected with the fetishisation of human skin. This played a recurrent and significant role when she was on trial, in addition to alleged adultery with other SS men and the mistreatment of prisoners. Ilse Koch's crimes were associated with sexually deviant behaviour and psychologised. Her conviction functioned as 'a catharsis for all "decent Germans"'.[54]

Anette Kretzer in her research on the representation of perpetrators in the first of the Ravensbrück trials in Hamburg also points to the fact that in public discussion on women in National Socialism, and in this case mainly in press reports of post-war trials in which female concentration camp guards were indicted, it was precisely crimes committed by women which appeared particularly enigmatic and were made into scandals or presented as pathological.[55] Kretzer refers to constructions of specifically female or male criminality and to corresponding gender-specific expectations of normality. Deeds committed by women count as especially brutal and abnormal; it is above all the 'unfemininity' of this behaviour which is emphasised. Kretzer traces this to certain expectations of normality in an idealised conception of femininity, which also serves as a means of distancing oneself from the cruel conduct of the guards. Like Duesterberg and Przyrembel, Kretzer points out that the other side of the coin to the construction of the 'female beast' is a 'collectively applicable counter-model' of a 'normality of innocence' amongst the mass of the unpersecuted German women.[56] The perpetrator is excluded from the construct of 'social normality' and in contrast to it constitutes an individual deviation which can be marginalised as pathological. Kretzer reveals that these images of gender and gender stereotypes determined the post-war discussion on female perpetrators and by demonising the perpetrators had the function of allowing commentators to evade a self-reflective consideration of the National Socialist past and to exonerate themselves.

Summary

It is clear then that recent researches no longer focus primarily on the question of whether women as a whole were perpetrators or more victims. It is taken as given that unpersecuted German women took part in the National Socialist system of government in the most diverse areas. Instead the discussion now centres on women's scope for action which, as recent studies show, did definitely exist and was exploited in the most varied ways. Attention is also being paid to National Socialist gender arrangements and to the gender images which after the war were projected above all on to female perpetrators.

The emphasis is not on the unambiguous assignment of persons to binary schemes, but on the most precise reconstruction possible of the modes of operation of the National Socialist system of government and the social conditions including the gender arrangements which permitted its repressive and criminal rule.

This end to unambiguous assignment is also oriented on the tendency of recent 'general' women's studies to regard the division into two genders not as 'natural', but as a social construct, and to deconstruct it. Once the division into two genders is questioned, then correspondingly all other binary divisions connected to it may also turn out to be constructs – thus too the victim–perpetrator duality so long maintained in research on women. If at the beginning of women's studies in relation to National Socialism it was decided in advance who should count as a victim and who as a perpetrator, and if later a distinction was drawn between a specifically female and a specifically male form of perpetration, it was now possible to take account of the multiplicity of women's roles. Enquiries above all about women's scope for action under National Socialism and about images of gender which operated during and after the National Socialist period proved and are proving to be fruitful both in considering women's role in National Socialism and in preventing the assumption of multiple roles from degenerating into an 'anything goes' approach.

Notes

*Translated by Richard Littlejohns

1. This chapter is also available, arranged differently and with other emphases, in Christina Herkommer, *Frauen im Nationalsozialismus – Opfer oder Täterinnen. Eine Kontroverse der Frauenforschung im Spiegel feministischer Theoriebildung und der allgemeinen historischen Aufarbeitung der NS-Vergangenheit* (Munich, 2000).
2. Joachim C. Fest, *The Face of the Third Reich* (Harmondsworth, 1979), 397.
3. Ibid., 400.
4. Ibid., 402.
5. Ibid.
6. Cf., for example: '... the over-excited, distinctly hysterical tone that quickly spread in all directions sprang in the first place from the excessive emotionalism of a particular kind of elderly woman who sought to activate the unsatisfied impulse within her in the tumult of nightly political demonstrations before the ecstatic figure of Hitler' (Fest, *Face*, 401).
7. Cf. Brigitte Brück et al., *Feministische Soziologie. Eine Einführung* (Frankfurt/Main, 1997), 20.
8. Cf. Annemarie Tröger, 'Die Dolchstoßlegende der Linken: "Frauen haben Hitler an die Macht gebracht". Thesen zur Geschichte der Frauen am Vorabend des Dritten Reichs', in *Frauen und Wissenschaft. Beiträge zur Berliner Sommeruniversität für Frauen* (Berlin, 1977), 327f.; Jürgen W. Falter, *Hitlers Wähler* (München, 1991), 140.
9. Cf. Petra Schomburg, 'Frauen im Nationalsozialismus. Ein Überblick über die historische Frauenforschung und die feministische Diskussion um Verantwortung und Beteiligung von Frauen am Nationalsozialismus', in

Ortrun Niethammer (ed.), *Frauen und Nationalsozialismus. Historische und kulturgeschichtliche Positionen* (Osnabrück, 1996), 44.
10. See also for the discrepancy between Nazi ideology and the needs of a society at war: Richard J. Evans, *The Feminist Movement in Germany 1894–1933* (London, 1976), 254; Timothy Mason, 'Zur Lage der Frauen in Deutschland 1930–1940: Wohlfahrt, Arbeit und Familie', in *Beiträge zur Marxschen Theorie*, 6 (Frankfurt/Main, 1976), 118–92.
11. Susanna Dammer and Carola Sachse, 'Kinder, Küche, Kriegsarbeit – Die Schulung der Frauen durch die NS-Frauenschaft', in Frauengruppe Faschismusforschung (ed.), *Mutterkreuz und Arbeitsbuch. Zur Geschichte der Frauen in der Weimarer Republik und im Nationalsozialismus* (Frankfurt/Main, 1981), 110; also Tröger, 'Die Frau im wesensgemäßen Einsatz', in ibid., 252f..
12. Gisela Bock, *Zwangssterilisation im Nationalsozialismus. Studien zur Rassenpolitik und Frauenpolitik* (Opladen, 1986), 17.
13. Ibid., 208.
14. Atina Grossmann, 'Feminist Debates about Women and National Socialism', *Gender and History*, 3 (1991), 354f.
15. Margarete Mitscherlich, *Die friedfertige Frau. Eine psychoanalytische Untersuchung zur Aggression der Geschlechter* (Frankfurt/Main, 1985).
16. Ibid., 11.
17. Ibid., 151f.
18. Ibid., 157. The assumption that women are provided with a 'weak super-ego' has been recognised – and refuted – as an example of androcentrism within Freudian theory (Karin Windaus-Walser, 'Gnade der weiblichen Geburt? Zum Umgang der Frauenforschung mit Nationalsozialismus und Antisemitismus', *Feministische Studien*, 1 (1988), 102–15).
19. Christina Thürmer-Rohr, *Vagabundinnen. Feministische Essays* (Berlin, 1987). Thürmer-Rohr refers less to National Socialism and above all to the nuclear threat and the destruction of the environment. Her thesis of joint perpetrators has nevertheless been discussed primarily in relation to the role of women in National Socialism.
20. Ibid., 51.
21. Ibid., 41f.
22. Claudia Koonz, *Mütter im Vaterland* (Freiburg im Breisgau, 1991).
23. Cf. Koonz, *Mütter*, 426.
24. Cf. 'Frauen gegen Antisemitismus: Der Nationalsozialismus als Extremform des Patriarchats. Zur Leugnung der Täterschaft von Frauen und zur Tabuisierung des Antisemitismus in der Auseinandersetzung mit dem NS', *Beiträge zur feministischen Theorie und Praxis*, 35(16) (1993), 77–89, here 83.
25. Angelika Ebbinghaus (ed.), *Opfer und Täterinnen. Frauenbiographien des Nationalsozialismus* (Nördlingen, 1987); see also Ute Frevert, *Frauen-Geschichte. Zwischen bürgerlicher Verbesserung und neuer Weiblichkeit* (Frankfurt/Main, 1986), 243.
26. Ebbinghaus, *Opfer*, 218ff.
27. Cf. Ebbinghaus, *Opfer*, 8; see also Gaby Zipfel, 'Verdrängte Erinnerungen, verdeckte Überlieferungen. Akteurinnen im Nationalsozialismus', *Mittelweg* 36(2) (1996), 69ff.

28. Cf. Petra Schomburg, 'Frauen im Nationalsozialismus', in Ortrun Niethammer (ed.), *Frauen und Nationalsozialismus. Historische und kulturgeschchtliche Positionen* (Osnabrück, 1996), 49.
29. Gisela Bock, 'Ein Historikerinnenstreit?', *Geschichte und Gesellschaft*, 18 (1992), 400–4.
30. Gisela Bock, 'Die Frauen und der Nationalsozialismus. Bemerkungen zu einem Buch von Claudia Koonz', *Geschichte und Gesellschaft*, 15 (1989), 563–79.
31. The main criticism of Ebbinghaus was made by Dagmar Reese and Carola Sachse. They criticise Ebbinghaus, for example, for employing a 'simple victim–perpetrator' – good and bad scheme which is oriented on legal concepts (Dagmar Reese and Carola Sachse, 'Frauenforschung zum Nationalsozialismus. Eine Bilanz', in Lerke Gravenhorst and Carmen Tatschmurat (eds), *TöchterFragen. NS-Frauengeschichte* (Freiburg im Breisgau, 1990), 73f.).
32. See on the established two lines of thought (the constructivist and the deconstructivist approach): Regina Gildemeister and Angelika Wetterer, 'Wie Geschlechter gemacht werden. Die soziale Konstruktion der Zweigeschlechtlichkeit und ihre Reifizierung in der Frauenforschung', in Gudrun-Axeli Knapp and Angelika Wetterer (eds), *Traditionen, Brüche, Entwicklungen feministischer Theorie* (Freiburg im Breisgau, 1992), 201–54; Judith Butler, *Gender Trouble: Feminism and the Subversion of Identity* (New York, 1990).
33. Gisela Bock, 'Ganz normale Frauen. Täter, Opfer, Mitläufer und Zuschauer im Nationalsozialismus', in Kirsten Heinsohn et al. (eds), *Zwischen Karriere und Verfolgung. Handlungsräume von Frauen im nationalsozialistischen Deutschland* (Frankfurt/Main, 1997), 246.
34. Christopher Browning, *Ordinary Men: Reserve Battalion 101 and the Final Solution in Poland* (New York, 1992).
35. Bock, *Ganz normale Frauen*, 268.
36. Carola Sachse, 'Frauenforschung zum Nationalsozialismus. Debatten, Topoi und Ergebnisse seit 1976', *Mittelweg* 36(2) (1997), 33.
37. Annette Kuhn, 'Dimensionen der Täterschaft deutscher Frauen im NS-System', in Annette Betrams (ed.), *Dichotomie, Dominanz, Differenz. Frauen platzieren sich in Wissenschaft und Gesellschaft* (Weinheim, 1995), 52.
38. Kirsten Heinsohn et al. (eds), *Zwischen Karriere und Verfolgung*, 13.
39. Cf. Sachse, *Frauenforschung*, 33.
40. Cf. Anna Maria Sigmund, *Die Frauen der Nazis* (Wien, 1998); or the TV series 'Hitler's Women and Marlene', now available also as a book: cf. Guido Knopp, *Hitlers Frauen und Marlene* (München, 2001).
41. Cf. Gudrun Schwarz, 'Frauen in der SS: Sippenverband und Frauenkorps', in Heinsohn, *Karriere*, 223–44; Gudrun Schwarz, 'SS-Aufseherinnen in nationalsozialistischen Konzentrationslagern 1933–1945', *Dachauer Hefte*, 10 (1994), 32–49.
42. At its inception the SS was not conceived as a kinship community of men and women. This changed in 1929 on the appointment of Heinrich Himmler as Reichsführer of the SS; then he presided over a growing membership and a reorganisation of the SS from a 'band of men' into a kinship community of

'racially' selected men and women whose task was to be the foundation of an 'elite race' (cf. Gudrun Schwarz, *Eine Frau an seiner Seite. Ehefrauen in der 'SS-Sippengemeinschaft'* (Berlin, 2001), 17ff.).
43. Cf. Gudrun Schwarz, 'Verdrängte Täterinnen. Frauen im Apparat der SS (1939–1945)', in Theresa Wobbe (ed.), *Nach Osten. Verdeckte Spuren nationalsozialistischer Verbrechen* (Frankfurt/Main, 1992), 203ff., 211ff.
44. Cf. Gudrun Schwarz, 'Das SS-Herrenmenschenpaar', in Helgard Kramer (ed.), *Die Gegenwart der NS-Vergangenheit* (Berlin, 2000), 304–13.
45. Schwarz, *Frau an seiner Seite*, 61.
46. Johannes Schwartz, 'Geschlechtsspezifischer Eigensinn von NS-Täterinnen am Beispiel der KZ-Oberaufseherin Johanna Langefeld', in Viola Schubert-Lehnhardt (ed.), *Frauen als Täterinnen im Nationalsozialismus* (Gerbstedt, 2005), 56–82.
47. Cf. Irmtraud Heike, 'Johanna Langefeld. Die Biographie einer KZ-Oberaufseherin', *WerkstattGeschichte*, 12 (1995), 14ff. See also her chapter in this volume.
48. Schwartz, 'Geschlechtsspezifischer Eigensinn', 58.
49. Ibid., 72.
50. Cf. ibid., 64; Johanna Langefeld was rebuked for this by the camp leadership. In one case she was even arrested on these grounds and brought to trial charged with having nationally prejudiced sympathies for Polish women. She was, however, cleared for lack of evidence (ibid., 78ff.).
51. Cf. Julia Duesterberg, 'Von der "Umkehr aller Weiblichkeit". Charakterbilder einer KZ-Aufseherin', in Insa Eschebach et al. (eds), *Gedächtnis und Geschlecht. Deutungsmuster in Darstellungen des nationalsozialistischen Genozids* (Frankfurt/Main, 2002), 227.
52. Ibid., 241.
53. Alexandra Przyrembel, 'Der Bann eines Bildes. Ilse Koch, die "Kommandeuse von Buchenwald"', in Eschebach, *Gedächtnis*, 245–67.
54. Ibid., 264.
55. Anette Kretzer, '"His or Her Special Job". Die Repräsentation von NS-Verbrecherinnen im ersten Hamburger Ravensbrück-Prozess und im westdeutschen Täterschaftsdiskurs', *Beiträge zur Geschichte der nationalsozialistischen Verfolgung in Norddeutschland*, 7 (2005), 134–50.
56. Ibid., 137.

5
Female Concentration Camp Guards as Perpetrators: Three Case Studies*

Irmtraud Heike

For a long time in studies of women under National Socialism guards in concentration camps received little attention. At best they were mentioned in separate studies of various concentration camps and satellite camps.[1] Recent years have seen a change in this respect, both in research and in the culture of memorials. Today there is an increasing volume of publication on the active involvement of women in National Socialism.[2] In this context individual biographies of guards are repeatedly an object of scrutiny,[3] although prominence continues to be given to descriptions of particularly spectacular examples, which on the whole prevents an objective examination of the deeds of the guards. The reconstruction of biographies of female guards is nevertheless indispensable, although the focus ought to be placed more on those women who constituted most of the guards and thus had a crucial influence on the prisoners' lives or their survival.

It is important to note in this connection that, while women were recruited to work in concentration camps as part of their obligatory service in the armaments industry, a series of women came forward for this work of their own volition. The question is: what made them apply voluntarily for employment as guards in a concentration camp?

Given that women volunteered as guards, there is a need to establish what role they played in the National Socialist annihilation policy. Did they in fact merely perform subordinate functions in the structure of the camps, as is frequently maintained in the testimony of former guards? Using a typical case, the biography of Johanna Langefeld,[4] a woman who served in the concentration camps from the early 1930s, we can trace the career of a Senior Guard (*Oberaufseherin*) and her involvement

Photo 5.1 Concentration camp Bergen-Belsen, Germany, 17 April 1945: Some captured female SS camp guards. The original caption reads: 'Some of the S.S. women whose bestiality and brutality was equal to that of their male colleagues.'

in the National Socialist policy of 'select and eradicate' in concentration camps.

Facts about female guards in concentration camps are available only from fragmentary sources. There are documents at administrative level which, however, are of a more general nature. Otherwise information about their activities in the concentration camps comes principally from evidence given in the post-war period by guards, either when indicted or as witnesses in investigations or trials initiated by the Allied forces either in West or East German courts. This applies to the life of Johanna Langefeld too. Only one interrogation of Langefeld, dating from 1946, is recorded at present: it is preserved in the National Archives in Washington.

Even in early trials instigated after the war by the Allies, above all in relation to the concentration camp of Bergen-Belsen[5] and the women's concentration camp at Ravensbrück,[6] former female guards were charged and convicted along with their male colleagues. These

Photo 5.2 Concentration camp Bergen-Belsen, Germany, circa 21 April 1945, after the liberation of the camp by British soldiers '[f]orcing former women camp guards and German mayors from surrounding towns to view mass graves in Bergen-Belsen concentration camp'.

proceedings and the choice of the accused have been widely and justifiably criticised, but the trials nevertheless sent out a clear signal that these crimes could not remain unpunished. It is evident, however, that Federal German legislation and criminal justice were unable to follow this example: in a state governed by the rule of law it was necessary to prove personal participation in a crime, whereas according to Allied guidelines the mere fact of membership of a unit responsible for crimes was sufficient to secure a conviction. This shift in tendency affected male suspects, but affected females to a greater degree. There were many reasons for this: the absence of legal foundations, the changed political framework in the Cold War, and not least the lack of willingness in postwar Federal German society to uncover the truth. A further difficulty was caused by changes in the social perception of female perpetrators and especially of female concentration camp guards in the course of time

Photo 5.3 Concentration camp Bergen-Belsen, Germany, 21 April 1945, after the liberation of the camp by British soldiers: 'The barracks of Bergen-Belsen concentration camp visible behind them, male and female camp personnel are lined up in front of a mass grave to hear a broadcast denouncing the Germans and their treatment of prisoners'.

from the foundation of the Federal Republic of Germany to the present day. This can be shown by reference to two examples, the prosecution of the former guards Lotte M. and Ingeborg Aßmuß and the enquiries conducted into their cases.

Female concentration camp guards: a survey

Women as well as men were persecuted and interned in concentration camps by the National Socialist regime. Female guards were responsible for women prisoners in various women's camps. The total number of female guards has not yet been established. Fritz Suhre, the former commandant of the female concentration camp at Ravensbrück, stated at the Nuremberg trials that from 1942 to 1945 some 3,500 such guards were trained in Ravensbrück, the central women's concentration camp, alone.[7] Although an exact figure for the number of female concentration camp guards is so far unknown, estimates suggest that only 10 per cent of the personnel in all concentration camps were women.[8] The reasons for this are to be found in the organisational structure of the concentration camps with its rigidly gender-specific lines.

Female guards belonging to the SS-Retinue (*SS-Gefolge*) guarded female prisoners for the first time in December 1937 in Lichtenburg castle in Prettin on the river Elbe which had been converted into a female concentration camp. It was there, and in the camp at Ravensbrück opened in May 1939 which was to become the central women's concentration camp, replacing the dismantled camp at Lichtenburg, that guard duties were shared between men and women for the first time. Whilst in both Lichtenburg castle and later in Ravensbrück the command staff, and thus the running of the camp, was entirely in the hands of men, women were supposed to guard the inside of the camp. As a result, women essentially determined the day-to-day existence of the inmates of the camp. The only exception within this strict hierarchy was the position of the female Senior Guard. Although she was a member of the command staff and the direct superior of all the female guards, she belonged like them to the SS-Retinue. This female SS-Retinue was presumably intended as a contrivance by which women, who were not supposed to become members of the SS, could be incorporated into it. On the one hand, women were clearly not meant to be integrated into this male-oriented elite organisation, but, on the other hand, such an affiliation was obviously necessary. Thus women in the SS-Retinue were subject like men in the SS to the so-called SS jurisdiction.[9]

From 1942 to September 1944 the women's concentration camp at Ravensbrück also served as the training camp for female guards. The reason for this was the opening of numerous women's sections within other concentration camps as well as the establishment of subsidiary camps for female prisoners. After completing their period of instruction in Ravensbrück the guards were in part employed in these new women's camps. In 1944 alone some 1,800 women, but probably still more,[10] were trained, at first in Ravensbrück and additionally from 1 September 1944, in accordance with a decision taken by group D of the SS Economic-Administrative Main Office (*SS-Wirtschafts-Verwaltungshauptamt, WVHA*), in other concentration camps with women's camps attached.[11] The guards were remunerated on the wage-scale paid to public employees. Their starting grade was Group IX and after three months' probation they progressed to Group VIII.

For an unmarried guard aged 25 in 1944 this meant a gross wage of some 185 Reichsmark per month and, after deduction of social insurance contributions and other charges such as board and lodging, a net salary of around 105 Reichsmark.[12] By way of comparison, the gross wage of an unskilled female worker in the manufacturing firm Osram in Berlin stood in 1944 at 165 Reichsmark per month, in other words it was lower.[13] The gross earnings of a domestic servant were even lower, on average around 30 to 40 Reichsmark plus free board and lodging. Even a trained cook did not receive more than 60 Reichsmark gross per month.[14]

Guards were also provided with their work clothing free of charge. They took their meals communally in the SS canteen, and dwellings and rooms for personnel were available in the SS village near the camp. However, the possibilities for making a career as a guard were more limited for females than for their male colleagues in the SS. 'With appropriate aptitude and hard work'[15] it was possible for guards to be promoted to Head Guard (*Erstaufseherin*) in a subsidiary camp or even to Senior Guard. Head guard was the title given to the female in charge of a subsidiary camp, whilst a Senior Guard was the direct superior of all female guards in a main camp. This brought an increase in salary. But how were female guards recruited, and what motives lay behind voluntary applications?

The route to becoming a female concentration camp guard

Advertisements for employment as a guard were typically placed in newspapers, and advisers in employment offices drew attention to vacancies in concentration camps.[16] On applying for a post as a female guard in Ravensbrück a woman would receive an information sheet in which the duties were extolled as 'light physical work'. The recruiting literature read as follows: 'In the Ravensbrück concentration camp women are detained who have committed offences against the people's community [*Volksgemeinschaft*] and now have to be isolated in order to prevent further harm. These women are to be supervised during their periods of work in the camp. For this work, therefore, you do not need any professional knowledge, since it is merely a matter of guarding the prisoners.'[17] Preference was given to applicants between the ages of 21 and 45.

From the biographies of guards which have come to light to date it emerges that women volunteered for a variety of reasons. Some of them obviously expected to gain financially from employment as a guard. It is noticeable that in stating their previous profession or employment a number of women said that they had previously worked as a domestic, a factory worker or some other unskilled occupation. Increased earnings, together with the security of working as a public employee and with the other benefits such as housing and work clothing, were apparent attractions, although there is nothing to suggest that these women acted out of economic necessity. Where applications to the concentration camp at Ravensbrück are concerned, it is also clear that a series of guards came from the immediate locality. Testimony given by former guards reveals that the camp at Ravensbrück was advertised as a new place of work within easy travelling distance.[18] Women also applied, however, who had previously followed a career in social welfare, seemingly seeing in the work as a guard some continuation of their previous employment.[19] Johanna Langefeld was one of these.

Johanna Langefeld: the biography of a concentration camp Senior Guard

Johanna Langefeld was born on 5 March 1900 in Kupferdreh near Essen and joined the NSDAP on 30 September 1937. In her application to join she stated that by profession she was 'matron in the workhouse [*Arbeitsanstalt*] at Brauweiler' near Cologne.[20] The provincial regional workhouse was one of the early camps for women. Johanna Langefeld worked there as a guard. The only source of information so far about her family, her origins and her early professional career was thought to be the autobiography of a former prisoner at Ravensbrück, Margarete Buber-Neumann. Detained in Ravensbrück from 1940 to 1945 and put to work on clerical tasks in the office of Senior Guard Langefeld, Buber-Neumann reports at length on the former guard.[21] In 1957 the two women met again, Johanna Lengefield seeking Margarete Buber-Neumann out in order to explain her behaviour in Ravensbrück to the former prisoner, presumably because she needed to talk about her past to someone involved.[22] Buber-Neumann writes that Langefeld came from 'a family of civil servants with a strict commitment to Germany as a nation' and felt 'the occupation of the Rhineland by the French in 1918...to be most profoundly shameful'. The family was reduced to poverty as a result of inflation, and Langefeld gave a euphoric welcome to the 'Renewal of Germany' proclaimed by Adolf Hitler. Widowed young, and with a child, she had no choice but to find a job. She decided to work in the prison service, 'in order to do good amongst the poorest of the poor'[23] – as Buber-Neumann's description of Langefeld says.

On 1 March 1938 Johanna Langefeld began work as a guard in the Lichtenburg concentration camp. According to her own evidence when interrogated in 1946, she was promoted to Senior Guard only a year later.[24] She did not record any reasons for this rapid rise. After the Ravensbrück camp was opened in May 1939 the inmates of the Lichtenburg concentration camp were transferred to the newly built camp. The entire body of guards moved with them. Johanna Langefeld now became the Senior Guard in Ravensbrück.

From 1940 onwards differences of opinion began to arise between Langefeld in her position as Senior Guard and the commanders of the camp, mainly the commandant Max Koegel.[25] Langefeld told Buber-Neumann that the disputes were caused by the 'crazy orders'[26] which Koegel gave. Amongst these, according to Langefeld, was the introduction of beatings as a punishment in Ravensbrück. Dorothea Binz, who from 1939 to 1943 was a guard and from 1943 to 1945 deputised as Senior Guard in Ravensbrück, testified in the first Ravensbrück trial in 1946 that in 1940 Koegel had given her an order to beat women prisoners with a stick. This happened, so Binz said, without the permission of Heinrich Himmler, the Reich Leader (*Reichsführer*) of the SS.[27] Even in the Lichtenburg camp there had been beatings, which constituted the severest form of punishment. When Himmler visited the Ravensbrück camp in 1940, Koegel took the opportunity to ask his permission to introduce beating as a punishment in Ravensbrück just as it had been before in the Lichtenburg camp. Langefeld reported to Buber-Neumann later that in the presence of Himmler she had protested energetically aginst the idea that women should be strapped to a frame and beaten. She alleged that Himmler had taken no notice of her objections.[28] Beatings were in fact introduced, although they required Himmler's personal authorisation.[29] Langefeld made the following comments on the practice of beating as a punishment in her interrogation in 1946: 'I'm no lawyer or pedagogue and so wouldn't like to be a judge or pass sentences. But just going on human feelings a large number of the punishments were too hard, in fact often much too hard. They often suggested casual handling of cases and even plain arbitrariness. Beatings with a stick had to be authorised by the *Reichsf.[ührers-SS Himmler]*. The commandant gave these orders. Since he had no legal knowledge, as far as I know, and was still less qualified pedagogically, such wrong sentencing was bound to occur.'[30]

Leaving aside the assumption that in interrogations the accused always seeks through their evidence to justify their own behaviour so as to avoid any possible prosecution, Johanna Langefeld apparently harboured the notion that concentration camps were legally sanctioned institutions of which the main aim was the 'improvement' and 'education' of the inmates. This National Socialist idea of education was in line with the ideology which Himmler himself professed but which remained no more than a theory in the concentration camps. Even in the early phases of the concentration camps they were devoted less to the education of political groups than to excluding political opponents, isolating social outsiders and terrorising the population. After the outbreak of war, the camps also had as primary functions the exploitation of prisoners as a workforce and the 'mass annihilation' of countless prisoners, and thus were still less designed as 'education camps'. It is also unclear whether Johanna Langefeld was anxious that female prisoners should be treated differently in concentration camps, based on the idea that the sexes were to be educated in different ways. In her interrogation in 1946 she expressed indignation above all about the random employment of 'the most incapable female guards' in the concentration camps. Such women, so she placed on record, had written arbitrary reports 'on insignificant matters which in their consequences had unacceptable repercussions'.[31] She thought that these women should be replaced by 'older work service leaders who had enough experience of life and whose morality and decency were in my view impeccable, so that they could do the job of guard in the way it needed to be done'. Her opinion was that 'nothing came of this idea ... because ... the leaders of the R.A.D. [*Reichsarbeitsdienst*][32] did not entirely agree with conditions in the camp, and especially not with the fact that women were to have such little influence over women's matters'.[33] These notions of 'reform', however unrealistic, do show that Johanna Langefeld was obviously hoping for a greater involvement of women in leading positions within the concentration camp organisation. Such wishful thinking was encouraged by a division of powers laid down in the organisational structure of the camps. The female Senior Guard was subordinate to the Protective Custody Camp Leader (*Schutzhaftlagerführer*),[34] but also directly to the commandant. She carried out tasks which in a men's camp were part of the remit of the Custody Camp Leader. The female Senior Guard was also supposed to support the Custody Camp Leader and 'assist him in an advisory capacity in all matters affecting women'.[35] The coexistence of the Custody Camp Leader and the female Senior Guard could, however, lead to frictions and arguments about areas of responsibility, an entirely deliberate 'multiple line system'. This decentralisation increased the flexibility of the organisation and allowed the individual sections considerable scope for independent initiatives. For the prisoners the organisational uncertainty and arbitrariness meant additional terror.[36]

That the rivalry between male members of the commandment staff and Johanna Langefeld was not confined only to the Ravensbrück camp, and the extent of her hopes for an extension of the powers of her position as Senior Guard, became clear after she had been transferred to Auschwitz in March 1942. She escorted 1,000 women when they were transported there from Ravensbrück, and they became the first prisoners in the women's section at Auschwitz. Johanna Langefeld was given charge of the camp.[37] When Himmler paid a visit to the camp in July 1942 she made complaints to him about her male colleagues, the Custody Camp Leader Hans Aumeier[38] and the commandant's adjutant Robert Mulka.[39] She describes this incident in her interrogation in January 1946: 'Consultation of some files and my subsequent complaint to the *Reichsführer* led to him [Himmler] giving the commandant, who was present on this occasion, the order that with immediate effect no SS leader, Sub-Leader [*Unterführer*] or man should be allowed to enter the women's camp. That in particular Aumeier, who had until then been the Custody Camp Leader, had no business with the external commandos [*Außenkommandos*]. As far as the Ravensbrück camp was concerned, Himmler said he would have the matter investigated.'[40]

The notes written after the war by the former commandant of the Auschwitz concentration camp, Rudolf Höss,[41] contain the following report: 'The Senior Guard at the time, Frau Langefeld, was in no way up to the situation, but stubbornly rejected all instructions given by the Custody Camp Leader. Acting on my own initiative I summarily put the FKL [= *Frauenkonzentrationslager*][42] under the authority of the Custody Camp Leader... However, since the Senior Guard considered herself to be an autonomous camp leader, she complained about being subordinate to an officer of an equal rank. And in the event I had to countermand my order... and I told him [Himmler] that Frau Langefeld would never ever be in a position to lead and strengthen the FKL Auschwitz properly, and furthermore requested that she be subordinate to the first Custody Camp Leader. He firmly declined to do this, despite the most conclusive proofs of the incompetence of the Senior Guard... He said that he wished a women's camp to be led by a woman and that I should assign an SS leader to assist her. But who of these leaders would want, so to speak, to subordinate himself to a woman?'[43]

Höss's remarks show clearly that the disputes between Langefeld and the commandant's staff involved not only the struggle for power which was normal in all concentration camps, but also the reluctance of SS leaders to be subordinate to a woman, especially when she was to receive greater powers of command than her male colleagues. Langefeld's complaint did, however, succeed initially. On 24 October 1942 the head of group D of the SS Economic-Administrative Main Office (*WVHA*) sent a letter to the camp commandants of the Ravensbrück, Auschwitz and Lublin concentration camps ordering them to assign elsewhere the previous Protective Custody Camp Leader of existing women's camps and in future to appoint the Senior Guard to carry out the duties they had performed.[44] Whether this instruction in fact brought about an extension in the powers of the Senior Guard is impossible to establish. Possibly the attempt failed again in the face of opposition from the male leaders in the commandant's staff in individual camps.

Johanna Langefeld returned to Ravensbrück in summer 1942 as Senior Guard. Soon afterwards she went to see the head of the *WVHA*, Oswald Pohl, to reiterate her criticism of the conditions in the women's camps at Auschwitz and Ravensbrück and to propose a possible reorganisation of the camps. However, this obviously met with rejection. On the contrary, Pohl reproached her with 'complaining to Himmler and running down the SS leader, Sub-Leader and even the guards', so she reported in her interrogation in 1946. In Ravensbrück too she encountered renewed hostility from the commandant and the Protective Custody Camp Leader, which led to her arrest in 1943.[45] Langefeld's reports and suppositions suggest that she may possibly have contravened important SS 'rules of the game', which obviously applied too to the SS-Retinue. It was characteristic of the SS organisation that it expected not only absolute allegiance and obedience but also a form of comradeship, a kind of complicity, whereby the members of the group covered for each other in the event of misdemeanours, concealed weaknesses, and practised a cohesion which closed ranks to the outside world. They formed a sworn community which stuck together even against other authorities in the SS.[46] By complaining about her colleagues Langefeld had presumably not only offended against the rules but also, as Pohl's annoyance makes it appear, gone over the heads of her direct superiors, the various commandants and Pohl himself. Her endeavour to gain more influence within the command structure of the camp hierarchy in her role as Senior Guard would also have been a further crucial factor in her dismissal.

Langefeld was initially held under house arrest, then came before an SS court and was dismissed from the service of the SS.[47] The SS had its own courts, whose supreme judge after Hitler was Himmler, and their punishments were less based on legal principles than on serving primarily as a means of disciplining members of the SS or the SS-Retinue. It was not so much persons who had done some objective harm who were pursued and punished as those who offended against the SS community.[48] Langefeld's 'offence' was punished by her exclusion.

She began by living in Munich and working for the Bavarian Motor Works (*BMW*). In 1946 she was arrested by the American military police. She was detained because her name was on lists of former guard detachments in a concentration camp. It emerges from the report on her arrest that at that time there were no concrete charges against her, and that she was picked up because she had been a member of the camp personnel. After short periods in prison in Munich and in Ludwigsburg, an assembly point for National Socialists imprisoned pending investigation, she was handed over to the Poles. She managed to escape from custody in a Polish jail, and she was able to disappear. She returned to Germany in 1958 and died in Augsburg in 1975.[49]

'The Senior Guard Johanna Langefeld had a reputation for decency amongst the prisoners. She didn't yell and she didn't hit people': this was Margarete Buber-Neumann's verdict on her.[50]

These testimonies are typical of the predominantly positive descriptions of the Senior Guard in the reports of former women detainees. Margarete Buber-Neumann evidently belonged to a circle of female prisoners with whom the Senior Guard occasionally held conversations. These were mainly women who were so-called 'political' prisoners.[51] Langefeld went so far in giving preferential treatment to some German 'political' prisoners that during Himmler's visit to Auschwitz in 1942 she suggested to him that a group of German women prisoners known to her from Ravensbrück should be released. The release was authorised, but did not take place until later.[52]

From the reports of prisoners it emerges that Langefeld at least once intervened to prevent the execution, normal in such cases, of two Polish women, on whom experiments in the form of operations had been carried out, an incident which occurred in March 1943. By telephoning the Protective Custody Camp Leader she saved the lives of both women. Encouraged by the Senior Guard's intervention, Polish women decided a few days later to go as a deputation to Langefeld's office and protest, with a view to preventing further scheduled operations. On this occasion Langefeld showed hesitation, avoided the women's complaints, and sent them back to their block. The experiments were continued.[53] Possibly she feared that a second interference with the orders of the Protective

Custody Camp Leader would intensify the rivalries, or perhaps the women's protest went too far for her.

At the same time Johanna Langefeld's reputation in the camp was that she was anti-Semitic. Johanna Sturm, an Austrian detained in the concentration camps from 1938, reports an incident in 1940. In the summer Johanna Langefeld had the Jewish women's block locked for three days. Hundreds of women were penned together, exposed to the heat, and left without food and water.[54] Bertha Teege, a former German prisoner, gave evidence in 1948 in the sixth Ravensbrück trial that women selected by the various commandants and local doctors for gassing had been assembled for transportation by Johanna Langefeld.[55]

There was no contradiction between Langefeld's preferential treatment of some groups of prisoners in Ravensbrück and her pronounced anti-Semitism. She acted perfectly in accord with the 'heritage and race doctrine' of National Socialist ideology. Her efforts to secure the release of German women indicate that she wanted once again to put into practice her notions of education which derived from the heritage and race doctrine. It followed that only those individuals could be educated who, to use the National Socialist terminology, belonged to the 'Nordic race'. On the basis of these 'doctrines' a hierarchy of prisoners had been constructed in the camps in which those who were 'racially' persecuted, Jews in particular, were right at the bottom of the scale.

Although the available prisoners' reports cannot give a representative picture of the prison society in Ravensbrück, it is nevertheless possible to see how great Langefeld's influence must have been on the lives and on the chances of survival of the imprisoned women. She could treat some groups of prisoners differently from others as the whim took her, and she had a decisive influence on the choice of women to fill responsible positions in the prisoners' self-administration.[56] The organisation of the camp gave her the right to decide whether, following a guard's report, a prisoner should be punished or not for some alleged offence.

Lotte M. and Ingeborg Aßmuß: former concentration camp guards prosecuted in West Germany

Records of trials, as has already become clear, are an indispensable source for acquiring knowledge about female concentration camp guards. Criminal investigations and trials in West Germany are thus of great significance, although they need to be examined critically against the background of Germans in the Federal Republic coming to terms with the National Socialist past.

In the early years of the Federal Republic there was no systematic and comprehensive prosecution of National Socialist crimes. The reasons are partly to be found in the prosecution system of the Federal Republic, but also in the initial unwillingness of the public prosecutors and judges involved to expose and punish crimes which had occurred in the Nazi era.

There was a lack of imagination and a male-oriented perspective in particular in relation to the role of women in the machinery for guarding prisoners in concentration camps. This can be demonstrated by reference to an example from the 1950s, which at the same time reveals the way in which the deeds of a former guard in the final phase of the war were played down in court. In 1951 Lotte M., who had been employed as a guard in an external part of the concentration camp of Neuengamme in the Porta Westfalica, part of the Weser valley (Hausberge), stood trial in the Hamburg regional court.[57]

From the beginning of March 1945 predominantly Dutch and Hungarian Jewish women had been accommodated at Neuengamme and made to work for the Phillips Works in an underground shaft system.[58] At the beginning of April 1945 the camp was dismantled and the prisoners forced into a so-called death march towards Beendorf near Braunschweig (Brunswick).[59] Transporting the female prisoners took place in part in closed goods trains. With another female, Lotte M. was assigned to guard this operation.[60] The transport went from Beendorf via Ludwigslust to Hamburg-Eidelstedt. On the way, further prisoners were added and soon there was extreme overcrowding. In the individual freight cars there were between 100 and 200 prisoners, and the provision of food as well as drinking water was extraordinarily bad, if not non-existent. Due to the catastrophic conditions several hundred people died during this transport.[61] The dead were either thrown from the train or buried on the spot in shallow graves during occasional stops.[62]

The former guard Lotte M. was charged with murdering two female prisoners. It was alleged that she had bludgeoned a Polish woman with a rifle butt and strangled another female prisoner with a cord. She was also accused of mistreating prisoners. On the first charge it was discovered that ten days after leaving Beendorf a Polish woman, who was obviously thirsty, had approached the guard. Lotte M., according to the charge, had then asked an SS sentry for a rifle and beaten the prisoner with it. The woman died as a result of the mistreatment. Evidence was taken from several witnesses, and the court concluded that the charge was not proven. The evidence of the witnesses 'did not agree on various points'.[63] In the second case it was alleged that the accused, during a low-level air attack on the train, had in the ensuing tumult strangled a female prisoner so tightly with a cord that she had very probably died as a result.[64] The regional court concluded that it was a case of attempted manslaughter, but not the offence of attempted murder, since there was no sign of cruel behaviour on the part of the accused, 'which occurs when a killing produces particularly severe suffering through the strength or the duration of the cause of the pain and when it arises from a callous and unmerciful disposition'. It was presumed instead that the accused 'had acted out of a certain annoyance that a general tumult had arisen which she could not control' and that 'to a certain extent her nerves got the better of her'. Moreover, the court said, 'it had involved the idea that on account of her position she was superior to the prisoners and could settle them down by draconian measures'. In its view the accused showed no tendency to brutality, and no base motives could be established. In two further cases Lotte M. was found guilty of mistreating female prisoners on the grounds of causing bodily harm whilst carrying out her duty as a concentration camp guard. The accused was found to be fully responsible for her actions. A medical expert had noted that the accused had a 'weak-willed, easily influenced, compulsive and in part still infantile personality'. In sentencing her it was also allowed in mitigation 'that the accused had not voluntarily taken up duty as a concentration camp guard' and had been 'obviously unsuited to this position'. Thus she had not been up to 'the demands of such position, which led to maltreatment of the kind described'. It was further noted in the accused's favour 'that the events took place in a disorderly and rather turbulent period, in which the accused's nerves were under great strain'. In calculating the sentence imposed on the accused it was, however, noted that she had 'assaulted' prisoners 'who were entrusted to her care and were more or less at her mercy'.[65]

Lotte M. was sentenced to a term of imprisonment of three years and six months in total.[66] However, the state prosecutor appealed on a point of law, claiming that the court had denied the characteristic of attempted murder or cruelty and that the legal grounds for the verdict were faulty. It was also suspected that the accused had acted from base motives, since possibly the deed had been decisively influenced by the thought that the SS had unlimited power over the prisoners and that as a guard the accused did not need to observe any mercy or sympathy towards prisoners.[67]

In summer 1952 the case again came before a jury in Hamburg. Now the court came to the view that in committing the deed the accused had not intended to kill the prisoner and also had not reckoned on the possibility of the woman dying as a result of the strangulation. The court also had grave doubts about the intention to kill, since 'all prisoners and of course the accused too knew that the war would soon come to an end and would finish with the total defeat of Germany'. The circumstances surrounding the transport, it said, had given too clear a signal. 'All parties therefore knew that the liberation of the prisoners was imminent and that it would also mean a reversal in the relationship between the prisoners and the accused.' It thus seemed to the court to be entirely illogical to assume that the accused had intended to kill a prisoner, since she would endanger herself by such an action. In deciding on the sentence it was noted in mitigation that the accused had been 'compulsorily' called up as a guard. She had, it was stated, received only a brief and inadequate training and at the time of her deeds had been working as a guard for only a few weeks. The court gave particular weight, however, to the fact that the events described had taken place in a situation of great tension, 'which could hardly have been handled by a mature and well trained man'. The accused, on the other hand, had found the situation difficult, since her whole personality seemed to make her unfit for such a duty and 'through the gruelling guard duties her nerves at the time were stretched to breaking point'. The sentence of 13 months' imprisonment now passed was counted as already served,[68] and the accused was released.

Above all in the early phase of trials in the Federal Republic there was a marked stereotyping of female involvement in the crimes of National Socialism, which is apparent in the case of Lotte M. Thus the question of the motive for her conduct was considered by reference to what were alleged to be specifically feminine traits. The 'character' of the woman concerned was discussed in detail and given emphasis. A much more intensive psychological examination of the accused and thus also of her deeds was undertaken than happened with male perpetrators.[69] In doing so, reference to the supposedly special burden placed on a woman serving in a concentration camp led to a gender-specific reduction to allegedly female characteristics.[70] It was also assumed that former female guards had no real position of power in the structure of National Socialist rule, but rather played a subordinate role, regardless of the fact that they exercised direct and immediate domination over the female prisoners and could thus decisively influence the lives of the detained women. Moreover, it was believed that the women were 'compelled' to work as guards, an assumption which has since been convincingly refuted.[71] The investigators and judges also had the idea that the women were in any case not up to dealing with the situation in a sphere which was more appropriate to men. So the former female guards appeared less culpable, as was taken for granted in the case of Lotte M. Hastily reached judgements based on such preconceptions obviously did not permit a detailed examination of the individual deeds in question and their background.

In many trials, of male as well as female National Socialist perpetrators, it was argued that there had been a diminution of individual responsibility, so as to reduce the moral burden placed on the accused, while isolating a few individuals from the mass of the German people and holding them responsible.[72]

Such tendencies operated just as much or even more so when dealing with former guards in criminal proceedings in the Federal Republic. In trials mainly conducted by the Allies in the post-war period a few female guards were prosecuted and thus formally demonised, being singled out as 'beasts' excluded from normal society.[73] By contrast, even in denazification courts in the post-war period[74] and above all in investigations and proceedings in the Federal Republic in subsequent years there was an extraordinary playing down of the guilt of female perpetrators in concentration camps. The founding of the Central Office of Regional Administration of Justice (*Zentrale Stelle der Landesjustizverwaltungen*) in Ludwigsburg in 1958 represented a break in the history of prosecutions in the Federal Republic. For the first time a determination prevailed to pursue the retrospective treatment under criminal law of the National Socialist past in a responsible and systematic way. Yet even after this turning point unrestricted pursuit of National Socialist perpetrators was still not possible. Although various debates in the Bundestag prevented the introduction of a statute of limitations for unsolved murders, many persons profited from this statute in respect of various other deeds such as manslaughter. Added to this, the increasing distance in time from the deeds made the question of proof in individual investigations and proceedings ever more difficult. The East–West conflict played a not inconsiderable role in this,[75] which worked to the advantage of the accused.[76] Delays and postponements in proceedings against female guards continued to be the order of the day.

After the collapse of the German Democratic Republic the investigators, especially those in Ludwigsburg, were able to gain new knowledge about former female guards. Here the files of the Stasi were an important source. Thus it was that the former guard Ingeborg Aßmuß, who lived for years in East Berlin, was traced. Ingeborg Aßmuß was, amongst other things, a guard in the women's concentration camp of Helmbrechts near Hof in Bavaria. In January 1945 there were some 680 prisoners in the camp, predominantly Jewish.[77] In April 1945 the SS forced the prisoners on a so-called death march, since the Allies were close to liberating the camp. Shortly after the end of the war survivors of the concentration camp testified that the SS had shot several of the prisoners during the evacuation. They alleged that Ingeborg Aßmuß had also been heavily involved in these killings. There was also the charge that in February 1945 she and other guards had beaten the woman camp doctor, a Russian, to death. Whilst her colleague Ruth Hildner was executed in 1947 in Prague, and the camp commandant, Alois Dörr, was sentenced to life imprisonment in 1969 in Hof,[78] Ingeborg Aßmuß lived in the GDR and could not be prosecuted. With the knowledge of the Stasi, she had assumed a different name.[79] Czechoslovakia sought extradition, but in vain, and the Federal Republic was unsuccessful in searching for her. It was not until 1994 that she was traced and the facts referred to the appropriate state prosecutor. In 1995, however, the proceedings were halted, since the killing of the Russian doctor was now covered by the statute of limitations. Nor did the local state prosecutor pursue the matter of the shootings on the death march, claiming that there was no reliable evidence from witnesses. A list of witnesses was available, most of them living in Israel and the USA, but it was not researched intensively enough.[80] It was only after criticism by the public that the state prosecutor resolved to re-examine the material which had been known for years, for signs of murder – obviously a matter for careful weighing up! 'Whether it is a case of murder or of manslaughter, is a question where the circumstances have to be assessed', the director of the state prosecutor's office stated. 'The crime of murder is based on the assumption that the deed is motivated by cruelty or base reasons. It's a difficult area.'[81] A few months later renewed investigations were halted following the death of the accused.[82]

Proceedings were started against less than 10 per cent of former female guards. Moreover, the majority of preliminary investigations were laid to rest in the course of the years 'in the absence of proof': with the increasing distance in time from the deed a quite unambiguous tendency to stop the enquiries can be discerned. In some cases long drawn-out investigations were finally 'completed' by the death of the suspect.[83]

The now advanced age and often frail health of accused persons meant an equally unsuccessful outcome even when more intensive efforts were employed to build up a comprehensive picture of Nazi crimes perpetrated by former female guards and to exact justice. The majority of a total of over 3,000 former guards received light sentences or were not convicted at all. Most of them lived unmolested in the Federal Republic of Germany.

Summary

From 1937 female guards belonging to the SS-Retinue guarded female prisoners in concentration camps. The female SS-Retinue was a construct by which female guards did not have to be integrated into the SS, but were nevertheless as much subject to SS jurisdiction as their male colleagues. There were career prospects for them, even if they were not comparable with those open to their male colleagues in the SS, and they could rise to Head Guard or Senior Guard. Female guards were recruited mainly in two ways. Some of the women, having been required to work in the armaments industry, were recruited for service in concentration camps, others volunteered for this work. Johanna Langefeld belonged to this second group. It is apparent from her remarks in her later interrogation and from accounts given by prisoners that it was her aim in the women's concentration camp at Ravensbrück to put into practice a concept of education based on National Socialist ideology. Little is known of her ideas, but she was obviously convinced that a women's concentration camp reorganised in this way could only be achieved through greater women's influence in the leadership of the camps. It would appear that at first these notions of hers were supported by Himmler, but they failed in the end due to the massive opposition of SS leaders amongst the commandants and their staff. However, it is recurrently stated in the reports of prisoners that Langefeld was thought by the imprisoned women to be a powerful person where her powers of decision were concerned. Her authority as Senior Guard was so extensive that she decisively influenced the everyday camp life of the female prisoners.

In contrast to Langefeld, who was able to elude a prosecution in Poland, Lotte M. faced trial in court in the Federal Republic in the 1950s and Ingeborg Aßmuß was the subject of investigations in the 1990s. Lotte M. escaped with a light custodial sentence, Ingeborg Aßmuß died before she could be charged. She had previously been able to live unpunished for years in the former GDR, and even after she was found the case was not examined seriously enough. Only a small number of former guards have had to answer to a court for their deeds. Fundamentally, the need prevailed to ignore or suppress the personal responsibility of individuals involved in Nazi crimes. It was Hitler and the male leaders surrounding him who had done the deeds, so it was implied, whilst the Germans and especially the women concerned were supposed to be amongst 'the victims and those led astray'.[84] However, the biographies of female guards again and again reveal that they had extensive scope for action despite the male-oriented hierarchy in concentration camps.

Notes

* Translated by Richard Littlejohns

1. See for example Isabell Sprenger, *Groß-Rosen: Ein Konzentrationslager in Schlesien* (Cologne, 1996); Hans Hesse, *Das Frauen-KZ Moringen: 1933–1938* (Göttingen, 2000); Alexandra-Eileen Wenck, *Zwischen Menschenhandel und 'Endlösung': Das Konzentrationslager Bergen-Belsen* (Paderborn, 2000); Bernhard Strebel, *Das KZ Ravensbrück: Geschichte eines Lagerkomplexes* (Paderborn, 2003).
2. See for example Irmtraud Heike, 'Johanna Langefeld: Die Biographie einer KZ-Oberaufseherin', *WerkstattGeschichte*, 12 (1995), 7–21; Gudrun Schwarz, 'Frauen in Konzentrationslagern: Täterinnen und Zuschauerinnen', in Ulrich Herbert et al. (eds), *Die nationalsozialistischen Konzentrationslager*, Vol. 2 (Frankfurt/Main, 2002), 800–22; Irmtraud Heike, 'Ehemalige KZ-Aufseherinnen in westdeutschen Strafverfahren', *Beiträge zur Geschichte der nationalsozialistischen Verfolgung in Norddeutschland*, 9 (2005), 89–102; Stefanie Oppel, *Die Rolle der Arbeitsämter bei der Rekrutierung von SS-Aufseherinnen* (Freiburg, 2006); Simone Erpel et al. (eds), *Im Gefolge der SS: Aufseherinnen im Konzentrationslager Ravensbrück* (Berlin, 2007).
3. See for example Daniel P. Brown, *The Beautiful Beast: the Life and Crimes of SS-Aufseherin Irma Grese* (Ventura, 1996).
4. The only names stated in full here are those which have already been published elsewhere.
5. See Alexandra-Eileen Wenck, 'Verbrechen als "Pflichterfüllung"?: Die Strafverfolgung nationalsozialistischer Gewaltverbrechen am Beispiel des Konzentrationslagers Bergen-Belsen', *Beiträge zur Geschichte der nationalsozialistischen Verfolgung in Norddeutschland*, 3 (1997), 38–56.
6. Zentrale Stelle der Landesjustizverwaltungen zur Aufklärung nationalsozialistischer Verbrechen in Ludwigsburg, *Frauenkonzentrationslager Ravensbrück: Eine Gesamtdarstellung* (Ludwigsburg, 1972, unpublished), 239–43.
7. This figure relates to Suhren's period as camp commandant in Ravensbrück. Cf. Suhren's testimony of 19 March 1946, Nürnberger Dokumente, Dok. 746b-D.
8. Bundesarchiv (BArch) NS 3/439.
9. Cf. Michael H. Kater, *'Das Ahnenerbe' der SS 1935–1945: Ein Beitrag zur Kulturpolitik des Dritten Reiches* (Stuttgart, 1974), 305; see also Kommandanturbefehl No. 3, 24 July 1942, BArch NS 4/RA.
10. Nationale Mahn- und Gedenkstätte Ravensbrück (AMGR) Ra Best. Lagergemeinschaft Band 39/893 und 40/899a.
11. Copy of a letter from Seitz, the head of administration, to the administrative offices of the relevant concentration camps, BArch NS 4/Bu 99.
12. BArch R 187/437.

13. 'Personal-Fragebogen' (personnel files) Hildegard K., 21 August 1944, BArch NS 4/Fl 10.
14. Decree of the Reich Trustee of Labour (Reichstreuhänders) for the economic district of Lower Saxony, 24 August 1942, Niedersächsisches Hauptstaatsarchiv Hannover (NdsHStAH) Hann 275/1065; see also [Ilse] Buresch-Riebe, 'Was verdient die Hausgehilfin?', *NS Frauen-Warte*, 10 (1941), 150.
15. BArch R 187/437. The style of writing in quotations has been preserved in accordance with the original.
16. See testimony of Jane B., BArch B 162/9807, Blatt 154–60 and testimony of Margarete Mewes, BArch B 162/9808, Blatt 510–23.
17. BArch R 187/437.
18. Cf. testimony of Margarete Mewes, BArch B 162/9808, Blatt 510–23.
19. Cf. testimony of Jane B., BArch B 162/9807, Blatt 154–60.
20. Application of Johanna Langefeld for the membership in the NSDAP, 30 September 1937; BArch (former Berlin Document Center, BDC) NSDAP-Zentralkartei (central file), Langefeld, Johanna, 05.03.1900.
21. Margarete Buber-Neumann, *Als Gefangene bei Stalin und Hitler: Eine Welt im Dunkeln* (Frankfurt/Main,1993).
22. Margarete Buber-Neumann, *Die erloschene Flamme: Schicksale meiner Zeit* (Munich, 1976), 30–43.
23. Ibid., 32.
24. Arrest Report Johanna Langefeld, NAW RG 338-000-50-11, Ravensbrück Vol. II, folder 3.
25. Cf. Johannes Tuchel, *Konzentrationslager: Organisationsgeschichte und Funktion der 'Inspektion der Konzentrationslager' 1934–1938* (Boppard, 1991), 380.
26. Buber-Neumann, *Die erloschene Flamme*, 31.
27. Testimony Dorothea Binz, Public Record Office, Kew (PRO) WO 235/310, 10.
28. Buber-Neumann, *Die erloschene Flamme*, 32–3.
29. Testimony Dorothea Binz, PRO WO 235/310, 10.
30. Testimony Johanna Langefeld, NAW RG 338-000-50-11, Ravensbrück Vol. II, folder 3.
31. Ibid.
32. German National Work Service.
33. Testimony Johanna Langefeld, NAW RG 338-000-50-11, Ravensbrück Vol. II, folder 3.
34. The Protective Custody Camp Leader was considered the deputy of the commandant, and also acted as the direct superior of the SS guards.
35. 'Dienstvorschrift für das F.K.L. Ravensbrück (Lagerordnung)' (camp regulations), AMGR Ra Nr. II/3-1-15.
36. Wolfgang Sofsky, *Die Ordnung des Terrors: Das Konzentrationslager* (Frankfurt/Main, 1993), 115–37.
37. Danuta Czech, *Kalendarium der Ereignisse im Konzentrationslager Auschwitz-Birkenau 1939–1945* (Reinbek, 1989), 189.
38. See Martin Broszat (ed.), *Kommandant in Auschwitz: Autobiographische Aufzeichnungen des Rudolf Höss* (Munich, 1979), 93.
39. See Bernd Naumann, *Auschwitz: Bericht über die Strafsache gegen Mulka und andere vor dem Schwurgericht Frankfurt* (Frankfurt/Main, 1965).
40. Testimony Johanna Langefeld, NAW RG 338-000-50-11, Ravensbrück Vol. II, folder 3.

41. See Broszat, *Kommandant*, 7–8.
42. Women's concentration camp.
43. Broszat, *Kommandant*, 118–19.
44. BArch (former NS-archive MfS), ZM 1491 file 1.
45. Testimony Johanna Langefeld, NAW RG 338-000-50-11, Ravensbrück Vol. II, folder 3.
46. Hans Buchheim, 'Befehl und Gehorsam', in Hans Buchheim et al. (eds), *Anatomie des SS-Staates*, Vol. 1 (München, 1989), 257; cf. Sofsky, *Ordnung des Terrors*, 122–5.
47. Testimony Johanna Langefeld, NAW RG 338-000-50-11, Ravensbrück Vol. II, folder 3.
48. Cf. Bernd Wegner, *Hitlers Politische Soldaten: Die Waffen-SS 1933–1945* (Paderborn, 1988), 319–33.
49. Buber-Neumann, *Erloschene Flamme*, 30–42.
50. Ibid., 35.
51. Buber-Neumann, *Als Gefangene bei Stalin und Hitler*, 324.
52. Cf. Czech, *Kalendarium*, 251; Broszat, *Kommandant*, 180. Testimony Johanna Langefeld, NAW RG 338-000-50-11, Ravensbrück Vol. II, folder 3.
53. Leokadia Kwiecinska, in Wanda Symonowicz (ed.), *Über menschliches Maß. Opfer der Hölle Ravensbrück sprechen...* (Warschau, 1961), 91–2.
54. Deposition of Johanna Sturm, BArch B 162/Dok.-Slg., Ordn. 451 h (interrogation 30 October 1947 and 15 March 1948 in JAG 334).
55. Deposition of Bertha Teege, BArch B 162/Dok.-Slg., Ordn. 451 h (interrogation 3 September 1947 in JAG 334).
56. The so-called 'self-administration' of the prisoners was a hierarchy devised by the SS and intended to relieve the SS personnel and organise everyday life in the camps.
57. Cf. AMGR Ra Best. Lagergemeinschaft Band 39/893 und 40/899a. Christiaan F. Rüter et al. (eds), *Die westdeutschen Strafverfahren wegen nationalsozialistischer Tötungsverbrechen 1945–1997: Eine systematische Verfahrensbeschreibung* (Amsterdam, 1998), 73; Adelheid L. Rüter-Ehlermann et al., *Justiz und NS-Verbrechen: Sammlung deutscher Strafurteile wegen nationalsozialistischer Tötungsverbrechen 1945–1966*, Vol. 9 (Amsterdam, 1972), 746.
58. Reinhard Busch, 'Zur Geschichte der KZ-Außenlager an der Porta Westfalica', in Pierre Bleton, *'Das Leben ist schön!' Überlebensstrategien eines Häftlings im KZ Porta* (Bielefeld, 1987), 9–11.
59. Katharina Hertz-Eichenrode (ed.), *Ein KZ wird geräumt. Häftlinge zwischen Vernichtung und Befreiung: Die Auflösung des KZ Neuengamme und seiner Außenlager durch die SS im Frühjahr 1945*, Vol. 1 (Bremen, 2000), 82.
60. Rüter-Ehlermann, *Justiz und NS-Verbrechen*, 757.
61. Busch, *Zur Geschichte der KZ-Außenlager an der Porta Westfalica*, 11.
62. Rüter-Ehlermann, *Justiz und NS-Verbrechen*, 756–7.
63. Ibid., 759.
64. According to the court the death of the female prisoner could not be established with absolute certainty. Cf. Rüter-Ehlermann, *Justiz und NS-Verbrechen*, 761.
65. Ibid., 763–8.
66. Bundesarchiv (branch Ludwigsburg), overview of the proceedings and sentences against Lotte M.

67. Rüter-Ehlermann, *Justiz und NS–Verbrechen*, 770.
68. Ibid., 753–4.
69. Cf. Insa Eschebach, 'NS-Prozesse in der sowjetischen Besatzungszone und der DDR: Einige Überlegungen zu den Strafverfahrensakten ehemaliger SS-Aufseherinnen des Frauenkonzentrationslagers Ravensbrück', *Beiträge zur Geschichte der nationalsozialistischen Verfolgung in Norddeutschland*, 3 (1997), 67.
70. Anette Kretzer, '"His or Her Special Job": Die Repräsentation von NS-Verbrecherinnen im ersten Hamburger Ravensbrück-Prozess und im westdeutschen Täterschafts-Diskurs', *Beiträge zur Geschichte der nationalsozialistischen Verfolgung in Norddeutschland*, 7 (2002), 143.
71. Irmtraud Heike, '"...da es sich ja lediglich um die Bewachung der Häftlinge handelt...": Lagerverwaltung und Lagerpersonal', in Claus Füllberg-Stolberg et al. (eds), *Frauen in Konzentrationslagern: Bergen-Belsen, Ravensbrück* (Bremen, 1994), 221–39.
72. Sigrid Weigel, *Bilder des kulturellen Gedächtnisses: Beiträge zur Gegenwartsliteratur* (Dülmen-Hiddingsel, 1994), 213–14.
73. Anette Kretzer, '"His or Her Special Job"', 134–50.
74. Kathrin Meyer, '"Die Frau ist der Frieden der Welt": Von Nutzen und Lasten eines Weiblichkeitsstereotyps in Spruchkammerentscheidungen gegen Frauen', in Ulrike Weckel et al. (eds), *'Bestien' und 'Befehlsempfänger': Frauen und Männer in NS-Prozessen nach 1945* (Göttingen, 2003), 117–38.
75. Anette Weinke, *Die Verfolgung von NS-Tätern im geteilten Deutschland: Vergangenheitsbewältigung 1949–1969 oder: Eine deutsch-deutsche Beziehungsgeschichte im Kalten Krieg* (Paderborn, 2002), 333–56.
76. Gerhard Werle, 'Der Holocaust als Gegenstand der bundesdeutschen Strafjustiz', in Bernhard Moltmann et al. (eds), *Erinnerung: Zur Gegenwart des Holocaust in Deutschland-West und Deutschland-Ost* (Frankfurt/Main, 1993), 103, 105–6.
77. Cf. Klaus Rauh, 'Helmbrechts: Außenlager des KZ Flossenbürg 1944–1945', *Miscellanea curiensia: Beiträge zur Geschichte und Kultur Nordoberfrankens und angrenzender Regionen*, 4 (2003), 117–49; Alexander Schmidt, 'Helmbrechts', in Wolfgang Benz et al. (eds), *Der Ort des Terrors. Geschichte der nationalsozialistischen Konzentrationslager*, Vol. 4 (Munich, 2006), 140–3.
78. SS Unterscharführer Alois Dörr was released after only a few months; cf. Michael Kasperowitsch, 'Doch Mord-Anklage?', in *Nürnberger Nachrichten*, 20/21 January 1996.
79. Peter Engelbrecht, 'Stasi versteckte Helmbrechtser KZ-Aufseherin', in *Bayerische Rundschau*, 25/26 November 1995.
80. Walter Wüllenweber, 'Nazi-Jagd im Aktenkeller', *Stern*, 48, 1995.
81. Michael Kasperowitsch, 'Tief erschüttert', in *Nürnberger Nachrichten*, 11 January 1996.
82. BArch B 162/43251-43255.
83. Cf. a synopsis of proceedings against former female KZ guards created by the author at the Bundesarchiv (branch Ludwigsburg).
84. Rudolf Schlaffer, *GeRechte Sühne? Das Konzentrationslager Flossenbürg: Möglichkeiten und Grenzen der nationalen und internationalen Strafverfolgung von NS-Verbrechen* (Hamburg, 2001), 162.

Part III
Psychological and Sociological Approaches

Part III

6
The Ordinariness of Extraordinary Evil: the Making of Perpetrators of Genocide and Mass Killing

James E. Waller

According to Jewish–Christian tradition, the first time that death appeared in the world, it was murder. Cain slew Abel. 'Two men,' says Elie Wiesel, 'and one of them became a killer.'[1] Throughout human history, social conflict is ubiquitous. Wars erupt naturally everywhere humans are present. As Winston Churchill said, 'The story of the human race is war. Except for brief and precarious interludes there has never been peace in the world; and long before history began murderous strife was universal and unending.'[2] Since the Napoleonic Wars, we have fought an average of six international wars and six civil wars per *decade*. An average of three high-fatality struggles have been in action somewhere in the world at any moment since 1900. The four decades after the end of the Second World War saw 150 wars, involving more than 60 member states of the United Nations, and only 26 days of world peace – and that does not even include the innumerable internal wars and police actions. Buried in the midst of all of our progress in the twentieth century were well over one hundred million persons who met a violent death at the hands of their fellow human beings in wars and conflicts. That is over five times the number from the nineteenth century and more than ten times the number from the eighteenth century.[3]

There is no sign that we are on an ascendant trajectory out of the shadow of our work of de-creation. Today, while the number of armed conflicts around the world has purportedly decreased, more than a quarter of the world's 193 nations still remain embroiled in conflict – a statistic that actually *under*estimates global violence since it only includes state-to-state conflicts or internal state conflicts while omitting asymmetrical conflicts, such as terrorist activity. The bipolar Cold War system has disintegrated into a system of 'Warm Wars', with randomised conflicts popping up in all corners of an interdependent world. Retired Army Major Andy Messing Jr., executive director of the conservative-oriented National Defense Council Foundation, warns that the growing proliferation of weapons of mass destruction and an increasing world population only add to the danger. In his words, 'It's going to be a very tough next 20 years.'[4] Even more liberal-leaning voices recognise that present-day population growth, unequal distribution of land and energy resources, and per capita consumption cannot be sustained without leading to even more catastrophic human conflict.

The greatest catastrophes occur when the distinctions between war and crime fade; when there is dissolution of the boundary between military and criminal conduct, between civility and barbarity; when political, social or religious groups embrace mass killing and genocide as warfare. I am not speaking here of isolated executions, but of wholesale slaughters. As collectives, we engage in acts of extraordinary evil, with apparent moral calm and intensity of supposed purpose, which could only be described as insane were they committed by an individual.

Aptly dubbed the 'Age of Genocide,' the past century saw a massive scale of systematic and intentional mass murder coupled with an unprecedented efficiency of the mechanisms and techniques of mass destruction. On the historical heels of the physical and cultural genocide of American Indians during the nineteenth century, the twentieth century writhed from the near-complete annihilation of the Hereros by the Germans in south-west Africa in 1904; to the brutal assault of the Armenian population by the Turks between 1915 and 1923; to the implementation of a Soviet man-made famine against the Ukrainian kulaks in 1932–3 that left several million peasants starving to death; to the extermination of two-thirds of Europe's Jews during the Holocaust of 1939–45; to the massacre of approximately half a million people in Indonesia during 1965–6; to mass killings and genocide in Bangladesh (1971), Burundi (1972), Cambodia (1975–9), East Timor (1975–9) and Rwanda (1994); and, finally, to the conflict that continues to plague the former Yugoslavia. All told, it is estimated that at least 60 million men, women and children were victims of genocide and mass killing in the last century alone.[5]

The dawn of the twenty-first century brought little light to the darkness. Since 1999, Russian armed forces have escalated their use of extortion, torture, violence and murder against Chechen civilians;

a wave of massacres in the early months of 2002 targeted Muslims in the state of Gujarat in India; at the close of 2003, Ethiopian government troops and local militia slaughtered more than 400 people of the Anuak tribe in the Gambella region of western Ethiopia. In Darfur, the western region of Sudan, at least 300,000 people have died as a result of a Sudanese government-sponsored campaign of violence and forced starvation that began in early 2003. Clearly, despite the end of the colonial era and the dismantling of the Cold War, the persistence of inhumanity in human affairs is incontrovertible.

There is one unassailable fact behind this ignoble litany of human conflict and suffering. Political, social or religious groups wanting to commit mass murder do. Though there may be other obstacles, they are never hindered by a lack of willing executioners. That is the one constant upon which they can count. They can always recruit individual human beings who will kill other human beings in large numbers and over an extended period of time. In short, people are the weapons by which genocide occurs. How are people enlisted to perpetrate such extraordinary evil?

Ironically, we know more about the broad mechanics of mass murder than we do about the mindset of people who carried it out. So, unlike much of the research in perpetrator behaviour, I am not interested in the higher echelons of leadership who structured the ideology, policy and initiatives behind a particular genocide or mass killing. Nor am I interested in the middle-echelon perpetrators, the faceless bureaucrats who made implementation of those initiatives possible. Rather, I am interested in the rank-and-file killers, the soldiers, police, militia (paramilitary) and civilians at the bottom of the hierarchy who personally carried out the millions of executions. These people were so ordinary that, with few exceptions, they were readily absorbed into civil society after the killings and peacefully lived out their unremarkable lives – attesting to the unsettling reality that genocide overwhelms justice. One point stands clear: to understand the fundamental reality of mass murder we need to shift our focus from impersonal institutions and abstract structures to the actors, the men and women who actually carried out the atrocities.

The goal of this chapter is to offer a psychological explanation of how ordinary people commit genocide and mass killing. It is an attempt to go beyond the minutiae of thick description ('who', 'what', 'when' and 'where') and look at the bigger questions of explanation and understanding: to know a little less and understand a little more.

The ordinary origins of extraordinary human evil

The origins of extraordinary evil cannot be isolated in the extraordinary nature of the collective; the influence of an extraordinary ideology; psychopathology; or a common, homogeneous, extraordinary personality type.[6] A myopic focus on the extraordinary origins of extraordinary evil tells us more about our own personal dreams of how we wish the world to work than it does about the reality of perpetrator behaviour. In that role, such explanations satisfy an important emotional demand of distancing *us* from *them*.

The truth seems to be, though, that the most outstanding common characteristic of perpetrators is their normality, not their abnormality; they are extraordinary only in what they have done, not in who they are. Perpetrators of genocide and mass killing cannot be identified, a priori, as having the personalities of killers. Most are not mentally impaired. Nor are they identified as sadists at home or in their social environment. Nor are they victims of an abusive background. They defy easy demographic categorisation. Among them, we find educated and well-to-do people, as well as simple and impoverished people. We find church-affiliated people as well as agnostics and atheists. We find people who are loving parents as well as people who have difficulty initiating and sustaining satisfying personal relationships. We find young people and old people. We find people who are not actively involved in the political, religious or social groups responsible for institutionalising the process of destruction as well as those who are. We find ordinary people who went to school, fought with siblings, celebrated birthdays, listened to music, and played with friends. In short, the majority of perpetrators of genocide and mass killing are not distinguished by background, personality or previous political affiliation or behaviour as being men or women unusually likely or fit to be genocidal executioners.

We are then left with the most discomforting of all realities – ordinary, 'normal' people committing acts of extraordinary evil. This reality is difficult to admit, to understand, to absorb. We would rather know Extraordinary Evil as an extra-human capitalisation. This reality is unsettling because it counters our general mental tendency to relate extraordinary acts to correspondingly extraordinary people. But we cannot evade this discomforting reality. We are forced to confront the ordinariness of most perpetrators of mass killing and genocide. Recognising their ordinariness does not diminish the horror of their actions. It increases it. As we look at perpetrators of genocide and mass killing, we need no longer ask who these people are. We know who they are. They are you and I.

There is now a more urgent question to ask. *How* are ordinary people, like you and me, made into perpetrators of genocide and mass killing? The importance of this question is only matched by the complexity of its answer. The precise 'how' of the transformation process remains veiled from us, as it may have remained veiled from the men and women who experienced it. The multiplicity of variables that lead an ordinary person to commit terrorism is difficult to pin down. It is impossible to establish general 'laws' that apply to all individuals in all contexts and at all times.

Regardless, we are now in a position to advance some hypotheses that may offer a solution more right than wrong. The remainder of this chapter outlines a general explanatory model (see Figure 6.1) of the making of perpetrators.[7] The model – drawing on existing literature; eyewitness accounts by killers, bystanders and victims from a wide range of genocides and mass killings; and classic and contemporary research in social and evolutionary psychology – is not an invocation of a single broadbrush psychological state or *event* to explain the making of perpetrators. Rather, focusing less on the outcome, it is a detailed analysis of a *process* through which the perpetrators themselves – either in committing atrocities or in order to commit atrocities – are changed.

The model recognises that human behaviour is multiply influenced and that any answer to the question 'Why did that person act as he

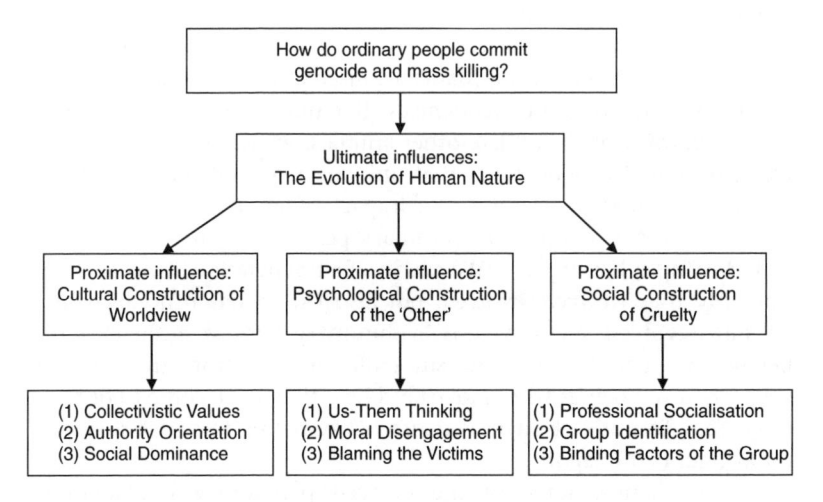

Figure 6.1 A model of how ordinary people commit genocide and mass killing

or she did?' can be examined at two levels of analysis – the proximate and the ultimate. As Pinker describes, 'A *proximate* cause of behavior is the mechanism that pushes behavior buttons in real time, such as the hunger and lust that impel people to eat and have sex. An *ultimate* cause is the adaptive rationale that led the proximate cause to evolve, such as the need for nutrition and reproduction that gave us the drives of hunger and lust.'[8] In other words, proximate influences refer to those immediate influences closest to the present moment: 'how' a behaviour occurs in the here and now. Ultimate influences, conversely, refer to those deeper influences from our evolutionary past: 'why' a behaviour evolved by natural selection. It is these ultimate influences that reveal the nature of human nature and, in so doing, help us understand the 'why' behind 'how' ordinary people become perpetrators of evil.

The concept of a human nature has returned to the front of academic conversation in the social sciences. Leading this charge is the field of *evolutionary psychology* (EP) – a marriage of the cognitive revolution in psychology of the 1950s and 1960s and the revolution in evolutionary biology of the 1960s and 1970s. Specifically, EP is a multidisciplinary approach within the Darwinian paradigm that seeks to apply theories of evolutionary biology in order to understand human psychology. The specific goal is to understand the design of the human mind in terms of Darwinian evolution. This is really engineering in reverse. In forward-engineering, we design a machine to do something. In reverse-engineering, we figure out what a machine – in this case, the human mind – was designed to do.

This approach says that human nature consists of a large number of evolved psychological mechanisms, or adaptations, that give rise to our natural instincts and tendencies. It reminds us that we are part of the natural world and, like other animals, we have our own particular psychological tendencies that animate many of our behaviours. We are obligated to examine the impact of *what* we are upon *who* we are in understanding how ordinary people commit extraordinary evil. As Singer has argued, 'We are the first generation to understand not only that we have evolved, but also the mechanisms by which we have evolved and how this evolutionary heritage influences our behaviour... For the first time since life emerged from the primeval soup, there are beings who understand how they have come to be what they are.'[9] To not seek such evidence is like failing to search a suspect for a concealed weapon.

At first glance, some of the evolved psychological adaptations appear to support our capacity for cooperative, caring, non-violent relations – love, friendship, cooperativeness, preferential and reciprocal altruism, nurturance, friendship, compassion, communication, a sense of fairness and, even, self-sacrifice – in short, the things that hold society together. In many ways, we owe our success as a species to these pro-social adaptations. Evolutionary psychology warns us, however, that self-congratulation about our human nature is premature. Beneath our social surface is a seamy underside of human nature that is much less flattering. For instance, our pro-social adaptations are qualified by the reality that we tend to reserve major doses of 'goodness' either for close kin or for non-kin who show signs of someday returning the favour. Underlying our acts of 'charity' for other organisms are strains of selfish and aggressive traits that are part of our inherently self-centred human nature; sometimes altruism and cooperation turn out to be the most effective ways to compete. Moreover, our Swiss Army knife of adaptations also includes some darker ultimate motives – such as intergroup competition for dominance, boundary definition, and fear of social exclusion – that often tear society apart.

In short, we have been endowed by evolution with a host of needs and desires, such that it is often difficult for one person to pursue his or her needs and desires without coming into conflict with other people. However deeply buried, the capacities for evil are within all of us. We have a hereditary dark side that is universal across humankind. Acts of evil are not beyond, beneath or outside ordinary humanness. Natural selection has left deep traces of design in our minds and at least some of those designs leave us evolutionarily primed with the capacity for evil – including the perpetration of terrorism.

While evolutionary psychology describes the ultimate evolutionary capacities common to all of us, this understanding must be couched in the context of the more proximate and immediate cultural, psychological and social constructions that converge interactively to activate these capacities. Building on these ultimate influences, the model emphasises three proximate, here and now constructions that impact individual behaviour in situations of collective violence. The *cultural construction of worldview* examines the influence of cultural models that are widely shared by the members of a perpetrator group. The *psychological construction of the 'other'* analyses how victims of genocide and mass killing simply become the 'objects' of perpetrators' actions. Finally, the *social construction of cruelty* explores the mechanisms used in creating an immediate social context in which perpetrators initiate, sustain and cope with their cruelty.

The cultural construction of worldview

All cultures leave their fingerprints on the members within them – most often through the transmission of a worldview. A worldview includes the presuppositions, intentions, meanings, rules, norms, values, principles, practices and activities through which people live their lives. Cognitive anthropology understands worldview in the rich theoretical context of cultural models. As Hinton describes, 'cultural models are largely tacit knowledge structures that are both widely shared by and mediate the understanding of the members of a social group'.[10] In other words, cultural models are the constituent elements of a worldview which give us the background, or lens, through which we interpret our social world and make judgements about appropriate responses. There are three specific cultural models – related to *collectivistic values*, *authority orientation* and *social dominance* – that are particularly relevant to understanding the making of perpetrators.

Collectivistic values of obedience, conformity, tradition, safety and order form a worldview in which group membership shapes and completes individuals. Group-based identity – whether centred on race, ethnicity, tribe, kin, religion or nationality – becomes a central and defining characteristic of one's personal identity and overshadows the self. Group goals become indistinguishable from individual goals. Conflict in a collectivistic culture is intergroup since group membership (often based on mythic blood ties or shared history) is enduring, stable and permanent and has an existence beyond the individual. When group membership is seen as impermeable and fixed, the potential to view other groups as perpetual threats is heightened.

Historically, genocidal regimes have emphasised collectivistic values that make group membership central to personal identity. Such regimes have been particularly adept at using such collectivistic values to highlight boundaries between in-groups and out-groups by making extreme categorical judgements based on the polar opposites of 'good us' versus 'bad them'. Our cause is sacred; theirs is evil. We are righteous; they are wicked. We are innocent; they are guilty. We are the victims; they are the victimisers. It is rarely *our* enemy or *an* enemy, but *the* enemy – a usage of the definite article that hints of something fixed and immutable, abstract and evil.

A cultural model of collectivistic values is often cultivated in concert with a highly salient cultural model of *authority orientation*, a way of ordering the social world and relating to people according to their position and power in hierarchies. This is a cultural model exemplified by a preference for hierarchical, vertical relationships with a clear delineation of spheres of power. Such a cultural model cultivates individuals who enjoy obeying authority and exercising power over those below them; who prefer order and predictability. While a certain degree of authority orientation is required in all social systems, a culture that inculcates an excessively strong authority orientation nurtures individuals who are less likely to oppose leaders who scapegoat, or advocate violence against, a particular target group.

Hinton has analysed the hierarchical nature of Cambodian society in relation to authority orientation. He argues that the vertical structuring of Cambodian society – where people are differentiated in terms of power, status and patronage – lays the groundwork for a cultural model of obedience to, and respect of, authority. Enculturation for this cultural model of obedience and respect begins at an early age and is reinforced by a wide range of social, political, linguistic, behavioural and religious conventions. As Hinton points out, even though the Khmer Rouge destroyed much of this traditional hierarchical system in Cambodian society, status differences continued to be structured vertically – and with more fixity – in the Communist regime. In this way, the Khmer Rouge was able to tap into a pre-existing – and, for many Cambodians, highly salient – cultural model of hierarchically based authority orientation to legitimate their power, goals, social structures of inequality and, even, mass murder.[11]

Finally, given the role of hierarchical systems in cultural models of authority orientation, it is necessary to examine the ultimate origins of hierarchies and how such hierarchies are perpetuated and legitimated. Aside from the sexual drive, evolutionary psychology suggests that one of the most universal and powerful motivating forces in animals is the desire for *social dominance*. This desire, leading to differences in rank and status, can be defined as the set of sustained aggressive–submissive relations among individual animals. In a group, these relations form a hierarchical structure, commonly called a social dominance hierarchy. In a social dominance hierarchy, some individuals within a group reliably gain greater access than other individuals to key resources – particularly resources that contribute to survival and reproductive success.

In addition to recognising the ultimate adaptive value of social dominance hierarchies, it is important to understand the real-time behavioural consequences of a psychological adaptation for social dominance and the ways in which cultural models of social dominance are often perpetuated and legitimated by ideologies, myths and symbols. Occasionally, our desire for social dominance has pro-social consequences as we realise that helping others creates friendships and coalitions that are useful in our struggle for power. At other times, however, our evolved desire for social dominance means that we have a predisposition to respond to certain kinds of situations aggressively (sometimes even violently) to get our way. Violence works as a means of getting some contested resource by increasing the cost of that resource to another individual. Moreover, once we get past initial inhibitions against aggressive and violence behaviour, such behaviour rapidly escalates and increases over time and seems, in part, to become self-reinforcing. In short, aggression and violence often function to increase our status and power within a social dominance hierarchy.

The psychological construction of the 'other'

Implied in these cultural models, and certainly inherent in a genocidal worldview, is the obliteration of a common ground between perpetrators and victims. How do victims simply become objects of the perpetrators' actions? How do perpetrators define the target of their atrocities in such a way as to 'excommunicate' them from a common moral community? There are three mechanisms central to understanding the psychological construction of the 'other' – *us–them thinking*, *moral disengagement* and *blaming the victims*.

Human minds are compelled to define the limits of the tribe. Kinship, however defined, remains an important organising principle for most societies in the world. Knowing who is kin, knowing who is in our social group, has a deep importance to species like ours. We construct this knowledge by categorising others as 'us' or 'them'. We have an evolved, universal capacity for us–them thinking in which we see our group as superior to all others and may even be reluctant to recognise members of other groups as deserving of equal respect.

Us–them thinking does not lead us to hate all outgroups. Social exclusion, let alone genocide and mass killing, is not an inevitable consequence of us–them thinking. We are reminded, however, that, once identified with a group, we find it easy to exaggerate differences between our group and others, enhancing in-group cooperation and effectiveness, and – frequently – intensifying antagonism with other groups. This process helps us understand how the suggestive message of us against them can be ratcheted up to the categorically compelling kill or be killed.

The *moral disengagement* that often results from us–them thinking is not simply a matter of moral indifference or invisibility. Rather, it is an active, but gradual, process of detachment by which some individuals or groups are placed outside the boundary in which moral values, rules and considerations of fairness apply. How do perpetrators regulate their thinking so as to disengage, or not feel, their moral scruples about harming others?

There is a variety of disengagement practices used by perpetrators to make their reprehensible conduct acceptable and to distance them from the moral implications of their actions. For instance, there is a moral justification in which mass murder is made personally and socially acceptable by portraying it as serving socially worthy or moral purposes. Perpetrators may believe this rationalisation to such an extent that their evil is not only morally justifiable (right to do), but becomes an outright moral imperative (wrong not to do it). Perpetrators can then justify their evil as essential to their own self-defence – to protect the cherished values of their community, fight ruthless oppressors, preserve peace and stability, save humanity from subjugation, or honour their national commitments.

Moral disengagement is also facilitated by the dehumanisation of the victims – categorising a group as inhuman either by using categories of subhuman creatures (that is, animals) or by using categories of negatively evaluated superhuman creatures (such as demons and monsters). Dehumanisation is most likely when the target group can be readily identified as a separate category of people belonging to a distinct racial, ethnic, religious or political group that the perpetrators regard as inferior or threatening. These isolated subgroups are stigmatised as alien and memories of their past misdeeds, real or imaginary, are activated by the dominant group.

The dehumanisation of victims helps perpetrators to justify their hurtful behaviour. A common form of dehumanisation is the use of language to redefine the victims so they will be seen as warranting the aggression. The surreal gentility of the euphemistic labelling of evil actions central to the moral disengagement of the perpetrators is complemented by a barbarity of language that dehumanises the victims. Perpetrators so consistently dehumanise their victims that the words themselves become substitutes for perceiving human beings. Before the Japanese performed medical experiments on human prisoners in the Second World War, they named them *maruta* – logs of wood. The Greek torturers studied by Gibson and Haritos-Fatouros referred to their victims as 'worms'.[12] The Hutu extremists called the Tutsi *inyenzi*, meaning cockroaches or insects. Haing S. Ngor, the late Cambodian doctor and actor who found fame for his role in *The Killing Fields*, notes of the plight of those persecuted by the Khmer Rouge: 'We weren't quite people. We were lower forms of life, because we were enemies. Killing us was like swatting flies, a way to get rid of undesirables.'[13] There is even a quantitative process of dehumanisation in which victims become mere statistics – bodies to be counted and numbers to be entered into reports. Reduced to data, dehumanised victims lose their moral standing and become objects requiring disposal.

Such dehumanisation often leads to an escalation of the brutality of the killing. Dehumanising victims removes normal moral constraints against aggression. The body of a dehumanised victim possesses no meaning. It is waste, and its removal is a matter of sanitation. There is no moral or empathic context through which the perpetrator can relate to the victim.

Perpetrators further facilitate moral disengagement by using euphemistic language to make their atrocities respectable and, in part, to reduce their personal responsibility for them. By masking their evil in innocuous or sanitising jargon, their actions lose much of their moral repugnancy. Mass murder becomes 'ethnic cleansing', 'bush clearing' or 'liquidation'. The camouflage vocabulary used by the Nazis to cover their extraordinary evil was especially striking – 'final solution', 'special treatment', 'evacuation', 'spontaneous actions', 'resettlement' and 'special installations', among many others.

Finally, the psychological construction of the 'other' feeds on itself and is driven by our brain's remarkable capacity to seek, and find, explanation in the events surrounding us, our actions, and the behaviours of people with whom we interact. We recognise that victims can be grouped in two broad categories – those who deserve their suffering and those who do not deserve their suffering. We know that bad things do happen to good people. To a large degree, we recognise the reality that it is not a just world.

But we do not so easily relinquish our hopeful illusion of a world that is fair and just. We hold on to that notion, however misguided, to give us the courage to go out into the world and to send our children out into the world. Our need to believe in a just world overwhelms our recognition that bad things can happen to good people. As a result, we often assume that victims deserve, and can be blamed for, their fates. Indeed, we show a hardy cognitive tendency to search for ways to blame individuals for their own victimisation. On the whole, the general tendency of *blaming the victims* for their own suffering is a central truth about human experience. For perpetrators, this tendency is invaluable in our striking propensity to devalue victims and their suffering. We will rearrange our perception of people and events so that it seems everyone is getting what they deserve. Victims must be suffering because they have done 'something', must somehow be inferior or dangerous or evil, or because a higher cause is being served. The belief that the world is a just place leads us to accept the suffering of others more easily, even of people we ourselves have harmed.

The social construction of cruelty

In addition to the cultural construction of worldview and the psychological construction of the 'other', a thorough understanding of how perpetrators are made requires an analysis of the real-time power of situational influences on individual behaviour. A social construction of cruelty makes each perpetrator believe that all people are capable of doing what they do. It is an inverted moral universe, shaped by a process of brutalisation, in which right has become wrong; healing has become killing; life has become death. A social construction of cruelty envelops perpetrators in a social context that encourages and rewards evil. We must borrow the perspective of the perpetrators and view their actions, not as the work of 'madmen', but as actions with a clear and justified purpose – as defined by a social construction of cruelty. There are three momentum-inducing features of a social construction of cruelty that enable perpetrators to initiate, sustain and cope with their cruelty – *professional socialisation, group identification* and *binding factors of the group*.

Newcomers to a social context of cruelty are typically in the position of someone who does not know his or her way around and knows it. It is natural for them to seek information from others to learn which behaviours are acceptable or not acceptable in the organisation. *Professional socialisation*, usually institutionalised in military or paramilitary organisations, often takes the form of a sequence of seemingly small, innocuous incremental steps – a series of escalating commitments. From 1967 through 1974, the process of escalating commitments was used by the military regime then in power in Greece to train torturers.[14] In a systematic process of escalating commitments, recruits underwent physically brutal initiation rites. At the same time as they were cursed, punched, kicked and flogged, they were told how fortunate they were to be invited into such an elite organisation. They were then subjected to torture themselves (as if it were a normal act), then assigned to guard prisoners, then to participate in arresting squads, then ordered to hit prisoners, then to observe torture and, finally, to practise torture in group beatings and a variety of other brutal methods. Once the training was complete, a carrot-and-stick strategy of special benefits coupled with threats and punishment for disobedience kept the perpetrators committed to their tasks.

Perhaps most relevant to professional socialisation, however, is a merger of role and person through which evil-doing organisations can change the people in them over time. When one performs the behaviour appropriate for a given role, one often acquires the attitudes, beliefs, values and morals consistent with that role and its behaviours. Seen in this light, the egregious brutality of terrorists does not automatically indicate an *inherent*, pre-existing brutality; not everyone playing a brutal role has to have sadistic traits of character. Rather, brutality can be a consequence, not only a cause, of being in a duly certified and legitimised social hierarchy committed to evil. In other words, the nature of the tasks of atrocity may have been sufficient to produce that brutality even if the perpetrators were not initially sadists. It may be a vicious social arrangement, and not the pre-existing viciousness of the participants, that leads to the cruel behaviours exhibited by perpetrators.

The merger of role and person has tremendous capacity for internalising evil and shaping later evil behaviours. Most of us easily slip into the roles society provides us. A person who becomes invested in the logic and practices of an evil-doing organisation becomes owned by it. In a self-perpetuating cycle of evil-doing, our behaviours and attitudes feed on each other as this altered psychological framework produces further changes in behaviour that lead to more profound alterations in our psychological framework.

As we saw in our discussion of collectivistic values, *group identification* – an emotional attachment to a group – is a potent influence on an individual's thoughts, emotions and behaviours. Group identification, whether centred on race, ethnicity, tribe, kin, religion or nationality, can become a central and defining characteristic of one's personal identity and may even overshadow the self. These group identities can even become such an important source of self-definition and esteem that other groups are perceived as threats – thus sowing the seeds for intergroup conflict by evoking suspicion of, hostility towards and competition with an out-group. At the extreme, group identification may be mobilised into collective violence or a genocidal imperative as it is used to forge in-group solidarity and undermine the normal inhibitions against killing out-group strangers. We can identify with a group, and against other groups, to such a degree that group identification comes to dominate our individual thoughts, emotions and behaviours, often against the interests and welfare of other groups.

Group identification carries with it a repression of conscience where 'outside' values are excluded and locally generated values dominate. Such a repression of conscience serves a self-protective function, as well as having a progressively desensitising effect on the perpetrators, and is facilitated in social contexts that promote diffusion of responsibility and de-individuation.

Diffusion of responsibility is accomplished by bureaucratic organisation into cells and columns as well as by a routinisation of bureaucratic sub-routines – a segmentation and fragmentation of the killing tasks – in which responsibility for evil is divided among members of a group. Such division of labour, in addition to making the killing process more efficient and effective, allows perpetrators to reduce their identification with the consequences of their evil. Once activities are routinised into detached sub-functions, perpetrators shift their attention away from the morality of what they are doing to the operational details and efficiency of their specific job. They are then able to see themselves totally as performers of a role – as participants *in*, not originators *of*, evil. It is easier for perpetrators to avoid the implications of their evil since they are focusing on the *details* of their job rather than on its *meaning*.

The segmented activities of bureaucratic organisations also provide a cloak of de-individuation that facilitates the commission of evil. De-individuation refers to a state of relative anonymity in which a person cannot be identified as a particular individual but only as a group member. The concept usually includes a decreased focus on personal identity, loss of contact with general social norms, and the submergence of the individual in situation-specific group norms. These are conditions that confer anonymity and increase the likelihood of evil as people partially lose awareness of themselves as individuals and cease to evaluate their own actions thoughtfully.

In addition, it is important for us to examine the ways in which group identification fulfils, and shapes, perpetrators' rational self-interests – both professionally and personally. Generally speaking, most perpetrators of genocide work within the context of a military or paramilitary organisation. In that context, there is a logic of incentives enmeshed with professional self-interest – ambitions, advancement and careerism – that certainly plays a role in understanding their behaviour. Moreover, there is often a mutually reinforcing, and deadly, compatibility of one's professional self-interests with a larger political, religious or social interest in annihilation of a specific target group.

Genocide and mass killing are replete with examples of perpetrators who used the situations of extremity to also advance their personal self-interest by claiming power, property and goods. The following account of a Hutu perpetrator from the Rwandan genocide is illustrative of this reality:

> A failed student turned killer, Shalom [Ntahobari] became a big man in Butare once the slaughter began. He swaggered around town with grenades hanging from his belt, often armed with a gun which he once aimed in insolent jest at a local burgomaster. One witness asserted that even military officers saluted Shalom. He controlled his own barrier in front of the family house near the university campus where he bullied his militia subordinates as well as passersby. One witness who had known Shalom as a fellow student witnessed him killing a man in order to rob him of his cattle.[15]

Finally, a social construction of cruelty relies on *binding factors of the group*, or cementing mechanisms that endow a social context with at least minimal stability. Such binding factors are the pressures that work to keep people within an evil-doing organisation or hierarchy. They constitute the social authority of a group and hold the individual tightly to a rigid definition of the situation, closing off the freedom of movement to focus on features of the situation other than its authority structure.

One significant binding factor is the explicit, or implicit, dynamic of conformity to peer pressure. Military science is replete with assertions that the cohesive bonds soldiers form with one another in military and paramilitary organisations are often stronger than the bonds they will form with anyone else at any other point in their lifetimes. Among people who are bonded together so intensely, there is a powerful dynamic of conformity to peer pressure – or 'mutual surveillance' – in which the individual cares so deeply about his comrades and what they think of him that he would rather die than let them down. Conformity to peer pressure certainly helps sustain perpetrators' involvement in evil. It is difficult for anyone who is bonded by links of mutual affection and interdependence to break away and openly refuse to participate in what the group is doing, even if it is committing atrocities.

What are the ultimate influences from our evolutionary past that make conformity to peer pressure so potent an influence on human behaviour? A wealth of psychological research supports the idea that conformity, while it may vary in degree across cultures and eras, is a human universal. Research on the socialisation of children suggests that we have an innate capacity to perceive and conform to group norms and behaviours. Asch's classic studies on group pressure gave us a compelling illustration of the degree to which people will conform – even when the correct, non-conforming response is unambiguous and there is no pressure (in the forms of rewards or punishments) to conform.[16] As Logan and Qirko conclude: 'There is considerable support for the suggestion that conformity is an evolved, nonrational human universal... ethnographic studies provide cross-cultural evidence for the importance of conformity.'[17]

Another significant binding factor is kin recognition cues that allow us to move from a biological definition of kinship to a social definition of kinship (that is 'fictive kin'). Such cues are important because kin recognition is so strongly related to altruistic behaviour in many species. Johnson has suggested that altruism for the benefit of non-kin can be fostered by cues of *association*.[18] In other words, we are evolutionarily primed to define kin as those with whom we are familiar due to living and rearing arrangements. So, genetically unrelated individuals can come to be understood as kin – and subsequently treated as such – if introduced into our network of frequent and intimate associations (for example, family) in an appropriate way. In addition, Johnson suggests *phenotypic matching* as another indirect kin recognition cue. By assuming a correlation between genotype (internally coded, inheritable information) and phenotype (outward, physical and behavioural characteristics), we can recognise likely kin by comparing our own phenotype with theirs. Though somewhat less reliable than the primary kin recognition cue of association, perceived phenotypic matching is still capable of eliciting altruistic behaviour on behalf of non-kin.

Because the kin recognition cues of association and phenotypic matching are indirect, they are subject to errors – as well as manipulation. It is the manipulation of kin recognition cues that gives us a new lens through which to view the mechanisms that military and paramilitary organisations use to bind individual members to the group and, subsequently, evoke the type of loyalty and emotional bonding that promotes the altruistic and self-sacrificing behaviours that are normally reserved for genetically related kin. The kin recognition cue of association is manipulated by military and paramilitary organisations through the training of recruits in extremely close and intense physical proximity that replicates natural kin contexts. In addition, the use of identifying and rhetorical language characterised by such kin terms as 'motherland', 'fatherland', the 'homeland', 'brothers-in-arms', and 'sisters-in-arms' encourages a social redefinition of kin through association. The supplemental kin recognition cue of phenotypic matching is manipulated by having individual members of a military or paramilitary organisation resemble each other as much as possible by means of uniforms, emblems, accoutrements, identical haircuts, weaponry, habits and mannerisms, tattoos and so on. In such ways, military and paramilitary organisations manipulate kin recognition cues to bind individual members to a larger group and, in so doing, to maintain and reinforce altruistic behaviour (such as volunteerism, risking one's life in combat and altruistic suicide) in a non-kin setting.

Conclusion

To resist the compelling cultural, psychological and social constructions that influence our behaviours requires a rare degree of individual strength – psychological, moral and physical. Regardless, we know that some people do resist, and it is in that knowledge that we both take hope and reserve the right of condemnation for those who perpetrate terrorism of any type. To offer a psychological explanation of how ordinary people commit genocide and mass killing is not to forgive, justify or condone their behaviours. We must not confuse explanation with exculpation; to explain behaviour is not to exonerate the perpetrator. There are no 'perpetratorless' acts of terror. Perpetrators of genocide and mass killing are not just the hapless victims of human nature, culture, psychology or their social context. On the road to committing atrocities, there are many choice points for each perpetrator. Sometimes the choosing may take place without awareness or conscious deliberation. At other times, it is a matter of very focused and deliberate decision-making. Regardless, what perpetrators decide to do makes a great difference in what they eventually do. In this way, the perpetrators, in wilfully failing to exercise their moral judgement, retain full moral and legal accountability for the atrocities they committed. No explanatory model, or 'psychological insight', will ever take that away.

It is arrogant to believe that we sit anywhere near the beginning of a world in which human evil – resulting either from anti-state or state terrorism – is dissipating. As conventional and unconventional warfare escalate across the globe, our hope for an increase in cooperative, caring, non-violent relations continues to fade away. We are left with the humbling and painful recognition that the persistence of inhumanity in human affairs is incontrovertible. It is hard to argue that we can do something beyond merely make the world a little less horrible.

My argument – that it is ordinary individuals, like you and I, who commit terrorism – is not an easy sell. None of us likes to be told that we are capable of such brutality. It is a pessimistic point of view that flies directly in the face of our sincere, but misguided, optimism that human evil can be obliterated by reforming society. We must not, however, avoid the hard task of trying to extract the comprehensible from the unthinkable. We must not let 'evil' be a throwaway category for the things we are afraid to understand. We must not let it be the impenetrable term we use when we come to the limit of human comprehension. We must not consider perpetrators so irrational, so atavistic, as to be beyond human understanding. We must not place human evil beyond human scrutiny. To do so is to give it the benefit of our ignorance. In this sense, our refusal to attempt to understand human evil is a wilful failure to know our own hearts and, if anything, only facilitates the continuation of evil in human affairs.

The lesson that ordinary people commit genocide and mass killing need not be compartmentalised only as 'bad news' – a disturbing, unsettling, disquieting truth about the human condition. The lesson does contain potentially 'good news' as well – the making of terrorists need no longer be a mystery. We are beginning to understand the conditions under which we can be transformed into killing machines. The more we know, and the more open we are to seeing ourselves as we are, the better we can control ourselves. It is only in accepting the limits of who we are that we have a legitimate chance to structure a society in which the exercise of human evil is lessened. Civility, after all, is a chosen state, not a natural condition. Ultimately, being aware of our own capacity for evil – and how to cultivate the moral sensibilities that curb that capacity – is the best safeguard we can have against future genocide and mass killing.

Notes

1. Cited in Lance Morrow, 'Evil', *Time* (10 June 1991), 52.
2. Quoted by R. Cooper in 'The Long Peace', *Prospect*, April 1999.
3. William Eckhardt, 'War-Related Deaths since 3000 BC', *Bulletin of Peace Proposals*, December 1991 and Ruth Leger Sivard, 'World Military and Social Expenditures', 16th edition (Washington, 1996).
4. 'Third of Nations Mired in Conflict', *Associated Press Report*, 30 December 1999.
5. Roger W. Smith, 'Human Destructiveness and Politics: the Twentieth Century as an Age of Genocide', in Isidor Wallimann and Michael N. Dobkowski

(eds), *Genocide and the Modern Age: Etiology and Case Studies of Mass Death* (Syracuse, NY, 2000), 21.
6. For a complete critique of the work of those who argue that the origins of extraordinary human evil lie not in ordinary individuals but in extraordinary groups, ideologies, psychopathologies or personalities, see James Waller, *Becoming Evil: How Ordinary People Commit Genocide and Mass Killing*, 2nd edn (New York, 2007).
7. Ibid.
8. Steven Pinker, *The Blank Slate: the Modern Denial of Human Nature* (New York, 2002), 54.
9. Peter Singer, *A Darwinian Left: Politics, Evolution and Cooperation* (New Haven, 1999), 63.
10. Alexander Laban Hinton, 'Why Did You Kill? The Cambodian Genocide and the Dark Side of Face and Honor', *Journal of Asian Studies*, 57 (1998), 93–122; here, 96.
11. Ibid., 98–101.
12. Janice T. Gibson and Mike Haritos-Fatouros, 'The Education of a Torturer', *Psychology Today*, 20 (1986), 50–8.
13. Haing S. Ngor, *A Cambodian Odyssey* (New York, 1987), 230.
14. Gibson and Haritos-Fatouros, 'Education of a Torturer'.
15. Quoted in Adam Jones, 'Gender and Genocide in Rwanda', *Journal of Genocide Research*, 4 (2002), 76.
16. Solomon E. Asch, 'Opinions and Social Pressure', *Scientific American*, 193 (1955), 31–5.
17. Michael H. Logan and Hector N. Qirko, 'An Evolutionary Perspective on Maladaptive Traits and Cultural Conformity', *American Journal of Human Biology*, 8 (1996), 615–29, here 625f.
18. Gary R. Johnson, 'Kin Selection, Socialization, and Patriotism: an Integrating Theory', *Politics and the Life Sciences*, 4 (1986), 127–40. Commentaries and an author's response follow on 141–54 in the same issue. See also his 'The Role of Kin Recognition Mechanisms in Patriotic Socialization: Further Reflections', *Politics and the Life Sciences*, 8 (1989), 62–9, in which he tentatively suggests 'location' as an additional, though less reliable, kin recognition cue.

7
On Killing and Morality: How Normal People Become Mass Murderers

Harald Welzer

In this chapter I would like to deal with the question of how it is possible for perfectly normal and average people to decide, in certain situations, to kill. In order to answer this question, I recently attempted to reconstruct the murderous career of a reserve police battalion, devoting special attention to the situative dynamics and the procedural aspects of the work of killing.[1] This analysis placed the process leading to mass killing within the context of the establishment of a 'National Socialist' morality, which began in 1933 and created a reality in which categorical differences between people became accepted as a condition of perception, interpretation and action. I would like to sketch out this social process in the first part of this chapter. Second, I will attempt a brief, process-oriented description of the first killing operation by Reserve Police Battalion 45. This shows that for the perpetrators killing was, in many respects, hardly such an abnormal procedure as it seems to us today, in view of the consequences of the Holocaust.

Crimes like the war of extermination (*Vernichtungskrieg*) and the Holocaust confront us with a brutality and cruelty that seem so much outside this world that we cannot find our way within them. When we ask how people were capable of committing all these atrocities – bestially murdering men, women and children – we tend to conceptualise the personalities of the participants in binary fashion: they acted morally or immorally, they were good or bad, they were perpetrators or victims, Nazis or anti-Nazis. But people are hardly this unambiguous. There were staunch Nazis who saved Jews, but one did not need to be a staunch National Socialist in order to kill Jews. A relationship to the intellectual content of German culture, to Beethoven, Mozart, Goethe and Keller, was often of real importance to the murderers, a deeply felt pleasure, part of their identity. The scientists who worked on eugenic experiments or who drafted plans for the settlement of the 'Eastern territories' (*Ostgebiete*) were not 'pseudoscientists', but cultivated people who used their internationally recognised qualifications for anti-human purposes. As Goetz Aly remarks: 'Catholic priests blessed the weapons for a crusade against godless Bolshevism, and at the same time resisted the crimes of euthanasia.'[2] Certainly more than a few Germans did not care for the Jews but nevertheless shopped in Jewish stores because they were less expensive. And, by the same token, there were certainly people who could wax indignant about the shameful treatment of Jewish judges and were ashamed of what was being done to these people, but nevertheless took advantage of the opportunity to buy a comfortable armchair or a pretty landscape where it was cheap: at the 'Jewish stalls' (*Judenkisten*) on Hamburg's 'Kamerun Quay', for example, where 'Aryanised' furniture expropriated from Belgian and Dutch Jews who had been deported or forced into emigration was sold off.[3]

Even if we think about ourselves, there are considerable discrepancies between our moral claims and our actions. Depending on the situation, we are all capable of acting, speaking and being interpreted in very different ways. We permit ourselves, for example, 'bad' behaviour in certain situations despite 'knowing better', and we master lies and contradictions, and disregard their opposites, trust, integrity and respect. Moreover, such self-examination immediately reveals something else. If we think about the patchwork of our moral existence, for every facet that seems morally somewhat questionable even to ourselves, we immediately try to legitimise *why* we did this or that against our better judgement, why we could not live up to our capacities, what the reason was for *having to* lie, cheat, betray or disappoint. Astonishingly, we generally find good reasons why behaviour felt to be wrong seems, in retrospect, to be sensible and thus, at least to ourselves, justified; and we need such reasons in order to do justice to our own moral claims, even if we acted against them 'in exceptional circumstances'. So how did the perpetrators perceive themselves? And how was it possible for them to do things that, only months before, they would have thought they could never do?

One of them said, 'I am not the monster I am made out to be. I am the victim of a fallacy.'[4] This remarkable self-assessment comes from Adolf Eichmann, one of the most grotesque figures in the panorama of Nazi perpetrators. He formulated it in his final statement at the Jerusalem trial. Like all perpetrators, Eichmann firmly denied that he had acted inhumanly – that is, beyond the moral categories of human society – although his tireless work essentially consisted in systematically killing those whom he and his kind had defined as outside human society. Eichmann understood the accusations against him no better than any of the other perpetrators, because the anti-human project to which he had devoted all his energies had established a moral universe in which there were reasons for mass murder that were obvious to the perpetrators. This was not personal, and Eichmann probably was referring to this when he characterised himself as the 'victim of a fallacy'. He simply did not understand what he was being accused of, and in this he was in accord with most perpetrators, for whom, to this day, the idea that they could be considered murderers is alien.

If we attempt to explain the behaviour of the perpetrators of extermination, we are faced with the problem that we are applying a moral framework to judge them that was not in force when they committed their crimes. This is not a statement that the perpetrators were unaware of the law or were acting on the mistaken assumption that refusing to kill would have serious consequences for them personally. No; first of all, they were perfectly aware of what they were doing and, second, they saw themselves, in their occasional feelings, as having to do something unpleasant, something essentially compliant with a social environment that expected them to take on the work of killing that was considered necessary. The radical nature of this viewpoint lies less in the fact that the individuals concerned took advantage of what Günter Anders called an 'opportunity for unpunished inhumanity' that was open to them – that they grasped sexual opportunities, enriched themselves personally and allowed themselves the entirely unfamiliar feeling of unlimited power and command.[5] All this is reprehensible, but not incomprehensible. Rather, what is far more difficult to understand is the fact that a social development had opened up to them precisely this surprising expansion of their personal scope of action – and that, of all things, it was a dictatorial, totalitarian system that granted them this incomparable expansion of their personal freedom.

If one views Nazism as a sort of operational accident in the history of modernity, as a society that went wrong and became a coercive system forcing itself into a collective process of radicalisation, I believe one fails to understand its central motivating force. The policy of extermination was not merely a phenomenon accompanying a totalitarian dictatorship that placed its hopes in the coercive formation of a community of those who belonged. This structure itself rested on a categorical definition of those who did not belong, and drew from this its seemingly irresistible and thoroughly sustainable attractiveness. The implementation of the anti-Jewish policy in many ways formed the centre of the developmental dynamics of the National Socialist society. Establishing a field for political activity that was able systematically to permeate all other fields of politics and thus society as a whole, set free enormous individual and collective energies, without which the gigantically destructive abilities of this regime cannot at all be understood.

The question is not only how men who had until then been recognised as perfectly normal could become murderers, starting in 1939 in Poland and especially in 1941 in Russia; but also how, beginning in 1933, an overwhelming majority of people who until then had been perfectly normal, could decide to take part in a process of active exclusion that happened with enormous speed and not see it as anything particularly bad – as anything that would dramatically depart from their value system.

It seems to me that one cannot understand all this unless one imagines that only one single coordinate in a social structure needs to be altered to change the whole system of coordinates – to establish a reality that is entirely different from the one that existed until the moment the coordinate was altered. This coordinate is called social belonging. Its alteration consists in the categorical redefinition of who belongs to one's own moral universe and who does not – who belongs to one's own group ('us') and who, as a member of a different group ('them'), is an 'other', a stranger, and ultimately a deadly enemy. Such an alteration of coordinates can be found not only in Nazism, where it was justified by racial theory – that is, by science; but also in Cambodia where it was based on class theory, and in ex-Yugoslavia and Rwanda where it was ethnically based. The unavoidable, absolute distinction between those who belong and those who do not is the one common characteristic shared by otherwise very varied, murderous societies – coupled with the phobia that the only solution to existing social problems consists in the complete elimination of the other, the non-belonging. This elimination can be seen first of all as territorial, as in the Nazis' Madagascar Plan or the territorial separation in ex-Yugoslavia. But the idea of elimination begets the practice of exclusion, expropriation and deportation, and that practice, along with the violence that accompanies it, transforms with horrifying regularity what was initially seen as 'resettlement' (*Umsiedlung*), or 'cleansing' (*Säuberung*) of the non-belonging into exterminating them.

This transformation is already inherent in the categorical definition of belonging. According to such a definition, what is to be done with the non-belonging is only a question of graduated expediency, not one of principle. In this spirit, Raul Hilberg stated that the fate of the European Jews was sealed the moment in early 1933 that a civil servant included in a decree a definition of who was 'Aryan' and who was not.[6] At that moment, that is, what had previously existed in a legally protected space of racial resentment and the desire for exclusion and elimination without being able to develop freely, became capable of being implemented in practice. Thus the definition first of all created entirely new possibilities – an offer to a majority to better itself socially, emotionally, and very rapidly and also materially at the expense of a minority. It raised needs felt by many people, even in other societies, from the status of wishes and potentials to the status of achievable and achieved reality. With this definitional act by the aforementioned civil servant, an essential, unbridgeable distinction between people became reality – a distinction that had already been constructed scientifically by racial biologists and had existed already, if only diffusely, in daily life in the form of prejudice, stereotypes and resentments.

The monstrosity of the National Socialist project lies in its explicit rejection of the universalist concept of humanity that had begun to prevail in bourgeois societies since the Enlightenment. What is often overlooked, is that, while the wrongs of the 'Third Reich' primarily targeted the 'them' groups such as Jews, Sinti and Roma, the opposition, the disabled and others, traditional concepts of morality and law continued to be in force for the members of the national community. The concepts of the *Herrenrasse* (Master Race) and the *Untermensch* (subhumans) were so attractive to average members of the German 'race' not because of the mere promise that this concept would make everything better, but because of the immediate practical implementation of the promise. Each step in the rapidly accomplished process of exclusion of the Jews not only worsened their objective situation, but at the same time improved the situation of non-Jewish Germans, not just gradually, but in every way. In his novel *Mephisto*, Klaus Mann had his not-fully-fictional character Hendrik Höfgen reflect as follows: 'But even if the Nazis remained in power, what had he, Höfgen, to fear from them? He belonged to no party. And he wasn't a Jew. This fact above all others – that he wasn't a Jew – struck all of a sudden as immensely comforting and important. He had never in the past estimated the true worth of this considerable and unsuspected advantage. He wasn't a Jew and so he could be forgiven everything.'[7]

Höfgen dreams the dream of an essential, unavoidable, non-negotiable, absolute superiority of the German 'race' over all other people. And this dream was achieved, directly and manifestly, by the practice of exclusion. The transformation of social coordinates made possible the almost total inclusion in the National Socialist project of all those who belonged. It also explains the largely unbroken approbation enjoyed by this project until the shock of the lost battle at Stalingrad. But this explanation still does not help us understand how so many people were able to decide not only to take part in the exclusion, which was not murderous at first, but ultimately also to participate in performing the work of killing that was considered necessary. After all, roughly three quarters of a million people were directly involved in the mass murders, and they all carried out their tasks – some reluctantly, some with an enthusiasm far beyond what was required. The key to understanding how this happened, lies in the fact that the National Socialisation of German society was not an ideological or propagandistic process – something one might think about and something to have an attitude to – but one that, in daily changes to lived practice, translated the anti-Jewish worldview of Nazism into a perceptible, tangible and lasting reality.

This reality consisted, for example, of the exclusion of Jews from all sorts of associations, unions, organisations and professions; of the passivity of the police towards anti-Jewish violence; of the perception, confirmed every day, that it was good not to be a Jew and that all of this was possible without anyone stopping these actually unusual occurrences, or even objecting to them; of Hitler's welfare state, which was due, not least, to the anti-Jewish policies. And it consisted of the constant increase of the prosperity of those who belonged, which was the reverse of the progressive exclusion and robbery of the others. As Götz Aly has shown, even in the final years of the war, the Germans enjoyed the highest standard of living in Europe, and German soldiers received the highest rate of reimbursement for loss of wages suffered due to call-up.[8] The fact that 'everyone was doing well' in the 'Third Reich' is even today part of what is passed down from generation to generation in German families.[9]

Every single, often incidental and inconspicuous step in social restructuring has consequences for the self-perception of the individual in the changing collective structure. In the social context formed jointly by those who belong and those who do not belong, a change of position on the part of the other also means a change in one's own position. 'As the aforementioned 80 million went in search of the feared Jewish grandfather,' wrote Hannah Arendt, 'a type of initiation ritual was achieved: each person came out of it with the feeling of belonging to a group of the "included", in contrast to an imaginary mass of the "excluded".'[10]

The advancement to 'Master Race' or to 'Aryan' is a question of emotion, but of an emotion that found an ever-firmer, irresistible counterpart in the changing reality of the 'Third Reich'.

The reality really did change in this way from day to day, and interviews with former members of the German *Volksgemeinschaft* give evidence to this day of the psychosocial attractiveness and emotional bonding force of this practical process of inclusion and exclusion. There is general agreement to this day among contemporaries that the 'Third Reich' can be described, at least until the Russian campaign, as a 'pleasant period': for many, this assessment held good until well into the war of extermination. And the argument, unchanged to this day, that people did not know about 'that thing with the Jews' cannot be attributed to repression, but to the fact that it was felt to be obvious that one now lived in a society that rightly consisted, and should consist, of non-Jewish Germans. The exclusion, persecution and expropriation of the others was not experienced as such, because these others, by definition, no longer belonged, and their anti-social treatment no longer affected the internal landscape of National Socialist collectivisation (*Vergemeinschaftung*) and morality. Eyewitnesses can no longer remember 'that thing with the Jews' because forcing them out, taking their possessions, and depriving them of rights was as obvious a part of Nazi reality as the fact that there were bread-rolls at the baker's and meat at the butcher's.

The penetrative force and rapid implementation (and incidentally also the staying power) of the Nazi project were based on the direct transformation of ideology into practice, which created 'Aryans' in the German reality as quickly as it created 'Jews'. Hannah Arendt wrote, in this spirit, that totalitarian propaganda is such that 'its content – at least for members of the movement and the population of a totalitarian country – no longer has to do with opinions about which one may argue, but has become as equally unassailable and real an element of their daily lives as two times two is four.'[11]

In establishing this new reality, the practical deprivation of rights and property of the inferior 'them'-group is just as essential to the practical construction of the new, superior 'we'-group as their absurd stylisation to a deadly enemy. As Peter Longerich has written, the ' "dejudaisation" of German society, and in the broader sense, the implementation of racist policies, provided ... the National Socialists with an instrument with which, bit by bit, to permeate individual aspects of life and subordinate German society to its claim of total power'.[12] This process itself had an enduring effect on the actors in the functional elite: the phantasm of a fundamental misfortune that emanated from the Jews and a future salvation promised by the vision of a racially pure society had, in the modus of its achievement, the character of unremitting self-affirmation. In other words, the creation of a new reality did not remain without consequence for the ideas of those who drove the National Socialist project.

Joseph Goebbels' diaries, for example, demonstrate impressively that he was really convinced of the existence of a world Jewish conspiracy and that this conviction was hardly a propaganda trick in which he himself did not believe. Himmler, Hitler, Goering and the numerous other pioneers and executors of the extermination at all other levels of hierarchy and function shared this conviction in more or less pronounced, but in any case sufficient, measure to set the gigantic project of the extermination of the European Jews in motion and bring it almost to completion. It makes no difference to the result whether someone has rational or irrational reasons for what he does. The results of his actions are as much an element of reality in the one case as in the other. The Holocaust is the most depressing and disturbing proof of this. And at the same time, the anti-Jewish policies prove the normative power of fact: every accomplished measure, every unpunished act of violence, every 'Aryanised' store, every deported family, every murdered Jew proved once again that this was not about ideology or propaganda, but about the creation of a reality of which every single *Volksgenosse* – member of the racial community – was a part. The most convincing thing for the individual must have been that all this really happened – that the sheer unlimited, unrestrained character of the process showed itself in the implementation of a social project that emancipated itself from traditional values, in such a radical way, without consequences or resistance of any kind.

This new reality formed the frame of reference against which the designated mass murderers measured themselves when they were called up, as part of the 1941 'Barbarossa' campaign, for police duty behind the advancing front. These duties also included – often to the surprise of the reserve policemen – so-called *Judenaktionen*, in which Jewish men, women and children were systematically shot. In so far as they had any contact with the judicial system in the post-war period, the perpetrators, often older men with civilian professions, generally defended themselves by referring to 'superior orders'; but we now know that refusing to take part in shootings brought no serious consequences, and that it was often not clear at all what the orders actually were. Written orders were issued down only to the commander level; further down, individual commanders were left free to decide whether to give their men the order to murder Jews.

In the case of Police Battalion 45, which I thoroughly researched, the teams were not given any general order in advance.[13] This battalion's first *Judenaktion* took place in Berdichev. One gunner later recalled: 'As far as I can remember the first operation, it was like this: we had to report early. The company chief, Paschke, then announced to the company that the company had to carry out an operation from the SS. He further told us that we had to get the Jews together, and then we'd find out the rest.'[14] Another member of the same company related that the actual order to shoot was only given on the spot: 'It's true that Klamm announced the order at the execution site, in the immediate vicinity of the ditch.'[15]

Such a gradual announcement of the order to shoot had several functional advantages. If one does not know what is going to happen next, one will not be nervous or excited, when nothing as unusual as a massive shooting has been ordered. On the other hand, such a casual treatment of the giving of orders counts on the existence of implicit knowledge among the men regarding the actual background of the diffuse orders; otherwise the preparatory acts – collecting the victims, cordoning off the shooting site, digging ditches, etc. – would not be carried out without question. Thus the gradual giving of orders is based on collectively shared knowledge and unspoken agreement about what is happening. At the same time, the unspoken nature of the actual order allows the individual to await what is to come with relative calm.

Karl Milz also relates how he was simply assigned to the ditch by Klamm as a gunner. That was the order to shoot. Another participant in the same event, Franz Bischof, describes the whole thing as follows: 'We stood right near a ditch. Here Klamm now designated me as a gunner, by saying more or less the following: "Bischof, you go into the ditch and shoot!" I had to follow Klamm's orders and went into the ditch. I was armed with a Russian rifle, loaded with 10 rounds of ammunition. While I went to the ditch, the first Jews were already being brought. The Jews were sent to the ditch one by one. There they had to lie down, and they were killed by me with a shot to the neck.' When asked by the prosecutors about how he knew how to kill the victims, Bischof answered: 'From Klamm. When the first Jews went by me into the ditch, Klamm grabbed the Jews by the neck with his hand or his fingers. Meanwhile he turned to me and said, more or less, "That's where you have to shoot".'[16]

The question of how the victims must have felt when they were used as demonstration dummies for their own murder cannot be answered here, and it is anyway impossible to imagine oneself in this situation of absolute debasement and threat. But one may ask what the perpetrators were experiencing in this situation. Once again, Karl Milz: 'Hardly had we reached the ditch when the first Jews arrived. We gunners looked at each other, because none of us knew what we were supposed to do or how and in what way the Jews were to be shot.'[17]

This is a decisive situation in which, once more, a decision had to be made about what to do. In the ditch, before the first shot, there was still theoretically the chance to stop, to refuse, to claim nausea, fear, incapacity. The gunners looked at each other – that is, they tried to measure themselves against each other, to figure out what the others were thinking, believing, intending. This social process of situative agreement on what kind of situation it is that one is in, was happening under pressure of time and action. The victims had already been 'brought' and something had to happen. In this situation it is the superior who solves the problem by narrowing it down to the practical level and showing them what to do. 'Klamm must have recognised our uncertainty, for he gestured to the arriving Jews that they should lie down in rows next to each other [sic]. When the Jews were already lying on the ground with their faces to the ground, Klamm walked up to me confidently, grabbed me by the neck with his hand and said, more or less, "This is where you have to shoot!" The other gunners were standing near me at the time, and they saw this. Then Klamm went to the victims lying on the ground – most victims, even during the later shooting, held their hands in front of their faces – stooped and shot these Jews with a pistol in the neck... It was several Jews in any case, more than five Jews in any case. After Klamm shot the Jews, we also had to start shooting.'[18]

By not only *showing* where they should shoot, but also shooting himself, Klamm creates facts. The shooting had already begun – there were already five or more victims – and had only to be continued. In this way, the shooting is already 'there', without the gunners having yet committed a murder. Each of the participants thus already finds himself within the murderous process, before he himself becomes active. Because Klamm started the process, the subjective responsibility of the others lies merely in 'imitating', or at most in 'going along', and that is different from 'trying out' and taking the initiative. At the same time, in a certain sense the crime has already been committed once Klamm finishes his demonstration; whatever comes next changes things quantitatively, but no longer qualitatively. 'Now the Jews kept on coming into the ditch, one after another. Klamm decided each time where they had to lie down. We gunners then had to start shooting on Klamm's orders. No command was given, but as soon as a Jew was shot, the next one had to lie down on top of him or next to him. I think that around three layers of dead Jews lay on top of each other before a new row was started.'[19]

Once the process has happened, no command is necessary; the work of killing proceeds automatically. One notes that in this description, the victims are viewed entirely instrumentally – in Karl Milz's view, they are objects of his work, components that are only interesting if they make no trouble. Here we see a dynamisation of the killing process, the suspension of personal responsibility through the quasi-automatic process itself, and the concentration of perception on the efficient performance of the work of killing. All these elements are made effective through the gradual style of command, which thus proves a highly efficient method of integrating the actors into the murderous activity.

Gradual command and the practical introduction to killing, which can be described as 'learning by doing', a step-by-step initiation into killing, provides advantages over direct orders: it gives both the commander and the team the opportunity to avoid explicitly moral conflicts. Up to a certain point, which essentially is in the ditch, the orders – collect the Jews, cordon off the road, etc. – are within the realm of police and military normalcy, as it could be defined and perceived at the time by the actors, if they wanted to perceive it that way.

Thus if one considers as a whole the context of events in an execution scenario that was, for most of the actors, a first-time experience, only the *last act* in the entire chain of actions falls within the format of the extraordinary. But by the time that point has been reached, the participants have already gone through a whole series of acts, the rightness of which would have been questioned if they had stopped, at this precise point, and considered their position in the action-structure. Here a familiar socio-psychological phenomenon, described as 'foot-in-the-door tactics', becomes evident.[20] The likelihood of getting someone to carry out a major favour increases if one begins by asking a small favour. This phenomenon played a role at various levels in the Milgram experiment – particularly at the point where the subject had essentially agreed to the experiment and thus made a commitment to the experiment leader; and, at a second stage, at the point where the subject began to give very low-level electric shocks to the supposed test person as 'punishment' for the wrong answer.[21] Examples like this show the extent to which a decision, once made, determines adherence to the same decisional trend in succeeding actions: James Waller coined the apt phrase, 'escalating commitments', to describe the process.[22]

In addition, the process of a 'Jew operation' (*Judenaktion*) involved a division of labour: the succession of actions was divided up. Part of the team evacuated the homes, others accompanied the victims to the collection points, others drove the trucks, others plundered those to be executed, and still others did nothing at all, some shot and others then filled in the ditches. These all represent various types of personal accountability, and every partial act in this chain of actions allowed various opportunities for modulation of the prescribed task – 'overlooking' victims, avoidance, but also taking initiative, consciously behaving brutally, etc. That is, at every step in the divided labour of execution there were opportunities for the individual to appropriate and define his task, and thus also various psychological spaces for assigning responsibility. Not for nothing do we find far more descriptions in the interrogation protocols of cordoning off an area than of executions. The reasons for this are mainly legal, but also psychological. For one thing, it means that the actors, to this day, do not see it as a contribution to the crime that they were 'only' members of an *Einsatzkommando* and in this capacity were 'only' cordoning off. For another, the fragmentation of the killing process provided the individual with the opportunity of seeing his actions, in comparison for example to those of the gunners, as 'something different' – and this distinction within the group extends to each perpetrator portraying each specific aspect of the crime as always 'more humane' than the 'more inhumane' acts of the other gunners, from whom the speaker separates himself by emphasising, for example, what type of victim he *didn't* kill. 'I myself,' says Karl Milz about a later shooting, 'was in the very fortunate situation that I at least did not have to shoot any infants with their mothers. The children that I had to shoot were already old enough for their mothers to hold them by the hand.'[23] The lack of empathy of such perpetrators leaves one speechless, and it allows us to easily overlook *why* they are saying this: because they do not want to fit in with the image of the unsympathetic killer that they fear prosecutors, judges and even their social sphere could have of them.

We may assume that, after the first shootings, the men in this battalion gained an initial, fundamental awareness: that the thing could be done, that the victims could be successfully fooled, and that most of them accepted everything that happened without visible resistance, until the final point when they were killed. The members of the battalion, regardless of which specific task they had been assigned, now knew how it was done, and they also knew that it wouldn't make much difference if they were assigned the task – generally seen as unpleasant – of getting into the ditch and shooting.

However, in the course of the 'orderly' execution, 'disruptive' moments repeatedly occurred – either weapons malfunctioned, or the wrong weapons were used, or the victims insisted they were not Jews, or the gunner became nauseous, or victims did not behave 'properly' and caused the men problems by attacking them verbally, spitting, handing them their children, or simply not dying quickly enough. Thus Franz Bischof, who, by his own estimation, shot some 100 people during the 'operation', reports that 'during the shooting blood (it could also have been bits of brain) spattered in my face'. At some point, it got to be too much for him: 'Then there was the penetrating smell of blood, and so at that point I left the ditch. I got nauseous, and after leaving the ditch I had to throw up.'[24] In retrospect, one tends to describe what happened there as an 'inferno' or 'hell' or 'chaos', but the real horror lies in the fact that the situation was not chaotic at all. Does one leave hell before throwing up? Franz Bischof, at any rate, would have thought it embarrassing to lose control over his body in this situation or violate rules of decency that he had learned, which indicates that social situations are structured by rules to a far greater degree than we generally realise. And it is important to be clear that situations experienced as new and unusual generally still contain a great deal that is familiar, so it is precisely the newness of the situation that engenders the need to cling to proven methods of orientation and behaviour. In other words, even the most unusual situations still contain, at the practical level, a great deal of 'normalcy' of perception, interpretation and action. This clinging to normalcy goes so far, as Stanley Milgram once noted, that people prefer to burn to death in a house-fire than run into the street with no pants on.

As horrible as the situation in the ditch is, it is not chaos. The actions are carried out systematically: the company chief gives orders, the team brings in new victims and waits by the ditch until the gunners are finished, an armourer stands ready to supply the gunners with fresh ammunition and exchange the weapons when the barrels get too hot. There is a field kitchen and breaks for breakfast and lunch. If someone feels nauseous, it is a problem for the ongoing operation, but not part of a chaotic, out of control process.

Because of the extreme violence employed, we tend to imagine the process as an 'inferno', but if we consider, in contrast, that the entire process was regularly completed in an 'orderly' fashion *even though* the gunners were spattered, *even though* the ditch was literally filled with blood, *even though* a gunner occasionally fell on top of the corpses, we realise that the framework within which all of this occurred remained intact. The operations had a beginning, a middle and an end, and they functioned, again and again. The frame of reference – that something was being done here that *had* to be done – remained in force primarily because everyone involved had decided, with greater or lesser difficulty, to take part.

The difficulties – for example the fact that a gunner might become nauseous – were concomitants of a process that many of the immediate perpetrators found unpleasant, but these difficulties were overcome. Strictly speaking, they merely served to constantly improve the situative setting, reducing the problems next time, or not permitting them to arise at all. But they were never a reason for questioning the operation as a whole, not even for the gunners themselves. As in Milgram's experiment, the prior decision to accept the given and, in fact, shared frame of reference made it progressively less conceivable that one could return to a starting point at which a decision might have been possible. The completion of the act provided common ground. The observers confirm by their presence that what is happening in the arena is appreciated or at least accepted. There is no outside intervention that might break up the pragmatic acquiescence in killing.

In conclusion, let me return to a more general perspective. The ease with which mass murder could be integrated into the felt normalcy of the 'Third Reich' can also be seen in the fact that all the institutions that had existed before 1933 could play a functional role in the National Socialist project: for them, for the *Reichsbahn* (German railway) officials, the heads of tax offices, the bank employees, the psychiatrists, the reserve police, it was as though nothing had changed in the least. The various professional requirements in the institutions left no room for special choice or training of personnel, as Raul Hilberg writes:

> Even the killing units and the killing centers did not obtain professional killers. Every lawyer in the RSHA was presumed to be suitable for leadership in the mobile killing units; every finance expert of the WVHA was considered a natural choice for service in a death camp. In other words, all necessary operations were accomplished with whatever personnel were at hand. However one may wish to draw the line of active participation, the machinery of destruction was a remarkable cross-section of the German population.[25]

Against this same background, Henry Friedländer once remarked that, despite an intensive search, he never found a job announcement in a German newspaper of the 1930s or 1940s in which the state sought experienced, qualified mass murderers.[26] But such an advertisement would have been unnecessary, since the machinery of destruction 'was structurally no different from organized German society as a whole; the difference was only one of function'.[27] Only the objective of all this familiar and usual behaviour was different from before: that is, it was an explicitly anti-human one. True, in the mind of the individual civil servant working on such a decree, the creation of rules for membership in the race that was begun immediately following the seizure of power was not yet a death sentence for those affected. One does not think so far in advance when dealing with an administrative task.

The fact that a person on one end of a chain of actions does not think about what happens at the other end of the chain is based in the division of labour and function that typifies the structure of activity in modern societies. But at every relay station in this dynamic structure, there are concrete people who know what they are doing – and connect this activity with a very conscious meaning. This means that we must understand our structure of social institutions and behaviours essentially as a *repository of potentials*, which, depending on the defined goal being pursued, can call up quite varied realities. Thus in asking questions about the perpetrators, and in the search to explain how they could do what they did, it is crucial to identify the potentials that are always available to open up collective and individual spheres of action in a variety of directions.

In addition, *under new circumstances* the potential needs of perfectly normal people can evolve. The entire secret of how National Socialism developed in such anti-human fashion lies in the surprising opening up of spheres of behaviour, in which things were suddenly permitted or even encouraged that had previously been forbidden. And with this I return to the behaviour of the immediate perpetrators which is apparently so inexplicable. It is only the absolutely horrifying nature of their behaviour, its inhumanity, which lies like an impenetrable screen before the appalling awareness of how easily these potentials can be unleashed.

Yet there seem to be clear differences between crossing the street upon encountering a Jewish acquaintance for fear of an embarrassing situation, and moving into an attractive apartment from which a Jewish family has been evicted, and ordering someone's death by signing a medical form, and designing crematorium ovens, and placing a gun against the neck of a child who is lying on the naked corpses of his parents. All these are qualitatively different thresholds, and some are harder to cross than others; but I fear that, in the end, they form a continuum, the beginning of which holds something apparently harmless and the end of which is marked by extermination. For most of us, it is only important to cross the first threshold in order to be able to cross the last. The perfidiousness of it all lies in the fact that when crossing the first threshold, the last one still seems intolerable, while there seem to be good reasons to take the first, not so terrible step. This is perhaps only a minor transgression against an already fragile inner conviction, against a morally unpleasant feeling. With each step, the moral threshold value, which had at first seemed to mark an insurmountable obstacle, sinks. And in the end, even the extermination of human beings can seem like something that one can and should do.

Notes

1. Harald Welzer, *Täter. Wie aus ganz normalen Menschen Massenmörder werden* (Frankfurt/Main, 2005).
2. Götz Aly, 'Ich bin das Volk', *Süddeutsche Zeitung*, 1 September 2004, 11.
3. See Frank Bajohr, 'The Beneficiaries of "Aryanization": Hamburg as a Case Study', *Yad Vashem Studies*, 26 (1998) 173–202.
4. Adolf Eichmann, in Hannah Arendt, *Eichmann in Jerusalem: a Report on the Banality of Evil* (New York, 1979), 248.
5. Günther Anders, *Besuch im Hades* (Munich, 1985).
6. Raul Hilberg, *The Destruction of the European Jews* (New York, 1961), 43, 45.
7. Klaus Mann, *Mephisto*, quoted in Saul Friedländer, *Nazi Germany and the Jews: the Years of Persecution 1933–1939* (London, 1997), 10.
8. The soldiers' families received 85 per cent of the last net income of the conscripted husband. See Götz Aly, *Hitlers Volksstaat. Raub, Rassenkrieg und nationaler Sozialismus* (Frankfurt/Main, 2005), 36.
9. Harald Welzer, 'Grandpa Wasn't a Nazi: the Holocaust in German Family Remembrance', *American Jewish Committee*, www.ajc.org (Berlin, September 2005); Harald Welzer, Sabine Moller and Karoline Tschuggnall, *Opa war kein Nazi: Nationalsozialismus und Holocaust im Familiengedächtnis* (Frankfurt/Main, 2003); Karoline Tschuggnall and Harald Welzer, 'Rewriting Memory: the Joint Production of the Past in Conversation', *Culture & Psychology*, 8(1) (2002), 130–45; Olaf Jensen, ' "One goes left to the Russians, the other goes right to the Americans" – Family Recollections of the Holocaust in Europe', in Martin L. Davies and Claus-Christian W. Szejnmann (eds), *How the Holocaust Looks Now: International Perspectives* (Basingstoke, 2006), 19–29.
10. Hannah Arendt, *Elemente und Ursprünge totaler Herrschaft* (Munich, 1996), 594.
11. Ibid., 573.
12. Peter Longerich, *Politik der Vernichtung. Eine Gesamtdarstellung der nationalsozialistischen Judenverfolgung* (Munich, 1998), 578.
13. The Police Battalion 45 was grouped in Aussig, a town in Sudetenland, in western Czechoslovakia. After an 'operation' in Poland the Battalion was regrouped and reservists were included in October 1940. Since then the Battalion was called Reserve Police Battalion 45, consisting of three companies

of 100–120 men each, devided into four platoons. Commander of the Battalion was Major Ulrich Gutmann (pseudonym), commander of the first company was Hauptmann Hans Paschke (pseudonym), commander of the second was Lieutenant Engelbert Klamm (pseudonym), commander of the third was Hauptmann Werner Appel (pseudonym). See Welzer, *Täter*, 91–7.
14. Bundesarchiv Ludwigsburg (BArch), B 162 / AR-Z 1251/65 Bd. B VII, Bl. 1203; in Welzer, *Täter*, 136.
15. BArch, B 162 / AR-Z 1251/65 Bd. B VII, Bl. 1475; ibid.
16. BArch, B 162 / AR-Z 1251/65 Bd. B VIII, Bl. 1496; ibid., 138.
17. BArch, B 162 / AR-Z 1251/65 Bd. B VII, Bl. 1477; ibid.
18. BArch, B 162 / AR-Z 1251/65 Bd. B VII, Bl. 1475; ibid., 139
19. BArch, B 162 / AR-Z 1251/65 Bd. B I, Bl. 171R; ibid., 140.
20. Jonathan L. Freedman and S. C. Fraser, 'Compliance without Pressure: the Foot-in-the-Door Technique', *Journal of Personality and Social Psychology*, 4 (1966), 195–202.
21. Stanley Milgram, *Obedience to Authority: an Experimental View* (New York, 1974).
22. James E. Waller, *Becoming Evil: How Ordinary People Commit Genocide and Mass Killing* (Oxford, 2002). See also his chapter in this volume.
23. BArch, B 162 / AR-Z 1251/65 Bd. B I, Bl. 152R; Welzer, *Täter*, 142.
24. BArch, B 162 / AR-Z 1251/65 Bd. B VIII, Bl. 1498; Welzer, *Täter*, 146.
25. Hilberg, *Destruction*, 649.
26. Henry Friedländer, lecture: 'Motive und Handlungsstrategien führender NS-Täter', Volkshochschule Hanover, Germany, 26 January 2001.
27. Hilberg, *Destruction*, 640.

Part IV
Perpetrators and Genocide

8
The Organisation of Genocide: Perpetration in Comparative Perspective

Donald Bloxham

Introduction: on the comparative study of genocide

The Holocaust, it is sometimes said, is unique. There are two possible meanings of the word 'unique' here. One is rather obvious and unarguable: the idea that all historical events are in some way unprecedented and unrepeatable in the precise combination of factors inducing and constituting them. Yet by that yardstick the Holocaust is only one unique episode amongst an infinite number. What scholars of the Holocaust tend to mean when they describe it as unique, or as 'uniquely unique', as some have averred, is that it has some metaphysical quality rendering it 'different' in a special way from any other historical event, including even extreme events such as other genocides.[1]

Since 'uniqueness' in the latter sense is a value judgement, however, it is not susceptible to proof by any proper means of testing. (Who is to decide what criterion constitutes the measuring stick, or to declare that any attempt to measure must by definition be flawed?) It remains an assertion, and, further, one stemming from the claim for attention to the subject when, prior to the 1980s and more particularly the 1990s, it was not a matter of universal interest. Academic suspicion of the very idea that something can be denoted 'unique' in this way should be further stimulated by the way that the term is so clearly invested with communal sentiment among the erstwhile victim group. In other words, it is a highly politicised term.

As a result of the battle about uniqueness, the comparative study of genocide has itself sometimes been used rather politically, in the sense either of 'proving' that the Holocaust was somehow qualitatively 'different' to all other genocides, or in proving that certain other select genocides were 'like' the Holocaust (see below). Neither of these ends is actually the function of comparative history as properly conceived, which is concerned equally with similarities and differences. The study of war, or revolution, or nationalism, or any number of other phenomena, has greatly benefited from the comparative approach with few of the attendant problems that have beset Holocaust and genocide studies.

Comparative study is not, however, only about the examination of broadly similar events occurring at different times and in different places with the intention of shedding light on those particular events themselves. The very act of identifying similar phenomena in different temporal and cultural contexts suggests that those phenomena – in this case, genocides – are not *sui generis*, or aberrations, but are somehow characteristic of or at least stimulated by wider historical patterns, wider trends in human development. In that sense, comparative study may at the same time be contextual even when examining ostensibly different sets of historical circumstances, just as it is possible to form empirically grounded theories of international and intergroup relations more generically. This sort of comparative-contextual work, as exemplified persistently by the work of Mark Levene and latterly by Michael Mann, is a highly useful way of explaining why genocides happen when and where they do, and, thereby, the mindsets of murderous elites as they embody the paranoias and hatreds of the genocidal moment.[2]

Comparative study may also be used to shed light on the internal dynamics of genocidal processes. For the purposes of this volume, it can be used to examine some of the circumstances in which individuals from outside the circles of ideologues and leaders – the grand decision-makers and tone-setters – participated in mass murder. In other words, this chapter examines not why genocide was chosen or happened-upon as a policy option, but how large numbers of people were incorporated into the execution of the policy without them necessarily subscribing to the letter of the ideology that inevitably guided the crime. It by no means proposes a comprehensive explanation, and, indeed, seeks to raise questions as much as answer them.

Comparing the perpetrators and perpetration of genocide

A problem confronting any student of genocide is that the incontrovertible evidence of mass participation in many instances of mass murder across time, space and culture lends itself to the conclusion that a killing potential actually resides within many, perhaps most humans. Arguments based on specific national or cultural histories as a way of explaining genocide – be these sophisticated discussions of the particular nature of German anti-Semitism, of the German 'special path' of historical development, or cruder, quasi-racist 'explanations' for genocide in Rwanda or Yugoslavia based respectively on stereotypes of brutal African tribal conflict or age-old Balkan enmities – are intrinsically limited because, while they may in some instances explain why a particular group was targeted, they do not necessarily explain why the explosion occurred when and how it did. More emphatically, they cannot explain a propensity to similar systematic mass slaughter, and mass participation in it, that is embodied in other cultural or national situations. (Consider that by some estimates, 200,000 'modern, civilised' Germans were involved at different levels in the murder of the Jews, and up to a million Rwandans out of a population of eight million in the 1994 genocide.) But the sad truth of the general potential to be drawn into murder need not make us throw up our hands, give up the task of differentiation and specific explanation by resort to grand generalisations about the flaws in some universal 'human nature'. The situational factor is always key: the *context* in which the killing occurs.

The very evidence of mass participation in most genocides shows that the context is generally more important than the disposition and beliefs of the individual perpetrator, since in the 'right' situation so many people of demonstrably different characters and values participate, and participate even in the most intimate and bloody forms of face-to-face killing. Context can mean legitimation, rationalisation and justification of acts that might otherwise seem illegitimate, irrational or unjustifiable – the determinants of the changing 'normative frame'. Context can also mean the sort of psychological distancing, perhaps by segmentation and routinisation of tasks, that can make involvement in extreme acts easier even for perpetrators without an ideological commitment to the task in hand – a condition facilitating mass murder even without changing the 'normative frame' for the individual agent in question.

This is not to disavow the significance of individual decision-making, character and conscience. Such matters remain vital, but unfortunately the evidence suggests that in only a small minority of cases does the ethical choice boil down to the proposition: 'to participate or not to participate'. Instead, while personal disposition and/or belief seem generally to be insufficient to forestall involvement in genocide or persecution if the 'right' socio-political context is in place, character and personal attitude assuredly can influence the zeal the perpetrator brings to the task, and the status he or she enjoys within the perpetrator hierarchy.

Meaningfully putting the emphasis on context is not easy, however. 'Context' is a slippery concept, since there is always more than one context in play in any given situation, and these are often the subjects of competing claims to primacy in determining behaviour. Anthropologists, sociologists, social psychologists and historians might all lay differing claims for the most significant context, be that the cultural norms and phobias of the society from which the perpetrators spring; the organisation and orientation of political structures within which the perpetrators operate; the behavioural and power relations between individuals in particular social situations; or the immediate physical circumstances of the act. Each of these perspectives is valuable, and any may have relatively more explanatory power for any given perpetrator than one of the other perspectives, but none on its own provides a total, generalisable explanation. There is, again, a banal reason for this, one based on the 'unique' make-up of any given person. On a different level, one of useful generalisation, we may extrapolate from Thomas Sandkühler's observation that the 'Final Solution' was *arbeitsteilig*: a crime based upon a division of labour.[3]

Since the reason for a division of labour is to bring people of different aptitudes together efficiently in the creation of a single end-product, it follows that the person(s) at each stage of the production process will have a different input and, probably, relationship to the finished product. There is no reason why all contributors across the board would have to have the same attitude to their task (a factory production-line worker in an armaments factory need not have a passion for the creation of armaments, simply a desire to make a living), and a similar disposition might not even be helpful, since more skilful workers, for instance, would not benefit in their delicate task from – say – the greater physicality involved in the work of a more rudimentary contributor. An entrepreneur, a middle-manager and a labourer cannot have the same balance of incentives, activities and aspirations. The interests of the shareholder differ again.

What is true for any individual organisation is also true for the overall political-economic system within which that organisation functions, since the overall system will divide tasks and responsibilities between organisations, meaning, in turn, that different organisations have a different ethos within which their own divisions of labour operate. The same goes for genocide. As roles, responsibilities and investments vary, so do actions, perspectives and motives, both at the inter- and intra-organisational levels.

The study of the overall system of genocide and of the system's contingent organisations are, therefore related. Both are fruitful areas of enquiry in assessing motivation for perpetration, since both shed light on the relationship between, on the one hand, power structures and 'high' ideology and, on the other hand, 'lower' social, cultural or psychological considerations. The macro-level study of the system sheds light on the relationship between genocidal elites (the ideological leaders and their spheres of direct activity) and the rest of the socio-political structure (organised society as a whole, to the extent that it is co-opted in the execution of genocide, or imbibes the spirit of the project). The meso- and micro-level study of the individual organisations sheds light on the relationship between the ethos and goals of any given organisation and character-based and psychological factors influencing the motivation of individuals within that organisation.

Since every genocide is by definition a large, complex and to some degree organised exercise, every genocide will to some extent employ principles of division of labour, a division that will both reflect and create different attitudes towards the task in hand, depending on the roles it assigns (or the roles different perpetrators assume). This means that within any given case of genocide there is no one profile of a perpetrator that even approximately fits all. Accordingly, while it may be possible to have a theory of genocide as a phenomenon, it is probably impossible to have a theory of the *perpetrator* of genocide. An approximate *taxonomy* or *typology* of the perpetrators of genocide may, however, be possible. And, thinking comparatively, it is possible to conduct at least as meaningful a study of perpetrators and perpetrator groups at roughly the same place in the division of labour across different historical instances of genocide as a comparative study of different groups of perpetrators at different positions within the same genocidal machinery.

Levene has observed that many genocides share approximately similar pyramidal structures (though this need not obtain for certain genocides perpetrated in colonial situations at a great distance from the metropolitan centre of the perpetrator polity):

> At the top a small group of core planners and directors in control of the key apparatus of state, government as well as army including military intelligence; below them a significantly larger group of administrators, army officers and police chiefs as well as, where appropriate, professional specialists... [and] finally at the bottom of the pyramid a mass of hands-on operatives.

[The final] much larger group always contains some or all of the following: the military, especially military police and elite units, secret or special police, and specially organised para-military militias recruited from party activists, particularly from closely aligned party youth movements and/or from criminal elements in society... These participants tend to represent the front-line strike-forces. But they are nearly always reinforced... by a range of other auxiliaries. The social composition of this element tends to be considerably more diverse. In addition to ordinary police it regularly includes units and militias recruited from displaced elements of the ethnic majority population, although also often from other ethnic or minority groups... Sometimes, these may be only nominally under central command and hence operate quasi-autonomously. Ordinary civilians may also participate on direction of the authorities or of their own volition.[4]

Using the language of economics, some of these organisational levels, or parts thereof, are *necessary* for the enactment of genocide (meaning that in their absence there would be no crime at all), some are *sufficient* (meaning that in their absence the crime would not take on its full dimensions or particular colouring). To consider for instance the genocide of the Jews, by the same token that SS and Nazi party offices (the *necessary*, ideological elements) would not have needed as they did to provide the policy lead if a general official consensus to extremism existed, the 'Final Solution' would not have been what it was without the participation of many of the regular organs of the German state, including face-to-face killers drawn from the ranks of ostensibly 'ordinary Germans', bureaucracies in Allied or satellite countries, and a number of private enterprises (the *sufficient*, structural elements). In the interests of a study of the motivation of perpetrators, what this means is that the core perpetrator organisations had to rely on others with less radical commitment to Jewish policy and, therefore, a different balance of internal motivations. Incidentally, this is not to suggest that the only leadership in Nazi Jewish policy came from SS or party circles. The genocidal elite, like others in other cases, was an open one, in the sense that individuals committed energetically to the policy but working outside such vanguard organisations could certainly partake of policy leadership. Personnel *within* each level of the process were to varying degrees interchangeable with each other, with a few individuals, most obviously the very highest leaders, but also the most specialised experts, the least so. Interchangeability *between* levels was again variable, but was generally lower than within levels.

This chapter seeks to shed light simultaneously on the organisation of the perpetration of the Holocaust and of other genocides by the examination of a case in which both useful comparisons *and* contrasts can be made with the 'Final Solution' and other instances. That case is the Armenian genocide ('Aghet' in Armenian), a mass murder that is invoked more frequently than any other in comparison with the murder of European Jewry. The philosophy underpinning the discussion is that outlined at the outset: namely to get away from ahistorical contentions about 'uniqueness' or 'non-uniqueness', and to treat the Shoah, like the Aghet, or the Porrajmos (the Romany word for the Nazi annihilation of their people), or the genocide of the 'Assyrian' people (an often overlooked crime perpetrated by the same regime that murdered the Armenians), or any other case, as residents on a historical *continuum* of organised mass murder, each instance of which has both its own peculiar features and some commonalities with others on the continuum. Correspondingly, the conclusions that follow do not imply any sort of hierarchy of genocides: just as comparison does not mean equation, differentiation does not mean either veneration or degradation.

The Armenian genocide: an overview

During the months from autumn 1914 to summer 1915 the government of the Ottoman Empire made a series of decisions resulting in the destruction of its Armenian Christian population. The pre-war Armenian community had been scattered throughout the empire. The majority belonged to the Armenian Apostolic church, though there were also Catholic and Protestant minorities. There were particular Armenian concentrations, though not demographic majorities except at the local level, in the historic Armenian settlements. These were Cilicia, to the north and north-west of the Gulf of Alexandretta on the Mediterranean coast, where Armenians had lived since the early middle ages, and the eastern provinces of Anatolia, where Armenian settlement dates back 3,000 years. The region of Anatolia itself is bordered by the Mediterranean, Cilicia, Syria, Mesopotamia, Persia, the Caucasus and the Black Sea. Together, Anatolia and Cilicia constitute most of the territory of modern Turkey.

During the First World War the Armenians of eastern Anatolia were either killed *in situ*, which was the fate of most of the men and male youths, or deported to the deserts of modern-day Iraq or Syria in the south. Along these deportation routes they were subject to massive and repeated depredations – rape, kidnap, mutilation and outright killing – at the hands of Ottoman gendarmes, paramilitary irregulars, local Muslim populations of varying denominations and some army units, while huge numbers simply perished from exposure, starvation and thirst. The kidnapped and other surviving women, and many orphans, were then subject to enforced conversions to Islam as a means of assimilation into the 'new Turkey'.

The deported Armenians of Cilicia and parts of western Anatolia were not subject to the same level of harassment on their journeys southward; they passed relatively unmolested to their desert fates or to exile from their homelands. Thus, though varying to an extent according to local conditions, these death marches served the same overall purpose – the destruction of significant collective Armenian existence on Turkish soil. Many of those who made it to the desert concentration centres were massacred in a series of attacks in 1916. Together, these events comprise the Armenian genocide. Some one million Ottoman Armenians died, half of the pre-war population and two thirds of those deported.

The primary perpetrators of the genocide were the leaders and central committee of the 'Committee of Union and Progress' (*Ittihad ve Terraki Cemiyeti*; CUP), the ruling faction in the Ottoman government. The CUP was formed out of the heterogeneous opposition groups collectively known as the Young Turks that developed in the late nineteenth century. The nationalism of the CUP became more pronounced and exclusive during the death throes of the Ottoman Empire in Europe in the Balkan wars of 1912–13, against the backdrop of a longer erosion of Ottoman territories, particularly in the last quarter of the nineteenth century. In justification of its deportation policy, the CUP pointed to Armenian nationalist agitation, contending that it aimed to tear apart by secession what remained of the empire. Given the history of Russian sponsorship of Balkan Christian independence or autonomy movements, and at a time of existential crisis for the empire during a war with its 'hereditary' Muscovite enemy, the CUP also suspected Russian-Armenian military collaboration in the Caucasus-Persian-Ottoman border regions. Thus, according to the CUP's professed logic, the Armenian deportations were a 'military necessity'.[5]

Yet while undoubtedly precipitated by the war, the deportations and massacres served the purpose of solving by violence what European diplomats had dubbed 'the Armenian question'. They enabled the CUP to remove a population depicted as a collective threat to continued

Ottoman rule over eastern Anatolia. Moreover, the events of 1915 cannot be seen in the isolation of the war years. The political agitation for reform or autonomy in the Armenian community from the 1870s had itself been exacerbated by large-scale massacres that had occurred across the empire in 1894–6 and in Cilicia in 1909, and was also influenced by the many everyday oppressions and discriminations that had intensified in many rural areas in the second half of the nineteenth century. While there is no straight line connecting the massacres of the 1890s with the genocide of 1915, for the guiding ideologies of the perpetrators were different, and the earlier killings were not conducted under the same sort of close centralised authority as their later counterparts, both occurred in the key context of the empire's terminal decline. Moreover the very fact of the 1894–6 and 1909 killings was a precedent, shaping the mindset of state and victims alike.

The organisation and organisations of the Armenian genocide

There are undoubtedly many points of real comparison between the Armenian genocide and the Holocaust, as scholars such as Robert Melson have pointed out.[6] One additional and rather politicised reason many scholars seek to co-identify the genocides springs from contemporary Turkish state denial of the former and the wish to gain legitimacy for recognition by association with a case (the Holocaust) that is universally recognised. For present purposes, one of the most important focuses of comparison with the Holocaust has been on the administration of destruction. Here some of the scholarship on the Armenian genocide has certainly crossed the line separating helpful comparative/contrastive study from the more-or-less complete co-identification of cases.

Vahakn N. Dadrian, the most prominent scholar of the Armenian genocide, has also been the main proponent of the argument for co-identification.[7] The most recent restatement of much of Dadrian's case is Peter Balakian's bestseller, *The Burning Tigris*. Balakian alights on the use of the telegraph system in the issuance of deportation and killing orders, and the use of trains for deportation of some Armenians through Syria, as evidence of the modernity of the destruction machinery. An accompanying recitation of the Ottoman chain of command and supervision is adduced as evidence that the genocide was perpetrated by a 'fine-tuned bureaucracy'. With the murderous combination of technology and bureaucracy thus 'proven', the implicit comparison with the 'Final Solution' becomes explicit when the reader is told that the Teşkilat-ı Mahsusa, the 'Special Organisation' that murdered many of the Armenian deportees, 'was similar to the Reich Security Main Office's Einsatzgruppen' (Wolfgang Gust has compared it to the SS), and that the civilian chief of the Special Organisation, Bahaettin Şakir, 'played a role not unlike that of Nazi Reich Security Head, Reinhard Heydrich'.[8] But it is difficult to reconcile Balakian's depiction with the wider realities of Anatolian society and power relations in the late Ottoman state.

Enough organs of the Ottoman state *were* involved in the destruction process, and enough of its interests vested in the removal of the Armenians by some means, for the genocide to be seen as a state project. Muslim Ottoman social and political elites had undoubtedly been radicalised in an anti-Christian direction by the massive territorial losses of the previous half-century, and by the accompanying abuse and ethnic cleansing of millions of Muslims by the newly emergent Christian states in the Balkans. Moreover, many state officials had been complicit in the pre-First World War massacres, and many would benefit materially from – and thus be implicated in – the First World War genocide, just as would many Muslim landowners and the Turkic-Muslim 'national economy' generally.[9] The state ideology under the Hamidian regime which preceded that of the CUP, was a neo-conservative attempt to unify Muslims into a more robust political unit, and implicitly acted to return Christians to their 'rightful', subordinate place in the socio-political hierarchy. Though this 'pan-Islamism' differed from the increasingly secular (if still religiously informed) brand of ideological complex driving the CUP to outright genocide in the First World War, in which Christians were placed completely beyond the pale, the successive ideologies shared an increasing suspicion of non-Muslim populations and a preparedness to use massacre as a means of combating putative secessionist threats. However, it is still debatable whether by the time of the First World War the most radical elements of the CUP were expressive of an exterminatory drive embodied in the established state infrastructure as a whole.[10]

The Interior Ministry housed the two bodies most closely involved in the ordering and administration of the major Armenian deportations during the First World War – that is, those deportations beyond the smaller ones ordered by the military from inside or within the vicinity of actual war zones – in the Directorate for the Settlement of Tribes and Immigrants (IAMM) and the Directorate for General Security (EUM). Parts of the Ottoman army and police forces are implicated in the killing of Armenians in eastern Anatolia *in situ* and during deportations, and the 'Special Organisation' (if we can use what may be a rather catch-all and imprecise term) was an irregular military formation, though directed in its killing actions by the CUP through members of the party's influential central committee.[11] Yet a number of important qualifying factors must be taken into account when assessing the character of the machinery of destruction and the relative roles of party, state, centre and periphery.

Firstly, if one index of the 'modernity' of a state is the extent of its control over its peripheries, then the Ottoman Empire even during the CUP period must be considered *modernising* rather than *modern*. The government was still very concerned to improve its communications and intelligence infrastructure and to increase its policing of heavily ethnically mixed border areas. The state's administrative apparatus in eastern Anatolia, where most Armenians lived, was relatively rudimentary, despite the obsession by the time of the Balkan wars with the ethnic make-up of the empire – an obsession that resulted in a programme of 'mapping' the empire according to its population profile.[12] The inadequacy, for instance, of the official machinery put in place in 1915 to administer the confiscation, sale and distribution of the property of the deported Armenians was illustrated by the high level of personal corruption attending the expropriation process.[13] The ongoing desire by the centre for closer control over the periphery would continue to be illustrated into the 1930s by the state's post-war assault on the eastern Anatolian Kurdish populations and their tribal networks and economies.

Secondly, the layer of central administration involved in issuing the major deportation orders in 1915 was comparatively thin, involving the higher echelons of Talaat, Minister of the Interior and CUP triumvir and his subordinates in the IAMM and EUM. Talaat might aptly be described as a micro-manager of the deportation process, regularly checking on the execution of his instructions and acquiring feedback on the process of expulsion of deportees and settlement of Muslims in their stead. He was aided by Şükrü Kaya of the IAMM, who frequently oversaw the enactment of the deportations in the provinces. The IAMM itself was established by the CUP in 1913 to marshal the settlement in Anatolia of Muslim refugees fleeing the Balkan wars and the new Balkan states, and as such was more closely identified with the ruling faction than were other state organs.[14] Meanwhile, party men, most notably the central committee member Bahaettin Şakir, also policed the Special Organisation actions 'on the ground'. Bahaettin Şakir himself frequently drove from province to province, exhorting his men to keep up the tempo of killing.[15]

Thirdly, and closely related to the second factor just enumerated, the murderous assaults on Armenian deportation convoys were distinctly under-bureaucratised. The perpetration machinery as whole was relatively 'bottom-heavy' in comparison with that of the 'Final Solution'. In some ways this was functionally useful. The exploitation of the telegraph system was a time-tested means of keeping the paper trail to a minimum, and of supplementing or supplanting paper orders; the latter aim was rather successfully achieved when we reflect on how the paucity of Ottoman documentation on the actual killing process (as opposed to the deportations themselves, which are reasonably well documented[16]) has sustained denialist historians. At the same time, the deployment of irregular forces for 'dirty work' was a time-honoured tradition in the Ottoman domains and in parts of the Balkans: their actions provided governments with a means of avoiding the blame for atrocities – 'plausible deniability'.[17] But another part of the explanation for the limited input from the state bureaucracy in the Armenian case was that the process was driven by the CUP within the state, to the extent that some cabinet ministers were kept in the dark about the true course of Armenian policy.[18] In the lead-up to war and genocide there was an attempt at fuller penetration of the state machinery by party representatives, as CUP emissaries were sent to the provinces and CUP members were appointed to the state posts of provincial governorships. Yet this 'coordination' – by a group that came to power by coup in 1908 and restored itself in 1913 during the crisis period of the Balkan wars – had not reached the levels achieved in the later 'totalitarian' states, and had to be pressed forward even during the genocide. Thus when general deportation had become policy in 1915 it was rigidly enforced by party agents with many provincial and district governors shadowed by watchful 'responsible secretaries' of the CUP to ensure appropriate execution of their central instructions.

The most enthusiastic killers in the provinces, men such as Dr Mehmed Reşid in Diyarbakir, who set the pace for mass murder even before the fully-fledged policy of genocide was in place, were recent appointments holding senior party posts and state posts (provincial and district governorships), as did many of the *Gauleiter* corps sent to govern parts of Nazi-occupied Eastern Europe.[19] Reluctant Ottoman officials were replaced by more enthusiastic ones, and some were killed.[20] All of this is suggestive of a concerted effort to maintain central direction of an extreme policy developed in a situation of wartime crisis by a regime paranoid about its hold on power and seeking to consolidate that hold.[21] The wartime genocide indeed served to accelerate the CUP's nationalistic penetration of the Ottoman case, in contrast, for instance, to the Nazi and Soviet cases, where greater penetration of the state machinery was conducted earlier as part of the conscious preparation for war that drove both regimes in the 1930s.

The CUP machinery of destruction also featured an overall contractual arrangement between ideological leaders and agents of execution somewhat different from its Nazi equivalent, notwithstanding the fact that the Nazis deployed some Eastern Europeans in the murder process under duress. Some of the manpower of the paramilitary forces comprised Muslim refugees from Russian rule in the Caucasus and former Ottoman territories in the Balkans. These were men who would aid in ethnic warfare and help stimulate Muslim insurgency in Tsarist territories, and many of them were strongly anti-Christian. But common criminals released from jail for the purpose figured very heavily, just as such people would be deployed in large numbers in ethnic cleansing and massacre in the 1990s in Serbian paramilitary forces. In both 1915 and the 1990s, such men were attracted to killing by the possibilities of enriching themselves from their victims, not to mention the opportunities for sexual and sadistic gratification. Historically, such bands had been expected to live off plunder. Similar motives influenced the various ordinary Muslims that also attacked Armenian deportation caravans once the tacit message had been transmitted from the CUP that the Armenians were fair game by the very fact of their removal.[22]

Conclusions

As we saw in the introduction to this chapter, in the Nazi-German state genocide was led by an ideologised core with strong party-political affiliations, often instrumentalising new, vanguard organisations fused onto the existing state structure. Heydrich's office would be a prime example of this phenomenon, blending the radicalism of the SS with the established authority of the state's police forces. There was a balance to be taken into account between the *ideological radicalism* provided by these vanguard organisations and the *legitimacy* provided by the command of the existing state structure. This was a shifting balance, however, and one that developed into a symbiotic relationship, as the Nazi penetration of the state machinery (via such acts as the 1933 'Law for the Restoration of the Professional Civil Service') over six years of successful rule prior to the Second World War simultaneously radicalised the state and enhanced the perceived legitimacy of the Nazis and their radical goals. Radicalism provided direction, while legitimacy helped facilitate mass participation by members of the populace and the civil service who themselves were not avid Nazis but were loyal citizens of the German state.

The sense of the legitimacy of the Nazi project as a whole, when compounded with division of labour principles, undoubtedly helps account for the fact that there is no recorded case of execution or even serious punishment for individual German functionaries refusing to participate in the most extreme aspects of that project – genocide. In fact, the evidence suggests that relative to many other cases of state-sponsored mass murder, the Nazi-German bureaucracy needed little goading to participate in genocide. The Nazi case might be contrasted, for instance, with the experience of the USSR in the 1920s and 1930s, when, in a regime with arguably less legitimacy in the eyes of its people, the bureaucracy itself was regularly exposed to violent purging as a way of disciplining it ideologically.[23]

In all states that have committed mass murder, the radical-ideological penetration of the public bureaucracy and, indeed, of the public sphere more broadly, has been a matter of degree. The same is true for the extent of the bureaucratisation of atrocity. As for the main subject of the above study, the Armenian genocide, this did have aspects of the bureaucratic about it, as is inevitable for any state project, but on a continuum of bureaucratised criminality it would fall some distance away from the 'Final Solution'.

The core perpetrators of the CUP acted ruthlessly to clear obstacles to their genocidal design, but they were also keen to avoid potential obstructions, as well as to keep the appearance of the innocence of the state. Ultimately they showed it was possible to circumvent parts of the state machinery and overcome a relatively underdeveloped administrative infrastructure by, on the one hand, micro-management from a committed central core, bolstered by a number of core agents infiltrating the provinces and sometimes using personal contacts to organise killing squads;[24] and, on the other hand, by the deployment of masses of executioners from outside the direct control of the regular state framework in the case of some local Muslims and, in the case of the criminals of the paramilitary organisations, beyond the boundaries of society altogether.

Shaping their system of murder thus made little difference to the victims, but it does cast some light on the incorporation and motivation of Ottoman officials and agents in the process. Indeed, whatever we are now discovering about the extent of corruption in the Nazi empire,[25] 'ordinary' criminal incentives for face-to-face killers in the Ottoman case were proportionately far more important than in the 'Final Solution'. Indeed, the irregular, mercenary basis on which many of these killers were recruited illustrates by absence and contrast the motive significance of the sort of institutionalised, hierarchical norms that helped some (but only some) salaried officials, employees and even policemen of many different sorts in Nazi Germany to partake in genocide as simply a part of their job.

Notes

1. Lucy Dawidowicz, 'The Holocaust was Unique in Intent, Scope, and Effect', *Center Magazine*, 14(4) (1981), 56–64; Yehuda Bauer, 'The Place of the Holocaust in Contemporary History', *Studies in Contemporary Jewry*, 1 (1984), 201–24; Emil Fackenheim, 'Why the Holocaust is Unique', *Judaism*, 5 (2001), 438–47. See also the sources detailed in the lengthy footnote in Steven T. Katz, *The Holocaust in Historical Context*, Vol. 1: *The Holocaust and Mass Death before the Modern Age* (New York, 1994), 27. Aspects of the arguments of this chapter have been made in greatly expanded form in Donald Bloxham, 'Organized Mass Murder: Structure, Participation and Motivation in Comparative Perspective', *Holocaust and Genocide Studies*, 22 (2008), 203–45.
2. Mark Levene, *Genocide in the Age of the Nation State*, 2 vols (London, 2005); Michael Mann, *The Dark Side of Democracy: Explaining Ethnic Cleansing* (Cambridge, 2005).
3. Thomas Sandkühler, 'Die Täter des Holocausts', in Karl Heinrich Pohl (ed.), *Wehrmacht und Vernichtungspolitik: Militär im nationalsozialistischen System* (Göttingen, 1999), 39–65.
4. Levene, *Genocide*, vol. 1, 99f.
5. For general histories of the genocide, see for instance the books cited in note 10 below.
6. Robert Melson, *Revolution and Genocide: On the Armenian Genocide and the Holocaust* (Chicago, 1992).
7. For example, Vahakn N. Dadrian, 'The Convergent Aspects of the Armenian and Jewish Cases of Genocide: a Reinterpretation of the Concept of Holocaust', *Holocaust and Genocide Studies*, 3(2) (1988), 151–69.
8. Peter Balakian, *The Burning Tigris: the Armenian Genocide and America's Response* (New York, 2003), 182f. See also ch. 14 as a whole ('Government-Planned Genocide'), 185f. ('A Fine-Tuned Bureaucracy'), and 190–5 ('The Railway'). See also Wolfgang Gust, *Der Völkermord an den Armeniern. Die Tragödie des ältesten Christenvolkes der Welt* (Munich, 1993).
9. On the idea of a Muslim-Turkic 'national economy', see Zafer Toprak, *Türkey'de 'Milli Iktisat' (1908–1918)* (Ankara, 1982); on plunder, Hilmar Kaiser, 'Armenian Property, Ottoman Law and Nationality Policies during the Armenian Genocide, 1915–1916', in Olaf Farschid et al. (eds), *The First World War as Remembered in the Countries of the Eastern Mediterranean* (Beirut, 2006), 49–71.
10. For different perspectives on the development of anti-Armenianism in the late Ottoman Empire, see Vahakn N. Dadrian, *The History of the Armenian Genocide* (Providence, 1995); Donald Bloxham, *The Great Game of Genocide: Imperialism, Nationalism, and the Destruction of the Ottoman Armenians* (Oxford, 2005). On the ideology of the CUP, see M. Şükrü Hanioğlu, *Preparation for a Revolution: the Young Turks, 1902–1908* (New York, 2001).

11. On the variety of police and paramilitary forces used by the Ottomans, see Edward J. Erickson, 'Armenian Massacres: New Records Undercut Old Blame', *Middle East Quarterly*, 13(3) (2006), 67–75.
12. Fuat Dündar, *Ittihat ve Terakki'nin Müslümanlari Iskân Politikası (1913–1918)* (Istanbul, 2001).
13. Christian Gerlach, 'Nationsbildung im Krieg: Wirtschaftliche Faktoren bei der Vernichtung der Armenier und beim Mord an den ungarischen Juden', in Hans-Lukas Kieser and Dominik Schaller (eds), *Der Völkermord an den Armeniern und die Shoah* (Zurich, 2002), 347–422, here 388.
14. Dündar, *Ittihat ve Terakki*; on Talaat as micro-manager, see Ugur Ü. Üngör, ' "A Reign of Terror": CUP Rule in Diyarbekir Province, 1913–1918' (MA thesis: Amsterdam, 2005).
15. Vahakn N. Dadrian, 'The Complicity of the Party, the Government and the Military: Select Parliamentary and Judicial Documents', *Journal of Political and Military Sociology*, 22 (1994), 29–96, here 59–60.
16. Many deportation orders are in the Prime Ministry, General Directorate of the State Archives of the Turkish Republic (ed.), *Osmanlı Belgelerinde Ermeniler (1915–1920)* (Ankara, 1995).
17. James J. Reid, 'Militarism, Partisan War and Destructive Inclinations in Ottoman Military History: 1854–1918', *Armenian Review*, 39(3) (1986), 1–21, here 6–11; Arnold J. Toynbee, *The Western Question in Greece and Turkey: a Study in the Contact of Civilizations* (London, 1923), 278–80.
18. Vahakn N. Dadrian, 'The Documentation of the World War I Armenian Massacres in the Proceedings of the Turkish Military Tribunal', *Journal of Political and Military Sociology*, 22 (1994), 97–132, here 98.
19. On the post-war trial of these 'responsible secretaries', see Annette Höss, 'Die türkischen Kriegsgerichtsverhandlungen 1919–1921' (PhD, Vienna, 1991). Also see Dadrian, 'Documentation'; on 'coordination', see Üngör, ' "A Reign of Terror" '; on *Gauleiter*, see Peter Hüttenberger, *Die Gauleiter: Studie zum Wandel des Machtgefüges in der NSDAP* (Stuttgart, 1969), 173f.
20. *Osmanlı Belgelerinde Ermeniler*, 140, Interior Ministry to Cemal, 26 April 1916 on the dispatch of an inspector to Marash because of leniency towards Armenians by the district governor. On killings, see Hilmar Kaiser, *At the Crossroads of Der Zor: Death, Survival, and Humanitarian Resistance in Aleppo, 1915–1917* (Princeton, NJ, 2001), 15f.
21. Donald Bloxham, 'The Armenian Genocide of 1915–16: Cumulative Radicalisation and the Development of a Destruction Policy', *Past and Present*, 181(1) (2003), 141–91.
22. Bloxham, *The Great Game of Genocide*, 42, 70, 93; Jacques Semelin, 'Analysis of a Mass Crime: Ethnic Cleansing in the Former Yugoslavia, 1991–1999', in Robert Gellately and Ben Kiernan (eds), *The Specter of Genocide: Mass Murder in Historical Perspective* (Cambridge, 2003), 353–70, here 366f.
23. See Part I of Henry Rousso (ed.), *Stalinism and Nazism: History and Memory Compared* (Lincoln, Nebraska, 2004).
24. On personal contacts, see Üngör, ' "A Reign of Terror" '.
25. Frank Bajohr, *Parvenüs und Profiteure: Korruption in der NS-Zeit* (Frankfurt/Main, 2001); Götz Aly, *Hitlers Volksstaat: Raub, Rassenkrieg und nationaler Sozialismus* (Frankfurt/Main, 2005).

9
International Law after the Nuremberg Trials and Rwanda: How Do Perpetrators Justify Themselves?

Gerd Hankel

Genocide, crimes against humanity and war crimes all have two things in common: the number of victims is very high and numerous perpetrators are involved. Thus, these are mass crimes in a double sense. Although according to legal definitions a single act of murder can constitute genocide, case law – in particular as it has been handed down by international criminal courts – categorises crimes as genocide only when it is apparent that the number of victims substantially exceeds the dimensions of normal crimes (even when precise numbers are not or not yet available).[1] The same holds in the case of crimes against humanity; here, the legal definition presupposes a widespread or systematic attack directed against a civilian population. And war crimes are especially abominable because they are generally committed on a large scale and as part of a plan or policy.

Perpetrators of mass crimes must be held accountable for their deeds. From a contemporary perspective and in view of the sheer dimensions of the crimes committed, this would seem to be an obvious demand and yet, for a long time, this was by no means the case. For perpetrators of mass violence were frequently members of a group – an army or militia unit for example – who acted on behalf and by order of a sovereign ruler or state. Independent of the form of rule, the sovereign state functioned as a kind of shield that protected the perpetrators from punishment. *Par in parem non habet iurisdictionem* is the legal principle that stipulates that a state may not exercise jurisdiction over another state. In the case of war crimes, exceptions occasionally were made, but it is questionable whether these occurred on the basis of an emerging sense of justice that recognised the need to limit state sovereignty in this context. It seems more likely that the underlying motive was the desire for revenge, for which demands for legal redress provided a convenient camouflage.[2]

A sense of justice that held that state sovereignty could not be invoked to justify all manner of crimes perpetrated in the name of the state did not begin to emerge until the First World War. Articles 227 to 230 of the Versailles Treaty stipulated that German politicians and military personnel who had allegedly committed war crimes or ordered others to perpetrate them were to be tried before military courts. Even former emperor Wilhelm II was to have been brought to trial before an international tribunal. Although this plan failed, it was this experience of failure which later prompted the Allies, in the aftermath of the Second World War, to have the National Socialist regime's military and civilian leaders stand trial before the International Military Tribunal established in Nuremberg for this express purpose. In the face of the enormity of Nazi crimes, it was inconceivable that the perpetrators might enjoy impunity, merely by arguing that they had acted on behalf of the sovereign German Reich. Although the Allies briefly considered summarily executing those considered guilty of the most horrific crimes, they quickly abandoned the idea since, as Thomas Mann rightly noted, such a policy would have been equivalent to 'emulating the methods of the Nazis'.[3]

What began with the Trial of the Major War Criminals and continued, from 1946 to 1949, with the second generation of trials in Nuremberg against various members of the Nazi military and civilian hierarchy (referred to in German as the *Nachfolgeprozesse*) was thereafter taken up – after a brief delay – on a national level: those suspected of genocide or war crimes stood trial before courts of law in numerous countries, i.e. those that had been occupied by the Nazi regime or joined forces against it. In all of these proceedings, the aim was to determine the guilt of individuals, rather than applying a notion of collective guilt to justify convicting all of the defendants. The success of this approach differed from one country to the next and often depended on each country's specific history of suffering under German occupation. In general, one might assert that there was a difference between the East and the West: courts in those countries with legal systems more deeply rooted in a Continental European or Anglo-American tradition were likelier to adhere to the principles of due process. In other words, these courts were more inclined to take into account mitigating evidence brought forward by the defendants in reaching their judgements.[4]

For survivors and victims of Nazi crimes, observing the application of such legal principles was no doubt a painful experience. Aside from the emotional strain associated with the legal proceedings, the victims had no choice but to accept the fact that there could be no punishment that paralleled the enormity of their suffering. Moreover, they were forced to recognise that, aside from a few pathological cases, the perpetrators of Nazi Germany's horrific crimes were not the monsters one might have anticipated but simply ordinary people. Nonetheless, if the legal process is to adhere to the standards of civil society and not to end in revenge, then there is no alternative to accepting the rules of due process. Just as victims or survivors have the right to insist that the state initiate criminal proceedings on their behalf, so do perpetrators have a right to a fair trial. The fact that this will all too often leave many questions unanswered and create an almost desperate sense of helplessness has been demonstrated in numerous trials of suspected Nazi perpetrators. Justice is a very difficult concept to grasp. This realisation has since been shared by those who still hope to see 'just punishment' delivered to the perpetrators of the Rwandan genocide.

I

But let us now take a closer look at the justifications employed by perpetrators of genocide and crimes against humanity. How, and with what arguments do perpetrators seek to justify their acts? What arguments are accepted by international law and result in a perpetrator either not being penalised or receiving a mitigated sentence? And, most importantly, in what cases can the validity of such justifications be verified and when is such verification outside the realm of the legal process?

One of the fundamental principles of law holds that a perpetrator's conduct that clearly fulfils the definition of a crime can nonetheless go unpunished, if the defendant succeeds in demonstrating that, under the given circumstances, this conduct can be justified or excused in a form that renders it socially acceptable. In these cases, the accused aims to show that any individual of ordinary moral sensibility would have acted in the same manner in a similar situation and thus, the conduct cannot be sanctioned. Furthermore, states that are governed by the rule of law are obliged to refrain from penalising, or punishing too severely, those whose behaviour does not constitute a threat to the normative framework on which the state is based. Essential for the stability of such a state is that its citizens accept its authority, and the precondition for this acceptance is the citizens' perception that they are being treated justly. The same can be said, incidentally, of the international community, which acknowledges certain key legal principles such as the presumption of innocence or the *in dubio pro reo* rule as well as an understanding of criminal law based on the idea of individual responsibility. If there is to be sustained global support for prosecution of those suspected of genocide and similar crimes before international courts (whether by ad hoc tribunals such as those established for the former Yugoslavia and Rwanda or by the new permanent International Criminal Court), then the entire context of each individual case must be examined and acknowledged and blanket convictions avoided.

Such demands are easily formulated and seem clear-cut at first glance. But the inherent problems become apparent in cases in which the accused present all manner of statements to explain their actions – statements that will be examined by the court and possibly overruled. In other words, as indicated briefly above, according to national and international criminal law, there are a number of justifications to which the accused have recourse. The decisive and difficult problem involved in assessing such defences is to ascertain whether the accused is presenting a legally valid answer to a criminal charge or merely seeking to avoid punishment and/or save face as a morally upright person.

One might add that there is a clear conclusion to be drawn on the basis of these arguments: those whose motives for murder, torture or rape are of a pathological nature are denied recourse to legally recognised justifications. (I am leaving aside recently discussed positions that question the existence of individual free will, based on purported neurobiological evidence; by attempting to disprove the idea of free will and individual responsibility, such standpoints repudiate the foundation of the social contract.)[5] These perpetrators may, in extreme cases, be considered not guilty of an illegal act, because they are unable to recognise the illegality of their conduct. But whether or not this is the case and whether or not the accused can be shown to be suffering from a 'defect', such individuals must be prosecuted and/or separated from society in one way or another (preferably by being committed to a psychiatric clinic). Otherwise, if their justification was acknowledged and their conduct not sanctioned, then society would actively contribute to eroding its own norms.

The following discussion therefore applies to normal offenders or the kind of 'ordinary men' referred to in the titles of recent books.[6] If we analyse the crimes of such individuals against the background of the

Nazi regime or the genocidal regime in Rwanda, one striking similarity between the two cases is that, in both instances, crimes of mass violence were committed in a context of war or civil war. And yet, there is no such thing as a war without the use of force and without violence, as evidenced by Immanuel Kant's use of the well-known and still timely Greek proverb, according to which war produces more evildoers than it eliminates.[7] But even in war, there must be limits to the use of force. This follows simply from the fact that states have always had an interest in ensuring that a war can be ended; otherwise, they would be far less likely to begin one. It is for these reasons that laws and customs of war, which aim to define the limits to the use of force during war, have evolved over the centuries, in particular in the modern period. Codification of these laws and customs began at the end of the nineteenth century and by the First World War they were already in place.

In this period, the definition of a crime against humanity was by no means unequivocal. In 1915 and once again in 1919 during the conference leading up to the Versailles Treaty, France and Great Britain demanded that those responsible for the genocide against the Armenians be punished, arguing that the genocide constituted a crime against humanity that threatened the foundations of human civilisation. The delegates of the United States, Robert Lansing and James Brown Scott, dismissed these demands by contending that the notion of humanity was so ill-defined that it could not serve as a basis for criminal proceedings.[8] Apart from a few exceptions, the high-ranking politicians and military men of the Ottoman Empire were never indicted for crimes associated with the mass death of the Armenian population.[9] The vast majority of suspected perpetrators were never forced to account for their actions. Today, there are few who would deny that the lack of a systematic criminal investigation has contributed significantly to the fact that a complex web of lies, denial and suspicions continues to shroud the Armenian genocide. However, this is merely by way of a passing remark. What is important for our discussion is that, since 1945, when the process of dealing with the consequences of Nazi crimes and injustice within the legal system began, crimes against humanity have been recognised internationally as just that: as crimes. (Moreover, this recognition was achieved despite initial vigorous protest from Germany, which held that this contravened the legal principle prohibiting *ex post facto* laws.) This issue of recognition was less significant on a national level, since the national courts could deal with the typical manifestations of crimes against humanity as crimes directed against individuals, such as murder or assault, within the framework of their existing penal codes. But this approach did not reflect the true dimensions of the crimes perpetrated by the National Socialist regime. Being charged with or convicted of murder or assault is obviously something quite different than being charged with and punished for genocide.

Meanwhile, however, this problem is no longer relevant, since most countries have formally incorporated paragraphs about mass crimes into national law. This is especially the case with genocide, which was previously considered one type of crime against humanity but is now understood to be a crime in its own right. There is, however, a problem raised here that is important for our discussion. While the charges of war crimes and crimes against humanity presuppose intent on the part of the perpetrators, a defendant cannot be found guilty of these crimes unless there is sufficient evidence not only of a general intent to kill but also of a specific intent, namely, the intention to kill members of a group of people as 'a national, ethnic, racial or religious group'.[10] In other words, convicting a suspect of genocidal murder is more difficult than convicting a war criminal or someone who has committed crimes against humanity. Although the same affirmative defences are available in the first case as in the other two, depending on the circumstances, such defences may prove to be much more effective either against or in favour of an individual charged with genocide.

II

After this rather technical remark, we can turn to the question of how defendants justify their actions by examining a case that attracted considerable attention in the German media in spring 2006, sixty years after the end of the Second World War. One of the country's major national daily newspapers printed an article in May 2006 headlined 'Indictment of former SS men called for'.[11] The article referred to an incident that occurred in Italy in 1944, in which members of an SS unit under *Wehrmacht* command were ordered to combat partisan resistance in the vicinity of Sant' Anna di Stazzema and subsequently massacred village residents. A total of 560 people, including 65 children under the age of 10, were killed.[12] Until the 1990s, both Italian and German authorities neglected, impeded or abandoned investigations of the massacre. Since then, however, Italian courts have convicted a number of the accused *in absentia* and officials in Germany, where the surviving suspects now live, have initiated enquiries. These events of the year 1944 raise a number of issues that are decisive in assessing the actions of the accused; among them: Was an order issued that unambiguously stipulated that the entire village population was to be killed? Was it possible for the German soldiers involved to refuse orders to combat partisan resistance? Does the obligation to obey superior orders represent a justification for these individuals accused of committing war crimes?

These questions lead us to the justifications formulated by those accused of committing crimes under the National Socialist regime to mitigate or even deny their responsibility for criminal acts. Whether a perpetrator acted out of conviction or was more or less indifferent or reluctant at the time of committing the crime is, for the moment, irrelevant. Some frequent defences, such as 'I was forced to obey orders', might be put forward by a perpetrator who identified with the order and accepted it without criticism because it came from superiors. But the same statement might be made by a perpetrator who was in no doubt about the criminal nature of the act demanded of him but who was convinced that he was unable to refuse to obey the order. Moreover, this statement usually provides no information as to the type of crime; it might be employed in reference to shooting of hostages within the context of combating partisans or with regard to executions of women and children who had absolutely nothing to do with partisans and were singled out simply because they were Jewish.

The most frequent and typical statements made to explain such actions by those involved in Nazi Germany's crimes were: 'I considered my actions to be justified. In war things are very different than they are in peacetime.' Or: 'I simply could not imagine that one of Hitler's orders could be criminal.' Or: 'We had to respond in the way we did, since otherwise the partisan threat would have spun out of control. A war against a malicious enemy cannot be fought according to the rules.' Or: 'I was obliged to follow orders.' Or: 'Orders are orders.' 'From a humane perspective, I did not agree with the things I had to do, but the orders left no alternative.' 'If I had refused to obey orders, I would have been killed myself. I had no choice.'

Some of these explanations might easily be applied to the context of the civil war and genocide in Rwanda and yet, owing to the differences in circumstances, other arguments must be included and shifted into the foreground, such as: 'I hadn't the least bit of doubt that the Tutsi were our enemies and sought our destruction.' Or: 'We, the Hutu, felt that we were threatened.' Or: 'I was forced to participate.' Or, more specifically: 'Had I refused, my family and I would have been killed.'

III

How are these characteristic explanations assessed and dealt with in legal proceedings? It is obvious that they cannot simply make the crimes in question disappear; the crimes have been committed and there are victims and perpetrators. But, as has been noted above, the issue is one of appropriate sanctions, and this depends on the extent to which the accused can be held individually responsible. And this, in turn, depends on the success of her or his defence. In the strictly legal sense, a defence is a response to a criminal charge. It denotes 'all grounds which, for one reason or another, hinder the sanctioning of an offence – despite the fact that the offence has fulfilled all definitional elements of a crime'.[13] The most significant defences generally recognised in international criminal law and national legal systems with respect to the issues discussed here are as follows:[14]

- *Superior orders*: This defence holds that there is no individual criminal liability (1) if the person in question was legally obliged to obey orders from a superior, (2) if the person did not know that the order was illegal, and (3) if the order was not manifestly illegal.
- *Duress, compulsion, and coercion*: the imminent threat of the use of force against a person deprives this person of any moral choice, so that the person asserts that there was no criminal intent at the moment the crime was committed. 'To establish the defence of coercion or necessity in the face of danger there must be a showing of circumstances such that a reasonable man would apprehend that he was in such imminent physical peril as to deprive him of freedom to choose the right and refrain from the wrong.'[15]
- *Self-defence*: an individual acts in legitimate self-defence when proportionate force is used to defend himself or another from imminent use of unlawful force. Self-defence is a recognised (e.g. in the European Convention of Human Rights) exception to the principle of respect for the right to life.
- *Mistake of law and mistake of fact*: both mistakes may be grounds for excluding criminal responsibility, if the accused lacks the required knowledge about the crime.
- *Reprisal and military necessity*: Reprisal is only justified if there has been a breach of international law by the adversary but the reprisal

must be proportional, otherwise it is not admitted as a defence. Military necessity may justify 'wanton destruction of cities, towns or villages, or devastation', nevertheless, it extends 'neither to killing of civilians nor to their deportation to concentration camps – actions that are never justified'.[16]

The *tu quoque* argument holds that the adversary committed similar atrocities, so that the conduct of the accused cannot therefore be indictable. This argument was recognised in Nuremberg as a defence, though only in connection with U-boat warfare.[17] Today, international humanitarian law considers *tu quoque* inapplicable because this law creates obligations (such as the prohibition of genocide or torture) that are *erga omnes*; that is, they must be adhered to by all parties. Indeed, it is difficult to imagine that an act of genocide should not be subject to prosecution because it was committed in response to a foregoing genocide.

The final point concerns the immunity of heads of state, ministers or diplomats. Immunity was denied such individuals in the Nuremberg trials and this rule continues to apply today to those charged with genocide. When a conflict arises between claims to immunity and criminal indictment, especially when crimes such as those presently under discussion are involved, invoking immunity is generally not accepted. It is, however, possible, that the criminal investigation is delayed until after the person has ended his period of office and thus immunity has ended.[18]

In all the above-mentioned defences, no distinction is made between justifications and excuses. Many legal systems (including, for example, the German system) differentiate between the two along the following lines: 'A justification speaks to the rightness of the act; an excuse, to whether the actor is accountable for a concededly wrongful act.'[19]

Today, however, international criminal law no longer makes this distinction explicitly but instead makes it implicitly when examining a given case. Grounds for an excuse are therefore more important in the context of mass violence and consequently most of the relevant 'defences' refer to these. In other words, murdering defenceless people in war is usually unjustified (the reprisals during the Second World War represent an exception) but can be excused, in which case the perpetrator is not subject to punishment. While we refer in everyday language to the perpetrators justifying their acts, in correct legal terms they actually excuse their behaviour and hope that society will respond by saying: 'That's right, in this situation you could not have acted otherwise, since you cannot be obliged to resist or act heroically.'

IV

If we now examine the judgements passed on National Socialist crimes and ascertain the extent to which they accounted for the perpetrators' statements and accepted their defences, significant differences become apparent. The international military tribunals, including the Nuremberg Tribunals, were particularly cautious in accepting the defendants' defences. In part, this was a consequence of the understanding of law at that time, as pointed out above. More important, however, was the unambiguous evidence against the defendants, most of whom were high-ranking officials. Those who were shown to have participated in the planning and implementation of National Socialist crimes could not plausibly cite political, military or legal constraints in order to deny their responsibility. The fact that some succeeded in doing so – the most prominent such defendant was Albert Speer – does not contradict this conclusion. Instead, this observation highlights a circumstance that was even more significant in trials before national courts: judgements and sentences depended upon the accused person, on the legal understanding of the respective court and, of course, on the available evidence. In itself, this is nothing new. And yet, when the crimes in question have not been fuelled by criminal energy but rather are the result of a ruthless sense of duty, a consequence of the brutalisation that can result from war, or are committed in a real emergency, these three elements can interact in such a way that the accused must be found partially or completely free of guilt.

Let us recall what observers of trials of Nazi perpetrators in West Germany repeatedly experienced. On the one hand, there were survivors who, confronted in court with the regime's atrocities, were under extreme psychological strain and hardly capable of reconstructing their personal ordeal. For those who had had to concentrate on survival every day, remembering precise details of what had occurred around them was a difficult task. On the other hand, there were the accused, who took advantage of the fragmentary or mistaken memories of the victims and, supported by their lawyers, hoped to secure an *in dubio pro reo* judgement or even an acquittal for lack of evidence. One witness, a former inmate of a concentration camp, remarked:

> The expectation is that, if we indeed were there, we must have seen and heard everything. But we were nearly paralysed with fear and terror and our senses hardly perceived a thing. They called on us to name the hour and the day; but in the camps no one had a clock,

no one had a calendar, and often we did not even know that it was Sunday or a holiday. We were told to describe how our executioners looked. But in their uniforms, all of them looked the same to us. And then, if we are mistaken in a single point, twenty years or more after the crimes, our entire testimony is discounted – lock, stock and barrel.[20]

If we then also taken into consideration that, in the post-1945 period, the Federal Republic of Germany was a state in which individuals who had held positions under the Nazis returned to positions of authority (and, indeed, in greater numbers in the judiciary than in the political sphere), then it will come as no surprise that so many trials of suspected Nazi perpetrators fell so disappointingly short of the mark, not only in the eyes of the victims.[21] Not that there would be any objection to an acquittal, were it based on an exhaustive examination of testimony and of the defendant's defence. The problem was, however, that the cases tried – for example, those in which duress, compulsion and coercion played a role – were quite diverse. First, there were cases in which the accused had, over a long period of time, carried out orders to kill without protest, indeed, with inner conviction – we only need recall that type of perpetrator with Nazi convictions – either because he wished to appear a good soldier in the eyes of his superiors, or because he was hoping for some personal advantage. Secondly, there were cases in which, initially, the accused sought to avoid carrying out the order to kill but then resigned himself to his fate and participated in the shootings. Thirdly, and finally, there were those cases in which the accused simply feared for his life and killed only after having first considered how he might avoid obeying orders.

The court's task was to determine which of these descriptions applied to a particular case. If the court perceived the accused in a manner that corresponded to one of the first two kinds of cases, he would be penalised. In such cases, defendants who presented arguments based on the duress, compulsion or coercion defence were deemed wholly unconvincing (when the offence was committed willingly) or only partially convincing (for defendants who acted out of resignation). But what exactly is the difference between committing an offence out of a sense of resignation and doing so out of fear for one's own life and for lack of an alternative (which is not sanctioned)? Judging this difference was made more difficult by the fact that fear for one's life did not necessarily have to be demonstrated by concrete factors such as an actual threat. It was sufficient – and this applied not only to German law but also to the criminal codes in other countries as well – for the perpetrator to have imagined or even mistakenly assumed a dangerous threat to his or her life. Thus, police officers who participated in executing Jewish inhabitants of Belorussian cities were acquitted because, in the opinion of the court, they demonstrated that refusing to carry out orders would have resulted in their own execution.[22] And rather than being an exception, such acquittals were the rule, especially in the first few years of trials before West German courts of individuals charged with participating in National Socialist crimes, especially when lower-ranking perpetrators were involved. What is remarkable about this is that, until today, there are no documented cases in which a soldier, policeman or member of the SS was indeed killed for defying an order to kill.[23] Thus, these cases reveal that a great deal depended on the court's perspective and its willingness to examine the past critically. Even if we cannot rule out the possibility that numerous Nazi perpetrators acted out of some imagined coercion, it is equally possible that similar numbers of Nazi perpetrators were much too generously granted the benefit of the *in dubio pro reo* principle.

The coercion-duress-compulsion argument also comes into play when defendants begin by submitting the superior orders defence. This followed from the provisions of section 47 of the German military penal code in force at the time, which applied not only to members of the *Wehrmacht* but also to SS and police units. According to this rule, the commanding officer was solely responsible if, as a consequence of his order, any part of the penal code was violated, for example by an order to kill that was not defined as a permissible act of war. Subordinates following such orders were only penalised if they recognised that obeying such an order constituted a criminal act. In other words, the subordinate had to be aware that the act was illegal, and this realisation had to be based on an average level of moral sensibility, rather than any special kind of knowledge. If the subordinate was found to be guilty of a minor offence, then according to paragraph 2 of section 47, he could be exempt from punishment. The following example illustrates the kind of cases considered to be in this category. During the 'evacuation' of a ghetto in the small town of Dünaburg, the accused, a police officer, had refused to obey his superior officer's orders to participate in rounding up and shooting the ghetto's Jewish inhabitants. He also refused to conduct a house-to-house search for Jews with his police dog. He was then ordered to join others in cordoning off the town so no one could enter or leave. He obeyed this order because, as he claimed, he could perceive no other means of avoiding participation in the operation. He testified quite convincingly that he did not have to make any use of his weapon.[24]

Cases such as these were rare, simply because, in the great majority of cases, the original order was carried out. Many of those who followed orders apparently felt they were issued directly by Hitler; as they asserted in court, Hitler was at the head of the legal order and his will was law. They did not know that there was any criminal intent behind the Führer's will, they claimed.[25] It is difficult to imagine adults with an average capacity to make moral judgements who attempted to explain mass executions or even the murder of individual children or old people simply by taking recourse to the 'Führer's will'. And yet they did exist and the judges of criminal tribunals, trained in a positivist legal tradition, apparently found repudiating these arguments a difficult task.[26] The fact that they finally did so had to do with a formula elaborated by Gustav Radbruch, a professor of law and, for a brief period during the Weimar Republic, German minister of justice. According to this principle, a legal rule should be considered invalid when 'a positive law contradicts justice to an extent that is so intolerable that it must be abandoned as "unjust law" in favour of justice'.[27] In other words, no one who is subject to the law can invoke a law that declares a crime to be the norm, no matter who created that law; he or she must know that criminal acts can never become lawful and therefore legal.

This recourse to natural law – which holds that human dignity is one of the highest possible goods to be protected – was facilitated by the fact that many of those charged with Nazi crimes admitted at these trials that, although they assume these were 'orders from the Führer', they had a sense that the acts they were ordered to commit were indeed 'somehow wrong'. Thus, the 'acting on orders' defence, which might otherwise have mitigated their guilt and the resulting sanctions, did not apply to their actions. And even judges – some of whom, as has been well documented, made frequent recourse to the argument about the Führer's will during the Nazi era – were no longer obliged to ask themselves uncomfortable questions about their concepts of justice. Whenever the accused revealed an awareness of the injustice of certain acts and was demonstrated to have committed those acts all the same, the courts could proceed as usual. The same applied to all those cases in which there was a sense of injustice but criminal acts were committed out of fear of the consequences of refusing orders. Here again, the issue became whether the defences of duress, coercion or compulsion were warranted or were merely being presented to mask or mitigate events and motives. This assessment applied to the majority of cases, since, as we have seen above, this was the only possible way to avoid or reduce punishment.

Although the superior orders defence at first proved to be of less practical importance during the Nazi crimes trials than the defence of duress, coercion or compulsion, this situation changed with passage of legislation by the West German parliament, after which the acting-on-orders argument gained considerable, albeit questionable, significance. Passed in 1968, this revision addressed the issue of the intent of someone committing an illegal act as a result of following an order. As noted above, according to section 47 of the military penal code, the subordinate could be held responsible and penalised if he was aware of the criminal intentions of the person who had issued the orders. Whether or not he himself had the intent to kill or commit other crimes was irrelevant. Following the revision enacted in 1968, the subordinate's homicidal intent at the moment the criminal act was being committed had to be established; otherwise, a conviction on a murder charge was impossible. Such defendants could only be convicted of less grievous offences such as manslaughter. For crimes committed during the Nazi regime, however, convictions on such lesser charges were no longer possible due to the statute of limitations. This meant that numerous subordinates would no longer be tried, much to the relief of numerous 'desk murderers' who, because they had worked relatively far away from the sites of the crimes, had a rather easy time of arguing that they did not fulfil the homicidal intent requirement.[28] They either argued that they had lacked comprehensive knowledge of events, or that they had only done their jobs and attempted, despite difficult circumstances, to help those whose lives were threatened by the Nazi regime. That the people they had ordered to be rounded up and deported were to be murdered was something they didn't know about, much less wanted to happen. In many cases, the charges were dropped because of the statute of limitations; the result was, in effect, nothing short of a barely disguised amnesty for white-collar Nazi criminals.

If we now turn to the next major genocide of the twentieth century, the genocide in Rwanda, which took place between April and July 1994, then several differences become apparent – if not immediately, then on closer inspection. The first is that, so far, there has been no amnesty for the crimes committed in Rwanda and whether there will be in the future remains an open question. Should this ever be the case, however, then it will not be the result of an unwillingness to investigate the crimes but rather due to the impossibility of prosecuting the large numbers of perpetrators with the means that the Rwandan judicial system has at its disposal. New suspects are being added to those already known each day; according to recent estimations, several hundred thousand new allegations are being raised by those accused in current trials, who assert: 'I did not act alone. X was also involved.'

The second difference is that defences such as those based on coercion, duress, compulsion or superior orders do not play any significant role in the trials dealing with the Rwandan genocide. In the proceedings before the International Criminal Tribunal for Rwanda in Arusha,[29] acting on the orders of a government or a superior can be recognised as a mitigating circumstance according to article 6, paragraph 4 of the court statutes. That this has hardly occurred so far is because numerous defendants were former high-ranking and influential persons, a similarity to the cases tried at Nuremberg. Claims by such individuals that they acted under duress or out of fear of the consequences of refusing to obey orders hardly seem credible. During proceedings before the Rwandan criminal courts or before the traditional *gacaca* courts,[30] in contrast, these defences are frequently recognised, since it is a generally acknowledged fact that many people perpetrated crimes under the threat of death. (This alone represents a significant difference between the events in Rwanda and the Holocaust.) Consequently, there was good reason to assume that some perpetrators (certainly not all, for there were also many in Rwanda who acted out of conviction) experienced real or perceived duress, coercion or compulsion. However, when the Rwandan courts recognise these defences, the perpetrators are not found not guilty and thus exempt from punishment as a consequence. Instead, defendants are ensured substantial reductions in their sentences if they confess to their crimes and elucidate the circumstances under which they occurred. The earlier such a confession is made, the greater the reduction of the respective sentence. Even in cases of multiple murders, prison sentences can be reduced in this way from the usual twenty-five to thirty years to only seven.[31] This procedure seeks to account for the fact that numerous perpetrators acted under coercion only when committing their first murder and later participated more or less voluntarily; the prospect of material gain (acquisition of the property of the victims) was a significant stimulus in this context.

The third and last difference is that perpetrators of the crimes in Rwanda frequently assert that, while they committed evil acts, they also did some good. They maintain that their efforts to save the lives of persecuted Tutsi are sufficient evidence of the fact that they participated in the murders only reluctantly and under extreme pressure.

Photo 9.1 One of the traditional courts near Butare, in the south of Rwanda in autumn 2002: the prisoners accused of acts of genocide are wearing pink-coloured prison-clothes.

During the trial of Juvénal Kejelijeli, the International Criminal Tribunal for Rwanda responded to such arguments by referring as follows to positions stated in another decision:

> (i) generally speaking, evidence of the character of the accused prior to the events for which he is indicted before the International Tribunal is not a relevant issue inasmuch as (a) by their nature as crimes committed in the context of widespread violence and during a national or international emergency, war crimes and crimes against humanity may be committed by persons with no prior convictions or history of violence, and the consequent evidence of prior good, or bad, conduct on the part of the accused before the armed conflict began is rarely of any probative value before the International Tribunal, and (b) as a general principle of criminal law, evidence as to the character of an accused is generally inadmissible to show the propensity of the accused to act in conformity therewith.[32]

Consequently, the court rejected Kejelijeli's argument. Rwandan courts also consistently reject comparable explanations ('I was not inhuman before; it was the apocalyptic circumstances that made me this way').

And justifiably so since, after all, Hutu and Tutsi lived together in one single state for a long time; under these circumstances, adopting an attitude that demonstrates respect for the life and dignity of others cannot be recognised as a special achievement.

V

Earlier in this chapter, legal defences were referred to as potentially problematic in different ways. From the point of view of the victims, legal defences can easily be perceived as allowing perpetrators to escape the punishment they actually deserve. From the point of view of the perpetrators, they offer an opportunity to account for the perpetrator's situation at the time the acts in question were committed. Frequently, however, as pointed out especially by Rwandan defendants, these considerations are felt to be inadequate. The question raised by the defendants is how they might have been expected to act otherwise, when confronted with a threat that left them with a deadly choice (i.e. their own death or that of another person).

These cases reveal the limits of the judicial system. Nothing can be done to redress the victim's loss; it is an irreversible fact. Family members, for example, are dead. The legal system also cannot deal with the perpetrators as if nothing has happened. The perpetrator has killed other persons and must be held responsible for his or her deeds. This means that, although the individual may have acted under extreme coercion, she or he will still face a prison sentence, although, as we have seen, there are exceptions to this principle. For example, a country's judicial system can be so deeply influenced by specific concepts of justice that influence its policies in dealing with its past that what might be perceived as a disproportionate degree of understanding for the real or supposed hardships of the perpetrators becomes apparent. Aside from this, however, and by the standards of international criminal justice, such exceptions are rare, since as article 31, paragraph 1 (d) of the statute of the new International Criminal Court stipulates, the essential precondition for these exceptions is that the perpetrator, when seeking to avoid the duress resulting from a threat of imminent danger, 'acts necessarily and reasonably to avoid this threat, provided that the person does not intend to cause a greater harm than the one he sought to avoid'. That this holds will be particularly difficult to maintain in cases of genocide and comparable mass crimes.

Thus, all things considered, the application of law to sanction perpetrators of genocide, war crimes or the like is a long and difficult matter.

That this process is about realising justice unduly complicates the issues. It may well be that justice exists in a metaphysical and religious sense, but it does not in a legal sense, neither for the victims nor for the perpetrators. What is possible is, on the one hand, to ascertain as precisely as possible what occurred and to do so with the greatest possible respect for the suffering and the interests of the victims and, on the other, to uncover the individual role of the perpetrators without denying their human dignity.

Notes

1. Cf. for example the trial of Bosnian-Serbian General Radislav Krstic before the UN's International Court of Justice in The Hague (IT-98-33-T), judgement of 2 August 2001, paras. 543, 581–3. In para. 586, the court cited the UN International Law Commission which asserts: 'It is not necessary to intend to achieve the complete annihilation of a group from every corner of the globe. Nonetheless the crime of genocide by its very nature requires the intention to destroy at least a substantial part of a particular group.'
2. For a more detailed discussion cf. Gerd Hankel, 'Kriegsverbrechen und die Möglichkeiten ihrer Ahndung in Vergangenheit und Gegenwart', in Bruno Thoß and Hans-Erich Volkmann (eds), *Erster Weltkrieg – Zweiter Weltkrieg. Ein Vergleich* (Paderborn, 2002), 669–71.
3. Thomas Mann, *Fragile Republik. Thomas Mann und Nachkriegsdeutschland*, ed. Stephan Stachorski (Frankfurt/Main, 1999), 45.
4. On questionable proceedings, for example against alleged German war criminals in the Soviet Union, cf. Andreas Hilger, 'Sowjetische Justiz und Kriegsverbrechen. Dokumente zu den Verurteilungen deutscher Kriegsgefangener, 1941–1949', *Vierteljahrshefte für Zeitgeschichte*, 3 (2006), 461–515.
5. On this problem see Gerhard Roth, 'Willensfreiheit und Schuldfähigkeit aus Sicht der Hirnforschung', in Gerhard Roth and Klaus-Jürgen Grün (eds), *Das Gehirn und seine Freiheit. Beiträge zur neurowissenschaftlichen Grundlegung der Philosophie* (Göttingen, 2006), 9–27.
6. The probably most discussed book is Christopher R. Browning, *Ordinary Men: Reserve Police Battalion 101 and the Final Solution in Poland* (New York, 1992); also Harald Welzer, *Täter. Wie aus ganz normalen Menschen Massenmörder werden* (Frankfurt/Main, 2005), which was written for a German-speaking readership and deals not only with Nazi crimes but also with the Rwandan genocide as well as other cases.
7. Immanuel Kant, 'First Supplement Concerning the Guarantee of Perpetual Peace', *Perpetual Peace* [1795] (London, 1917), 151.
8. La Paix de Versailles, *Responsabilités des auteurs de la Guerre et Sanctions* (Paris, 1930), 538; Robert Lansing, 'Some Legal Questions of the Peace Conference', *American Journal of International Law*, 8 (1991), 631–50.
9. Cf. Taner Akçam, *Armenien und der Völkermord. Die Istanbuler Prozesse und die türkische Nationalbewegung* (Hamburg, 1996), 77–121.
10. Cf. the following extract from the Genocide Convention of 1948: 'In the present Convention, genocide means any of the following acts committed with the intent to destroy, in whole or in part, a national, ethnical, racial

or religious group, such as: (a) Killing members of the group; (b) Causing serious bodily or mental harm to members of the group...'
11. Matthias Arning, 'Anklage gegen frühere SS-Männer gefordert. Antifaschisten halten Staatsanwaltschaft Verschleppung vor/Bundesweite Aktionen zum 8. Mai', *Frankfurter Rundschau*, 6 May 2006, 4 (translation G.H.).
12. Cf. Friedrich Andrae, *Auch gegen Frauen und Kinder. Der Krieg der deutschen Wehrmacht gegen die Zivilbevölkerung in Italien 1943–1945* (Munich, 1995), 208–10.
13. Cf. the definition in William A. Schabas, *Genocide in International Law* (Cambridge, 2000), 314.
14. Ibid., 316–44; Christiane Nill-Theobald, *'Defences' bei Kriegsverbrechen am Beispiel Deutschlands und der USA. Zugleich ein Beitrag zu einem Allgemeinen Teil des Völkerstrafrechts* (Freiburg/Breisgau, 1998), 57–61; Kai Ambos, *Der Allgemeine Teil des Völkerstrafrechts. Ansätze einer Dogmatisierung* (Berlin, 2002), 111–13, 543–5, 825–7; Gerhard Werle, *Principles of International Criminal Law* (The Hague, 2005), 138–40.
15. *United States v. von Leeb* ('German High Command Trial'), (1949) 11 LRTWC 1 (United States Military Tribunal), quoted from Schabas, *Genocide*, 333–4.
16. Albin Eser, 'Defences in War Crime Trials', in Yoram Dinstein and Mala Tabory (eds), *War Crimes in International Law* (The Hague, 1996), quoted from Schabas, *Genocide*, 341.
17. Ibid., 341f., note 167.
18. Cf. Werle, *Principles*, 173–5.
19. George Fletcher, *Rethinking Criminal Law* (Boston, 1978), 759; quoted from Schabas, *Genocide*, 315.
20. Quoted from Adalbert Rückerl, *NS-Verbrechen vor Gericht. Versuch einer Vergangenheitsbewältigung* (Heidelberg, 1982), 253.
21. Nor did East Germany undertake sustained efforts to prosecute perpetrators of Nazi crimes. Although the German Democratic Republic, as it was officially called, presented itself as a model anti-fascist state, Nazi crimes were not prosecuted if the persons responsible for them happened to be important for the state and its ruling Sozialistische Einheitspartei; cf. Henry Leide, *NS-Verbrecher und Staatssicherheit. Die geheime Vergangenheitspolitik der DDR*, 2nd edn (Göttingen, 2006), 27–131, 413–18.
22. Cf. *Neue Juristische Wochenschrift*, 16 (1964), 731.
23. Cf. Rückerl, 285, 288. The author of this article was part of the team that created and organised an exhibition entitled 'Vernichtungskrieg. Verbrechen der Wehrmacht 1941 bis 1944' (presented from 2001 to 2004). In the course of research in that context, the exhibition team was unable to find evidence of a single case in which a refusal by a member of the German *Wehrmacht* to carry out orders ended in superiors ordering that the soldier in question be executed.
24. This example in discussed in Rückerl, *NS-Verbrechen*, 288.
25. Cf. Anton Roesen, 'Rechtsfragen der Einsatzgruppen-Prozesse', *Neue Juristische Wochenschrift*, 4 (1964), 133–6; Hans Welzel, 'Gesetzmäßige Judentötungen?', *Neue Juristische Wochenschrift*, 12 (1964), 521–3.
26. Intense debate on what constituted injustice and what did not during the twelve years of the Nazi regime began in Germany immediately after the end of the war in 1945. Cf. Clea Laage, 'Die Auseinandersetzung um den Begriff

des gesetzlichen Unrechts nach 1945', in Redaktion Kritische Justiz (ed.), *Die juristische Aufarbeitung des Unrechts-Staats* (Baden-Baden, 1998), 265–97.
27. Quoted from ibid., 268.
28. Cf. Heribert Ostendorf, 'Die – widersprüchlichen – Auswirkungen der Nürnberger Prozesse auf die westdeutsche Justiz', in Gerd Hankel and Gerhard Stuby (ed.), *Strafgerichte gegen Menschheitsverbrechen. Zum Völkerstrafrecht 50 Jahre nach den Nürnberger Prozessen* (Hamburg, 1995), 78–9.
29. This international court was created by a UN Security Council Resolution in November 1994, cf. Resolution 955, *International Legal Materials*, 33 (1994), 1598. The court, which is located in Arusha in neighbouring Tanzania, is charged first and foremost with bringing those to justice who organised and planned the genocide.
30. The idea of the traditional *gacaca* courts was reactivated in Rwanda in order to deal with the large numbers of defendants, after it became apparent that they could not be tried in a reasonable period of time by the regular courts. In the *gacaca* courts, there is neither a prosecutor nor a lawyer for the defence; instead, the local population determines whether the accused is innocent or guilty. Following the tradition of the *inyangamugayo* or wise men, the verdicts are spoken by men and women who are recognised in the community. The *gacaca* judgements emphasise the notion of redress or compensation rather than punishment.
31. Cf. Article 73 of the Loi Organique No. 16/2004 from 19 June 2006 on the structure, jurisdiction, and the procedures of the *gacaca* courts, in J.O. (de la République du Rwanda) no. spécial du 19/6/2006.
32. Cf. Case No. ICTR-98-44 A-A, *Judgement*, 23 May 2005, para. 301.

Index

Aachen, 76, 81
Abu Ghraib, 1, 3, 18
Achim, Viorel, 94
Adam, Uwe Dietrich, 31, 49
Adorno, Theodor W., 34, 71, 77
Aghet (Armenian genocide), 191
Akçam, Taner, 218
Akkerman (Cetatea-Alba), 84
Allen, Michael Thad, 52
Aly, Götz, 13, 20, 39–40, 51, 52, 166, 170, 180, 200
American Indians, 16, 146
Améry, Jean, 32
Anatolia, 191–2, 195
Ancel, Jean, 95
Anders, Günter, 167, 180
Andrae, Friedrich, 219
Angrick, Andrej, vii, xiii, 5, 13, 14, 52, 78, 93, 94, 95, 96
Ansbacher, Heinz L., 26, 48
anti-Jewish, 17, 42, 82, 168, 170, 172
anti-Semitism, xiv, 14, 32–4, 37–9, 43, 45, 57–8, 74, 86, 102–3, 106, 111, 132, 187
Antonescu, Ion, 79, 93, 95
Applebaum, Anne, 2, 19
Arendt, Hannah, 5, 13, 32–4, 49, 50, 170–1, 180
armed SS, *see Waffen-SS*
Armenia, Armenian genocide, xiii, 13, 17, 146, 191–200, 205
Arning, Matthias, 219
Arnold, Klaus Jochen, 95–6
Artzt, Heinz, 94
Arusha, 215, 220
Asch, Solomon, E., 161, 164
Asher, Harvey, 53
Aßmuß, Ingeborg, 15, 123, 132, 136–8
Aumeier, Hans, 129

Auschwitz, Auschwitz-Birkenau, concentration camp, 15, 30, 33–4, 42, 50, 51, 129–31, 140
Austria, 27, 32, 40

Babel, Ludwig, 28–29
Bach-Zelewski, Erich von dem, 69
Baden, 59
Bajohr, Frank, 51, 180, 200
Balakian, Peter, 193–4, 199
Balta, Sebastian, 93
Baltic nations, 35
Bangladesh, 146
Bankier, David, 77
Banks, Curtis, 19, 51
Barlad, 83, 96
Bartov, Omer, 36, 51, 58, 76
Bauer, Udo, 19
Bauer, Yehuda, 199
Bauman, Zygmunt, 34, 50
Baumeister, Roy F., 8–9, 20
Beendorf, 133
Beethoven, Ludwig van, 165
Belarus, 35, 37, 43, 53
Belzy, 83
Benedict, Ruth, 76
Benz, Wolfgang, xiv, 142
Berdjansk, 85
Bergen-Belsen, concentration camp, ix, 30, 42, 121–3, 139, 142
Bessarabia, 79, 83
Best, Werner, 40
Bey, Cevdet, 196
Biess, Frank, 53
Binz, Dorothea, 114, 127, 140
Birn, Ruth Bettina, 53, 96
Bischof, Franz, 173, 177
Bleton, Pierre, 141
Bloxham, Donald, viii, xiii, 11, 13, 17, 185, 199, 200

Bock, Gisela, 35, 41, 50, 52, 101–2, 107–11, 117, 118
Böhler, Jochen, 76, 92
Bohn, Robert, 92
Bolgrad, 84
Boog, Horst, 94
Bracher, Karl-Dietrich, 31, 49
Braham, Randolph L., 95
Braunschweig, 133
Brauweiler, 126
British Foreign Office, 25
Broszat, Martin, 33, 35, 49, 140, 141
Browder, George, 45, 52, 53
Brown, Daniel P., 139
Browning, Christopher, 5–6, 8, 13, 20, 33, 37–8, 40, 45–6, 49, 50, 51, 53, 56–7, 71, 76, 77, 92, 96, 118, 218
Brück, Brigitte, 116
Buber-Neumann, Margarete, 126–7, 131, 140, 141
Buchbender, Ortwin, 50, 77
Buchenwald, concentration camp, 29, 30, 114, 119
Buchheim, Hans, 49, 141
Budjennowsk, 85
Bukovina, north, 79
Burdick, Charles, 77
Burke, Joanna, 20
Burundi, 146
Busch, Reinhard, 141
Buss, David, 9–10, 20
Butare, x, 160, 216
Butler, Judith, 118

Cambodia, 8, 146, 153, 156, 164, 168
Caucasus, 79, 85, 191–2, 197
Central Office of Regional Administration of Justice (*Zentrale Stelle der Landesjustizverwaltungen*), 136
Chiari, Bernd, 53
China, 8
Chotin, 83
Churchill, Winston, 145
Cilicia, 191–3
Cologne, 126
Commichau, Alfred, 55, 69

Committee of Union and Progress (*Ittihad ve Terraki Cemiyeti*; CUP), 192, 194–8, 199, 200
Cooper, Robert, 163
Cosmides, Leda, 9, 20
Creighton, M. R., 76
Criminal Investigation Division (CID), 2
Cüppers, Martin, 52, 93
Czech, Danuta, 140, 141
Czechoslovakia, 137, 180
Czechstochwa, ix
Czernowitz, 83, 88, 94

Dachau, concentration camp, 30, 42
Dadrian, Vahakn N., 193, 199, 200
Dammer, Susanna, 117
Darby, Joseph M., 1, 2, 19
Darfur, 16, 147
Darwin, Charles, 150
Davies, Martin L., xv, 180
Dawidowicz, Lucy, 32, 49, 199
Dean, Martin, 43, 48, 53, 96
Deletant, Dennis, 93
Demant, Ebbo, 50
Dicks, Henry V., 50
Diefendorf, J. M., 52
Dilic, Tomislav, 92
Dinstein, Yoram, 219
Directorate for General Security (EUM), 194–5
Directorate for the Settlement of Tribes and Immigrants (IAMM), 194–5
Diyarbakir, 196
Dobkowski, Michael N., 163
Dollwet, Joachim, 77
Doneson, Judith, 34
Dubossary, 84
Duesterberg, Julia, 114–15, 119
Dünaburg, 212
Dündar, Fuat, 200
Duntley, Joshua, 9–10, 20

Ebbinghaus, Angelika, 106–8, 117, 118
Eckhardt, William, 163
Eichmann, Adolf, 13, 30, 33–4, 166–67

Einsatzgruppe(n), xiii, 13, 14, 28, 30, 35, 40–1, 48, 50, 52, 55, 57, 69, 78–81, 83–92, 93, 94, 96, 194, 219
Einsatzkommando(s) (Ek), 5, 14, 40, 81, 84, 94, 176
Eisenbach, Arthur, 48
Elista, 85
Engelbrecht, Peter, 142
England, Lynndie, 1, 2, 19
Erber, Ralph, 21, 53
Erickson, Edward J., 200
Erpel, Simone, 139
Eschebach, Insa, 119, 142
Eser, Albin, 219
Essen, xiv, xvi, 126
Ethiopia, 147
euthanasia programme/T-4, 40, 42, 102
Evans, Richard J., 117
evolutionary psychology (EP), 9, 20, 149, 150–1, 153

Fackenheim, Emil, 199
Fahlbusch, Michael, 49
Falter, Jürgen W., 116
Farnbacher, Fritz, 67–9, 76, 77
Farschid, Olaf, 199
Feldman, Gerald D., 52
Fest, Joachim, 100–1, 116
Final Solution, 5, 14, 28, 30, 39, 82, 85, 156, 188, 190–1, 194, 196, 198
Fletcher, George, 219
Förster, Jürgen, 94
France, 27, 57, 205
Frank, Dorothee, 10–12, 20, 95
Fraser, S. C., 181
Frederick, Ivan L., 1, 3
Freedman, Jonathan L., 181
Frei, Norbert, 93
Freikorps, 60, 89
Freud, Sigmund, 102–3, 117
Frevert, Ute, 117
Friedländer, Henry, 178, 181
Friedländer, Saul, 47, 51, 54, 180
Funke, Manfred, 49

Galicia, 37
Garbe, Detlef, 50
Gellately, Robert, 21, 200

Gentile, Carlo, 95
Georgijewsk, 85
Gerlach, Christian, 51, 93, 95, 200
German Democratic Republic (GDR), xv, 34, 136–8, 219
German Federal Republic (FRG), 38
Germany, ix, xiii, xv, 4, 7–8, 12, 17, 25–9, 34–6, 38–9, 41, 47, 58–62, 66, 75, 78–9, 89–90, 101, 106, 109, 111, 121–3, 126, 131–2, 135, 137, 199, 203, 205–7, 210–11, 219
Germany (West), 28, 34, 109, 132, 210
Gestapo, 28, 40, 42, 74, 78, 80–1
Geyer, Michael, 77
Gibson, Janice T., 155, 164
Gildemeister, Regina, 118
Gleichmann, Peter, 48, 95
Goethe, Johann Wolfgang von, 165
Goldhagen, Daniel Jonah, 13, 37–8, 40, 46, 51, 57, 76
Göring, Hermann, 172
Gottwald, Alfred, 94
Götz, Aly, 20, 39–40, 51, 52, 166, 170, 180, 200
Graner, Charles A., 1
Great Britain, 79, 205
Greece, 85, 157
Gross, Jan Tomasz, 47
Groß, Werner, 69, 77
Grossmann, Atina, 102, 117
Grün, Klaus-Jügen, 218
Gust, Wolfgang, 194, 199
Gypsies/Sinti and Roma, 35–6, 50, 69, 85, 95, 169, 191

Haar, Ingo, 49
Haffner, Sebastian, 63
Halder, Fritz, 70
Hamburg, xiii, xiv, 37, 56, 81, 115, 133, 134
Hampson, Rick, 3, 19
Haney, Craig, 19, 51
Hankel, Gerd, x, xiii, 5, 13, 17–18, 201, 218, 220
Haritos-Fatouros, Mike, 155, 164
Hartmann, Christian, 75, 93
Hausleitner, Mariana, 93, 94
Hecht, Cornelia, 51

Heike, Irmtraud, xiii, 13, 15, 113, 119, 120, 139, 142
Heim, Susanne, 39, 51
Heinsohn, Kirsten, 52, 111, 118
Hellfeld, Matthias von, 76
Helmbrechts, concentration camp, 15, 136
Herbert, Ulrich, 29, 34–5, 39, 49, 50, 51, 52, 54, 139
Herbst, Ludolf, 93
Herf, Jeffrey, 77
Herkommer, Christina, xiv, 5, 13, 15, 99, 116
Hersh, Seymour, 1, 18, 19
Hertz-Eichenrode, Katharina, 141
Herzog, Dagmar, 53
Heschel, Susannah, 47, 52, 54
Hesse, Hans, 139
Heydrich, Reinhard, 29, 80–3, 94, 194, 197
Higher SS and Police Leaders (HSSPF), 81, 86, 94
Hilberg, Raul, 5, 13, 19, 32–4, 49, 50, 169, 178, 180, 181
Hildner, Ruth, 137
Hilger, Andreas, 218
Hillgruber, Andreas, 95
Himmler, Heinrich, 5, 29, 78, 80–1, 86, 91, 118, 127–31, 138, 172
Hinton, Alexander Laban, 152–3, 164
Hitler, Adolf, 10, 25, 28–30, 33, 36, 63–4, 66, 69, 73–4, 100–1, 116, 126, 131, 138, 172, 213
Hochhuth, Rolf, 32
Höfgen, Hendrik, 169
Holocaust/Shoah, ix, xiii, xiv, xv, 5–6, 10–18, 25–8, 30–9, 41, 43–4, 47–8, 56–8, 67, 72, 93, 146, 165, 172, 185–6, 191, 193, 200, 215
Höss, Annette, 200
Höss, Rudolf, 15, 33, 129
Hürter, Johannes, 93
Hutu, 155, 160, 207, 217

India, 147
Indonesia, 146
infantry regiment(s), 55, 59, 69, 71
Institute for Contemporary History (Institut für Zeitgeschichte), 30–1
International Court of Justice in The Hague, 218
International Criminal Tribunal for Rwanda, 215–16
Ioanid, Radu, 95
Iraq, 1, 3, 18, 192
Irish Republican Army (IRA), 10
Italy, 85, 206

Jäckel, Eberhard, 49, 94
Jacobsen, Hans-Adolf, 49, 77
Jäger, Herbert, 31, 49, 95, 96
Janowitz, Morris, 58, 76
Jellonek, Burkhard, 35, 50
Jensen, Olaf, xiv, 1, 19, 180
Jerusalem, 30, 33, 166
Jews/European Jewry, 5, 8, 27–39, 41–2, 45, 48, 55–9, 67, 69, 72, 78, 82–5, 90, 103, 112, 132, 146, 165–6, 169–75, 177, 187, 190, 191, 212
Johannsen, Ernst, 76
Johnson, Gary R., 161, 164
Jones, Adam, 164
Jureit, Ulrike, 75, 93

Kaiser Friedrich III, infantry regiment, 59
Kaiser, Hilmar, 199, 200
Kaiser, Wolf, 53, 93, 94
Kant, Immanuel, 218
Kasperowitsch, Michael, 142
Kassel, 81
Kater, Michael H., 139
Katz, Steven T., 199
Kaya, Şükrü, 195
Keitel, Wilhelm, 70
Kejelijeli, Juvénal, 216
Keller, Gottfried, 165
Kershaw, Ian, 49
Kertsch, 85
Khmer Rouge, 8, 153
Kiernan, Ben, 21, 53, 200
Kischinew, 83
Kislowodsk, 85
Klamm, Engelbert, 173–4, 181
Klee, Ernst, 35, 50, 77
Klein, Peter, xiii, 93, 94
Klinkhammer, Lutz, 95
Knapp, Gudrun-Axeli, 118

Index

Knopp, Guido, 118
Koch, Ilse, 29, 114, 119
Koch, Karl, 114
Koegel, Max, 127
Kogon, Eugen, 13, 28, 48
Koonz, Claudia, 41, 52, 53, 105–8, 112, 117, 118
Kosovo, 12
Krasnodar, 85
Krausnick, Helmut, 49, 50, 92, 93, 94
Kreissler, Kurt, 73
Kretzer, Anette, 48, 115, 119, 142
Krimtschaken, 85
Krstic, Radislav, 218
Krutscha, 55
Ku Klux Klan, 8
Kuhls (Lieutenant), 55, 69
Kuhn, Annette, 110, 118
Kühne, Thomas, xv, 5, 11, 13–14, 27, 41, 48–52, 55, 75, 76, 95
Kunz, Norbert, 95
Kwiecinska, Leokadia, 141
Kwiet, Konrad, 94

Labour Service (*Reichsarbeitsdienst*, RAD), 63, 128
Langefeld, Johanna, xiv, 15, 113, 119, 120–1, 126–32, 138–41
Lansing, Robert, 205, 218
Larsen, Stein Ugelvik, 51
Lehnert, Esther, 52
Leide, Henry, 219
Leningrad, 79
Leszczynski, Kazimierz, 96
Levene, Mark, 21, 186, 189, 199
Levi, Primo, 32, 37, 51, 67, 76
Levin, Nora, 32, 49
Lichtenburg, concentration camp, 42
Lifton, Robert Jay, 1, 18
Lithuania, 42
Little, Alastair, 12
Littlejohns, Richard, 75, 92, 116, 139
Logan, Michael H., 161, 164
Longerich, Peter, 30, 47, 49, 51, 53, 54, 77, 171, 180
Lublin, 37, 51, 130
Lüdtke, Alf, 34
Ludwigsburg, 131, 136

M., Lotte, 15, 123, 132–6, 138
Maccoby, Hyam, 96
MacLean, French L., 94
MacQueen, Michael, 42–3
Majdanek, concentration camp, 42
Mallmann, Klaus-Michael, 41, 48, 52, 53, 92–5
Mann, Klaus, 169, 180
Mann, Michael, 52, 186, 199
Mann, Thomas, 202, 218
Manoschek, Walter, 92
Manuila, Sabin, 94
Mariupol, 85
Mason, Timothy, 117
Matthäus, Jürgen, 46, 48–51, 53
Matzke, Frank, 62–3, 73, 76
Mauthausen, concentration camp, 42
Maykop, 85
Melcher, Hermann, 76
Melitopol, 85
Melson, Robert, 193, 199
Mesopotamia, 191
Messing Jr., Andy, 146
Meyer, Kathrin, 142
Meyer, Klaus, 96
Michlic, Joanna, 54
Milgram, Stanley, 5–7, 20, 37, 51, 57, 175, 177–8, 181
Military Intelligence (MI), 1, 3, 189
Miller, Arthur, 3, 19, 20
Milz, Karl, 173–4, 176
Minerlynie, 85
Mitscherlich, Margarete, 102–3, 117
Modersen, Gerhard, 65, 76
Moeller, Robert G., 29, 49
Mogilew, 69
Moller, Sabine, xvi, 180
Moltmann, Bernhard, 142
Mommsen, Hans, 35, 51
Moringen, concentration camp, 42
Morrow, Lance, 163
Mory, Carmen Maria, 29
Moscow, 79
Mozart, Wolfgang Amadeus, 165
Mulka, Robert, 129
Müller, Bruno, 14, 81, 84, 86
Müller, Rolf-Dieter, 52
Müller-Hill, Benno, 35, 50

226 Index

Munich, 30, 131,
Musial, Bogdan, 51
Muslim(s), 10, 147, 192, 194–5, 197–9

Narodnyj Komissariat Wnutrennych Del (NKWD), 88
National Archives, Washington, 121
National Association of Disabled Soldiers, Veterans, and War Dependants (*Reichsbund der Kriegsbeschädigten, Kriegsteilnehmer und Kriegshinterbliebenen*), 61
National Defense Council Foundation, 146
Naumann, Bernd, 140
Naumann, Klaus, 77
Nebe, Arthur, 69
Neuengamme, concentration camp, 15, 133
Newman, Leonard, 21, 44, 53
Ngor, Haing S., 156, 164
Niethammer, Ortrun, 117, 118
Nikolajew, 84–5, 90–1
Nill-Theobald, Christiane, 219
Niven, William, 36, 50, 51
Noga steppe, 85
Northern Ireland, 12
Nosske, Gustav, 81
Nuremberg, 4, 202, 215
Nuremberg Trials, 13, 17, 28, 89, 123, 201–2, 209–10, 215

Oberheuser, Herta, 29
Odessa, 84
Ogorreck, Ralf, 93
Ohlendorf, Otto, 14, 28–9, 79–81, 83, 86, 88–9, 91
Oldenburg, Manfred, 95
Operation Barbarossa, 79
Oppel, Stefanie, 139
Orth, Karin, 52
Ostendorf, Heribert, 230
Ostmark, 81

Paschke, Hans, 173, 181
Paul, Gerhard, 33–4, 48, 53, 92, 94
Perels, Joachim, 48
Persia, 191–2
Persterer, Alois, 81

Pinker, Steven, 150, 164
Pjatigorsk, 85
Pohl, Dieter, 48, 49, 51, 53, 93, 96
Pohl, Karl Heinrich, 49, 199
Pohl, Oswald, 130
Pohl, Rolf, 95
Poland, ix, 5, 8, 27, 37, 47, 57, 71, 78, 138, 168, 180
Poliakov, Léon, 50
police battalion(s), 5, 8, 16, 37–8, 56, 71, 80, 85, 165, 173, 180, 218
Polonsky, Antony, 54
Porrajmos, 191
Posen, 5
Potsdam, 25
Prague, 137
Prettin, 124
Pretzsch, 81–2
Przyrembel, Alexandra, 114–15, 119

Quinkert, Babette, 93
Qirko, Hector N., 161, 164

Radbruch, Gustav, 213
Rauh, Klaus, 142
Ravensbrück, concentration camp, 15, 29, 42, 115, 121, 123–7, 129–32, 138
Reese, Dagmar, 118
Reich Security Head Office (RSHA), 14, 40, 78, 80–2, 86, 178
Reichenau, Walter von, 70
Reichswehr, 66
Reid, James J., 200
Reitlinger, Gerald, 28, 50
Remarque, Erich Maria, 76
Reşid, Mehmed, 196
Rhineland, 126
Richter, Heinz A., 92
Röder, Werner, 94
Roesen, Anton, 219
Röhm, Ernst, 66
Rohwer, Jürgen, 94
Romania, 79, 83–4, 87–8
Roseman, Mark, 53
Rosmus, Anna, 47
Rossino, Alexander B., 92
Rostov on the Don, 85
Roth, Gerhard, 218

Rousso, Henry, 200
Rückerl, Adalbert, 219
Rüter, Christiaan F., 141
Rwanda, x, xiii, 11–12, 17–18, 146, 160, 168, 187, 201, 203–5, 207, 214–18, 220

Sachse, Carola, 110, 117–18
Sachsenhausen, concentration camp, 42
Şakir, Bahaettin 194–5
Salzburg, 81
Sandkühler, Thomas, 49, 188, 199
Sant' Anna di Stazzema, 206
Schaack (vicar), 59
Schabas, William A., 219
Scheffler, Wolfgang, 93, 94
Schenckendorff, General Max von, 69
Schlaffer, Rudolf, 142
Schmidt, Alexander, 142
Schmuhl, Hans-Walter, 35, 50
Scholtz-Klink, Gertrud, 105
Schomburg, Petra, 116, 118
Schutzstaffel (SS), ix, 14–15, 28, 30, 35, 38–40, 42, 55, 57, 66, 69, 80–1, 83, 85, 91–2, 112–14, 118, 121, 124–5, 127, 129–31, 133–4, 136–8, 140, 141, 142, 173, 190, 194, 197, 206, 212
Schwartz, Johannes, 113, 119
Schwarz, Gudrun, 42, 52, 112–13, 118, 119, 139
Schwinge, Erich, 75
Scott, James Brown, 205
Security Police (Sipo), 40, 78, 94
Security Service (SD), 40, 78–81, 83
Seetzen, Heinz, 81, 83
Segev, Tom, 51
Seibel, Wolfgang, 52
Semelin, Jacques, 200
Sereny, Gitta, 50
Shalom [Ntahobari], 160
Shapiro, Paul A., 95
Shaw, Martin, 21
Shepherd, Benjamin, 76
Shils, Edward, 58, 76
Shoah, *see* Holocaust
Sibille (Lieutenant), 55, 69, 71, 75
Sigmund, Anna Maria, 118

Simferopol, 85
Singer, Peter, 150, 164
Sivard, Ruth Leger, 163
Smith, Rober W., 163
Smolensk, 55
Sobibor, concentration camp, 33
Sofsky, Wolfgang, 140, 141
Sonderkommando(s) (Sk), 81, 83–6, 94
Sontag, Susan, 18
Sosmus, Anna, 54
Soviet Union (SU), *see* USSR
Special or Task Commandos, *see Sonderkommandos (Sk)*
Special Squads, *see Einsatzgruppe(n)*
Special Units, *see Einsatzkommando(s) (Ek)*
Speer, Albert, 210
Spielberg, Steven, 36
Sprenger, Isabell, 139
Stalin, Josef, 8, 36, 89
Stalingrad, 170
Stanford, prison experiment, 3, 5, 37
Stangel, Franz, 33
Staub, Ervin, 19, 20
Stauffenberg, Claus Schenk, Graf von, 36
Stavropol, 85
Stein, Marcel, 51, 95
Sterz, Reinhold, 50, 77
Stoenescu, Alex Mihai, 95
Stokes, Lawrence D., 94
Stone, Dan, 48
Storm Troopers, *see Schutzstaffel* (SS)
Strebel, Bernhard, 139
Streckenbach, Bruno, 81
Streit, Christian, 31, 49
Stuby, Gerhard, xiii, 230
Sturm, Johanna, 132, 141
Sudan, 147
Suhre, Fritz, 123, 139
Sydnor, Charles W., 51
Symonowicz, Wanda, 53
Syria, 191–3
Szejnmann, Claus-Christian W., xv, 5, 13, 20, 25, 180

Taake, Claudia, 52
Tabory, Mala, 219
Taganrog, 85

Index

Talaat, Mehmed (Minister of the Interior; Ottoman Empire), 195
Taliban, 8
Taman peninsula, 85
Teege, Bertha, 132, 141
Teşkilat-ı Mahsusa ('Special Organisation'), 194
Thomsen, Erich, 92
Thoß, Bruno, 218
Thürmer-Rohr, Christina, 104, 117
Tighina (Bendery), 84, 87
Timor, East, 146
Tooby, John, 9, 20
Toprak, Zafer, 199
Toynbee, Arnold J, 200
Transnistria, 84
Treblinka, concentration camp, 33
Tröger, Annemarie, 116
Tschuggnall, Karoline, xvi, 180
Tuchel, Johannes, 140
Tudosse (Tuodossi), 83
Turks, 146, 192
Tutsi, 155, 207, 215, 217

Ueberschär, Gerd R., 52
Ukraine, 38, 43, 79, 84
Ulm, 30
United Nations (UN), 145, 218, 220
United States Holocaust Memorial Museum (USHMM), Washington DC, ix
USA, 7, 137
USSR, 8, 27, 41, 53, 57, 66–7, 79, 81–2, 94, 198, 218

Valentino, Benjamin A., 21
Verhoeven, Michael, 54
Versailles, Treaty of, 61, 75, 202, 205
Vietnam, 7
Vohs, Kathleen D., 8–9, 20
Volkmann, Hans-Erich, 218
Volksgemeinschaft, 12, 125, 171

Waffen-SS, 2, 40, 52, 57, 69, 80–1, 93,
Waller, James E., xv, 4, 9, 13, 16, 19, 43, 53, 145, 164, 175, 181, 141
Wallimann, Isidor, 163
Wegner, Bernd, 141
Wehner, Joseph M., 76
Wehrmacht, ix, xiii, 13–14, 28, 31, 36–8, 40–1, 49, 51, 55–8, 64, 66–7, 69–72, 75, 76, 77, 92, 93, 95, 96, 199, 206, 212, 219
Weigel, Sigrid, 142
Weimar Republic, 44, 59, 213
Weinke, Anette, 142
Weiss, Peter, 76
Weitbrecht, Dorothee, 92
Weizsäcker, Richard von, 34
Wellershoff, Dieter, 65, 76
Welzel, Hans, 219
Welzer, Harald, xvi, 12–13, 16–17, 19, 43, 53, 54, 95, 165, 180, 181, 218
Wenck, Alexandra-Eileen, 139
Werle, Gerhard, xiii, 61, 142, 219
Wetterer, Angelika, 118
Wheatley, Ronald, 93
Wiesel, Elie, 145
Wieviorka, Michel, 20
Wildt, Michael, 45, 52, 78, 86, 92–4
Wilhelm II (German emperor), 202
Wilhelm, Hans-Heinrich, 35, 50, 92, 96
Wippermann, Wolfgang, 96
Wobbe, Theresa, 119
Wodie, 85
Wüllenweber, Walter, 142
Wyman, David, 50

Young, James E., 50
Yugoslavia, 10, 27, 146, 168, 187, 200, 204

Zapp, Paul, 81, 84, 94
Zimbardo, Philip, 3–5, 7, 19, 20, 51
Zimmermann, Michael, 36, 50
Zimmermann, Moshe, 54
Zitelmann, Rainer, 49
Zöllner (*Einsatzgruppe D*), 90–1